The Relevance of Bernard Lonergan's Notion of Self-Appropriation to a Mystical-Political Theology

american
university
studies

Series VII
Theology and Religion

Vol. 267

PETER LANG
New York • Washington, D.C./Baltimore • Bern
Frankfurt am Main • Berlin • Brussels • Vienna • Oxford

Ian B. Bell

The Relevance of Bernard Lonergan's Notion of Self-Appropriation to a Mystical-Political Theology

PETER LANG
New York • Washington, D.C./Baltimore • Bern
Frankfurt am Main • Berlin • Brussels • Vienna • Oxford

Library of Congress Cataloging-in-Publication Data

Bell, Ian B.
The relevance of Bernard Lonergan's notion of self-appropriation
to a mystical-political theology / Ian B. Bell.
p. cm. — (American university studies. VII, Theology and religion; v. 267)
Includes bibliographical references and index.
1. Lonergan, Bernard J. F. 2. Catholic Church—Doctrines—History—
20th century. 3. Theology, Doctrinal—History—20th century. I. Title.
BX4705.L7133B45   230'.2092—dc22   2007051210
ISBN 978-1-4331-0072-7
ISSN 0740-0446

Bibliographic information published by **Die Deutsche Bibliothek**.
Die Deutsche Bibliothek lists this publication in the "Deutsche
Nationalbibliografie"; detailed bibliographic data is available
on the Internet at http://dnb.ddb.de/.

The paper in this book meets the guidelines for permanence and durability
of the Committee on Production Guidelines for Book Longevity
of the Council of Library Resources.

Printed in the United States of America

The Relevance of Bernard Lonergan's Notion of
Self-Appropriation to a Mystical-Political Theology

Ian B. Bell

E   R   R   A   T   A

Regrettably the wrong series volume number was printed for this book. Necessary corrections will be made in subsequent printings. The correct information follows:

aUS

american
university
studies

Series VII
Theology and Religion

Vol. 284

This work is dedicated to my loving wife, Melissa.
You are the inspiration for all that I do.

TABLE OF CONTENTS

ACKNOWLEDGMENTS

The author acknowledges with gratitude permission to reprint portions of the following texts:

Jon Alexander, "What Do Recent Writers Mean by Spirituality?" *Spirituality Today* 32 © 1980. Reprinted by permission of the publisher. All rights reserved.

Ian Bell, "An Elaboration of the Worshipful Pattern of Experience in the Work of Bernard Lonergan," *Worship* 81 © 2007. Reprinted by permission of the publisher. All rights reserved.

Robert Doran, "Psychic Conversion." In *Theological Foundations*, 2 vols. Milwaukee, WI: Marquette University Press, © 1995. Reprinted by permission of the publisher. All rights reserved.

Gustavo Gutiérrez, "Toward the Fifth Centenary," trans. Dinah Livingstone, in Gustavo Gutiérrez, *The Density of the Present: Selected Writings*. Maryknoll: Orbis Books, © 1999. Reprinted by permission of the publisher. All rights reserved.

Bernard Lonergan, "Healing and Creating in History," in *A Third Collection*, ed. Frederick E. Crowe. New York: Paulist Press, © 1985. Reprinted by permission of the Bernard Lonergan Estate. All rights reserved.

Bernard Lonergan, *Method in Theology*, 2nd ed. Toronto: University of Toronto Press, © 1996. Reprinted by permission of the author. All rights reserved.

Mark D. Morelli, "Horizonal Diplomacy," in *Creativity and Method: Essays in Honor of Bernard Lonergan*, ed. Matthew L. Lamb. Milwaukee, WI: Marquette University Press, © 1981. Reprinted by permission of the publisher. All rights reserved.

James Robertson Price III, "Lonergan and the Foundation of a Contemporary Mystical Theology," in *Lonergan Workshop*, vol. 5, ed. Fred Lawrence. Chico, CA: Scholars Press, © 1985. Reprinted by permission of the author. All rights reserved.

Strange Freedom: The Best of Howard Thurman on Religious Experience and Public Life by Earl Fluker. © 1998 by Walter Earl Fluker and Catherine Tumber. Reprinted by permission of Beacon Press, Boston. All rights reserved.

INTRODUCTION

While pursuing my Master's degree at the College of St. Catherine in St. Paul, MN, a colleague of mine once said to me, "If everybody were mystics, nothing would ever get done." Although she made this comment respectfully after encountering such individuals as John of the Cross and Teresa of Avila, whose writings often focus on the interior spiritual development of the soul, something about her comment struck me as a little off. If Christians are called to live with one another in love, then should not the mystical union with Divine love be able to inform Christian persons profoundly as to the manner in which they live with one another? As this question continued to pursue me throughout my doctoral studies, I began to realize that my colleague was not alone in her perception of a distance between spiritual matters and the affairs of the world. Rather, this is an old problem that has plagued the Christian tradition since at least the 12th century, and at its heart lies what Tad Dunne calls a 'split soul' mentality in which spirituality is cordoned off as a special category of experience, separate from the concerns of every day life.[1]

The prominence of the split soul is especially remarkable considering the world at the beginning of the 21st century. People everywhere are experiencing a hunger for spiritual fulfillment that would provide meaning in their lives. Writers produce books on spirituality and the great mystics of history at a rapid pace, and people are reading them in an effort to increase their consciousness of the Divine or to satisfy their spiritual hunger. People visit monasteries and make pilgrimages to holy places seeking to encounter more deeply the presence of God. Assuming that these experiences fail to have an effect on the manner in which people live their everyday lives would be ill advised considering the number of individuals involved in such pursuits.

In addition to this increased attention to spirituality in the late 20th and early 21st centuries, Christians have recognized the relation of the interior life to exterior behavior from the very beginnings of the church. The synoptic gospels speak of Christ's identification between love of God and love of neighbor in the greatest commandment (Mt 22:34-40; Mk 12:28-34; Lk 10:25-28) as do the Johannine literature (1 Jn 4:7-21) and the Pauline writings (1 Cor 13:8). Moreover, even though Paul opposed matters of the flesh (*sarx*) with a life of the Spirit (*pneuma*), no such distinction was present in his concept of *soma*, the body in right relation with God. For Paul, the spiritual life and the bodily life were in fact one life, lived in the Spirit of God.[2] //

The question remains, then, as to how the split soul mentality came to prevalence. According to Walter Principe, the Pauline sense of spirituality may be found in Christian writers through the 13th century. During the ninth century, however, an exception occurred when an individual by the name of Candidus began to use the term *spiritualitas* in an "entitative-psychological sense" rather than the Pauline moral sense. Here *spiritualitas* is opposed to *corporalitas* or *materialitas*. In other words, with Candidus, the conception of spirituality as a distinct element of the human person came into being. In his theology, the spiritual life is not conceived as integrally connected with the exterior world, but rather as an interior reality that is superior to the physical world in which persons live. Although the Pauline meaning of spirituality continued to dominate for the next few centuries, Candidus's new usage became more widely present in theological discussion, and in the 12th century the psychological sense of the term became more widespread through the writings of Gilbert of Poitiers, Gundissalinus, and Gerard of Cremona. In the 13th century, according to Principe, the use of the term in opposition to worldly concerns became widespread.[3]

Principe claims that the medieval debate regarding ecclesiastical jurisdiction only exacerbated the situation. In this discussion a distinction was drawn between spiritual and temporal lords. The spiritual lords were to hold sway over the interior and religious life of the individual, and the temporal lords were to hold authority regarding exterior and civil matters. Eventually, *spiritualitas* came to designate church property while *temporalitas* referred to the property of a civil ruler.[4]

Gradually, a wedge was driven between the spiritual and the temporal, which became concrete both in theological discourse and the lives of the people of the medieval period. This split between spirituality and the world came to expression in the no-longer Latin world in France in the 17th century as 'spiritualité' became increasingly associated with the devout religious life. Moreover, in philosophical circles matter and corporeality began to be defined in opposition to spiritual reality. But perhaps the greatest blow to the Pauline understanding of spirituality came as writers began to use the term in a pejorative sense to attack the spiritual life of Madame Guyon and Fénélon.[5] These individuals belonged to the spiritual movement known as 'quietism' in which individuals placed such emphasis on being silent before God that all other concerns melted away. This perspective reached its zenith in an indifference towards ecclesial pronouncements regarding the path to salvation. Such concerns as charity and participation in the sacramental life of the church were perceived as unnecessary because the goal of the spiritual life was understood as remaining still before God and allowing God to speak to the innermost depths of the soul.[6]

After a lapse in usage of 'spiritualité', the opposition between spiritual and worldly matters worsened in the 20th century, possibly because of the influence of French theologians in the early and middle parts of the century.[7] The end result of these centuries of theological movement is that Principe is able to make the claim that "no English dictionary has been found that gives anything more than 'the quality or condition of being spiritual; attachment to or regard for things of the spirit as opposed to material and worldly interests.'"[8] Principe's identification of the rift between spirituality and the affairs of the world echoes in the work of the philosopher Louis Dupré. In his *Passage to Modernity*, Dupré identifies a centuries-long process of separating the realm of the transcendent from the human sphere of reality that culminates in the philosophical movement known as "modernity."[9] Dupré begins his work with an examination of the Greek philosophy, which, he claims, included an understanding of reality in which the cosmos consists of an order that is divinely given from above. Therefore, the quest for meaning involved the identification of the manner in which objects or events fit into the divine order.[10] Later thinkers altered this view of the cosmos by coming to view their role as improving or perfecting the forms that appeared in this order. Meaning was no longer to be found solely through observation, but also through the creative imagination.[11] In other words, philosophers began to view the cosmos not only as the reality in which human persons acted, but also as an external object to be studied and in some cases altered by human activity. This development, coupled with the scientific work of Copernicus, Galileo, and Bacon eventually led to an instrumental view of the cosmos in which individual persons could shape their own reality, in other words, to make their own meanings.[12] Dupré writes:

> Bacon's call for unlimited control over nature rested on the assumption that nature possessed no purpose of its own... This placed the responsibility for conveying meaning and purpose to the world entirely on the human person, the only creature endowed with purposiveness.[13]

The significance of conceiving the human person as maker of meaning lies in its accompanying notion of freedom. The actions of individuals are no longer viewed in light of the divine order. Rather than merely participating in a reality ordained by the divine, each person is free to create their own reality. This freedom, however, is in direct tension with the notion of a transcendent source of the universe. The freedom of the contingent is limited in light of the freedom of the divine, and when this difference is viewed in light of the Christian doctrine of the fall, in which a ruptured relationship between God and humanity comes into being, and the nominalist[14] notion of an incomprehensible deity, a complete separation between creator and creation is a short step.[15] According to Dupré, the difficulties associated with this separation led to the modern age.[16]

Dupré proposes that prior to the modern age the focus of philosophical thought was the reestablishment of a union between the two spheres. Driven by the doctrine of the Incarnation in which the human is joined to the divine, this search for unification lies behind such theories as Aquinas's medicinal notion of Grace[17] and Luther's tension between justification and sin.[18] Of these attempts at unification, the Baroque period was the last, and here Dupré ends his historical survey. Hereafter, the thinkers of the modern age would strive to recognize and articulate this separation rather than search for a resolution of the tension.[19]

The coming of the split soul to prominence may also be found in Jon Alexander's article on the manner in which recent writers have used the term "spirituality." Alexander notes that in the 17th and 18th centuries, writers tended to reserve this word for discussions of matters considered divine or supernatural in nature or to reference such notions as incorporeality.[20] Although use of the term was generally limited to free religious groups in the 19th century, perhaps because of the association of the word with antinomianism[21] and unorthodoxy, some Roman Catholic thinkers did engage in a discussion of spirituality the participants of which fell into one of two positions.

> One view saw a fundamental division in the spiritual life between (1) ordinary growth in the moral life through stages of observing the commandments, undergoing purgation, practicing asceticism, and progressing toward fulfillment of the counsels of perfection, and (2) the extraordinary state of mystical prayer and other phenomena, such as visions, inner locutions, perhaps miracle-working, and the like. All the latter were attained by, and meant for, only a few.[22]

In other words, the spiritual life did not necessarily involve other elements of life. For most individuals, spirituality was indeed connected with the moral life, but for those rare individuals who experienced the mystical life, the spiritual life was a matter solely of the interior life.

The second position in this debate, as identified by Alexander:

stressed the unity and continuity of the spiritual life, maintaining that mystical prayer is the goal to which every Christian is called and for which he or she is offered grace, although, in fact, many, and perhaps even most, do not attain it... The latter is an ordinary outcome of Christian life well lived...[23]

From this perspective, spirituality and mysticism are directly connected to the manner in which human persons live their lives. If they lead a Christian life informed by their spirituality, they will encounter the mystical experience of the Divine. No clear distinction between spiritual and moral issues in such an understanding.

Alexander asserts that this latter position has gained the upper hand in recent discussions of spirituality, for the term "spirituality" has taken on a more experiential connotation as the expression of the interior life is recognized in concrete human situations. Such a trend would seem to resist the split soul mentality. However, Alexander notes this increased emphasis on the experiential element of spirituality has been accompanied by a tendency to use the term in a more generic fashion, as the expression of religious existence.[24] This is a far cry from previous identifications of spirituality with the specific practices of obeying the commandments or pursuing asceticism. Thus, according to Alexander, spirituality has become an abstract notion of religiosity rather than being rooted in a specific context.

With specific attention to mysticism, the articulation of this lamentable rift finds its classic expression in the work of the early 20th century North American philosopher William James who emphasizes the transiency of the mystical experience. The mystical encounter with God, he claims, has a definite starting and ending point. This union comes to an end, and the mystic must return to "ordinary" experience. Even though the mystical experience often infuses individuals with knowledge or wisdom that is applicable to the world, the sphere of human experience in which this understanding is communicated is somehow qualitatively different from everyday life.[25]

Yet despite the appearance of the divorce between spirit and world documented by Principe and Dupré and given systematic expression by James, the aforementioned affection and reverence for the great spiritual leaders and exemplars of the past and the search for spiritual fulfillment continues in synagogues, mosques, and churches today. At the same time, the world of the early 21st century is rife with the destructive influence of social and economic structures driven by acquisitive materialism, self-advancement and aggrandizement, rather than by the spiritual wisdom that is the legacy of the mystical tradition. As a Christian theologian, I believe that the interior life, though it continues to play a significant role in the lives of believers today, is an underutilized resource for the amelioration of the social ills that plague human communities today.

I am convinced that this underutilization of the mystical tradition is a direct result of the split soul mentality in which matters of interior spiritual development are understood as belonging to a distinct category of human experience that is kept apart from matters of everyday life. The result is that individuals who find spiritual fulfillment or wisdom in moments of mystical experience of union with the Divine or in encounters with the spiritual legacies of those who have gone before us attempt to "transfer" what they have learned in their spiritual lives to their practical living with one another, which stands in opposition to a notion of spirituality in which the interior life forms an integral element of living.

Thomas Merton proposes such a system of transference as he seeks to find a place for the contemplative life in a world that measures success by quantifiable achievements. In his *Contemplation in a World of Action*, he argues that the monastic life serves a prophetic function insofar as it demonstrates to the world the importance of spending time with God. In the examples set by the men and women who live the monastic life, the world is reminded that the acquisitive culture of today can not provide the inner peace that can only be found by spending time with God.[26] Merton writes:

> [A]s we all know too well, those who are completely immersed in the world with its violence and confusion may certainly have a very real experience of its problem, but they may also see these problems so close at hand that they lose their perspective. Their view of things needs to be completed by the perspective of those who see life from another angle.[27]

The role of contemplatives, then, is to communicate the presence and love of God to the world through their life of prayer and dedication to the Divine. Men and women visit spiritual masters and places to gain wisdom, and then return to ordinary life. They may be invigorated by the experience, or be inspired to be more of a person of God, but the fact remains that they leave the monastery or close the book. What is lacking is a description of the manner in which those individuals who are inspired by contemplatives take their wisdom and inspiration into the ordinary life.

To be fair here, I must be clear that Merton himself did not see his system as establishing such a sharp distinction between the contemplative life and that of the world; indeed, the contemplative cooks and cleans, repairs and refurbishes, travels and recreates. Rather, Merton hoped that the new found openness of the cloister to the world emphasized in the monastic renewal of Vatican II would inspire people to incorporate their relationship with the Divine more deeply in their daily lives in the world.[28] My point is simply that Merton's system, by locating the contemplative life as somehow separate from the everyday affairs of the world without the corresponding element of the manner in which this transference of wisdom takes place is incapable of fully responding to the split soul mentality that is the concern of this book. Merton's work must be complemented by further investigation.

When the mystical tradition and its interpreters are examined more deeply to develop a complement that succeeds in resisting the split soul, the split soul mentality is by no means unreasonable. The writings of the mystics and subsequent theologians can easily be used to support the notion that mysticism stands in opposition to the affairs of the world, and that those individuals who encounter the Divine in mystical union only do so by renouncing the world to concentrate solely on the interior life. To be more concrete, the escape from the world that characterizes the writings of mystics such as John of the Cross[29] and Thérèse of Lisieux[30] are at times interpreted as a concentration on spiritual affairs to the neglect of matters of the world.[31] Moreover, the sometimes brutal ascetic practices of such mystics as Henry Suso[32] and Francis of Assisi[33] are often taken as a rejection of the body and the affairs of the 'physical' world.

However, I contend that such an interpretation of the lives and writings of these mystics is an inadequate understanding of the mystical tradition, for the goal of mysticism, as identified by the early 20th century Anglican theologian, Evelyn Underhill, is to engage Reality as it truly exists. I capitalize the "R" here because Underhill makes a distinction in her work between reality with a small "r" and Reality with a capital "R." The former represents an encounter with the world in which persons lack an awareness of deeper levels that can only be accessed through a profound awareness of the presence of the Divine. She uses the latter to designate Reality in all of its depth and complexity. Thus, if human persons gain an appreciation of Reality, they are not fooled by the illusions and distortions which are characteristic of the human condition.[34] Therefore, according to Underhill's theology, mysticism is not necessarily an escape from the world but rather an experience of union with the Divine that enables individuals to encounter the world without being deceived by the shortcomings and distortions created by focusing their lives on things other than their relationship with the Divine. Moreover, the mystical encounter with the Divine provides individuals with a profound awareness of the love Christian persons are to have for one another, and I believe mystics, equipped with such an appreciation of Divine love, rather than escaping from the world and leaving it to its own affairs, instead possesses an extraordinary resource for addressing social ills.

Moreover, in light of Underhill's work on mysticism, I question James's notion that mystical experience is transient in nature. Underhill documents the lives of the mystics as progressing in four stages. The first part of the mystical path, she claims, is a conversion toward the mystical life in the heart of the individual. The great Christian mystics hear a divine call to a life lived in which the interior life becomes the primary focus of the person. After hearing this call, a period of purgation is necessary in which those aspects of their personality or society that inhibit the acceptance of the approach of the Divine are removed. This is followed by a time marked by mystical illumination in which God approaches the individual, and nothing stands in the way of the approaching the Divine. In this stage, the mystical life does indeed match the analysis of James because these mystical encounters are temporary. They may be remarkably frequent, but the mystic does return to ordinary experience. This is not, however, the final phase of the mystical journey, for the time of illumination is followed by a life lived in union with the Divine. Finally, the mystic lives at all times in mystical union with God.[35]

If Underhill's portrayal of mysticism is examined in light of the manner in which we inhabit the world, I believe that the basis for asserting that the mystical life not only bears on the world, but is only authentically lived with the world in mind may be found. To provide an example, Underhill writes the following in her *Practical Mysticism*.

> [T]he galloping race-horse, with legs stretched out as we are used to see it, is a mythical animal, probably based on the mental image of a running dog. No horse has ever galloped thus: but its real action is too quick for us, and we explain it to ourselves as something resembling the more deliberate dog-action which we have caught and registered as it passed. The plain man's [*sic*] universe is full of race-horses that are actually running dogs.[36]

In other words, through the gift of union with the Divine, the mystic is equipped to know the manner in which things actually exist, not just as they appear. The mystic may find the galloping race horse of the North American dream that the free democracy of the United States is based on equality and opportunity for all is actually a running dog. Factors such as gender, ethnicity, socio-economic background, or whom one knows prevent the race-horse of equal opportunity for all from being anything more than a mythical creature. Given the dehumanizing effects of the gross disparities found in the socio-economic fabric of the United States, can a mystic who has experienced loving union with the Divine say that the current situation is in accordance with the gospel's message to love our neighbors? Moreover, the applicability of mystical wisdom to worldly affairs is not limited to critical examination of societal affairs, but also aids the mystics as they actively participate in worldly matters. Teresa of Avila serves as an example of a mystic whose spiritual life played a significant role in her involvement in the politics of 15th century Spain.[37] In Underhill's theology of mysticism then, that which is lacking in Merton's contemplatives may be found. For Underhill, the mystical relationship of union with the Divine cannot help but become an aspect of the manner in which human beings inhabit the world and deal with their fellow human beings. Mystics are only truly alive when they listen to the voice of Love and obey.[38]

Mysticism so understood may serve as an informative source for a "political theology." Political theology has its contemporary roots in the work of such figures as Dorothee Sölle and Gustavo Gutiérrez. A more complete discussion of their work will appear in Chapter One, but for the purposes of this introduction describing political theology as theology concerned with the implications of the Christian faith for the manner in which Christian persons live with one another suffices. The call of the gospel to live with one another in love bears directly on the social, economic, and political structures societies erect as Christian persons seek to answer this call. Do these structures reflect the love that people are to have for one another, or do the basic human needs of certain individuals or groups go unmet? Do some people live on the so-called margins of society where human dignity is assaulted by the manner in which the social order is configured? Do certain groups pay the economic, social, and political price for the continued success of a privileged group? If this is so, and I believe that an honest examination of the world today tells us that it is, then what is an appropriate response for the church, and what are the theological underpinnings to such a response?

The attempt to link mysticism with such a political theological project by no means has its origin with my work here in this book. I have already briefly described the attempts made by Thomas Merton and Evelyn Underhill to elucidate the connection between mysticism and the world. More recently, Howard Thurman notes that the often extraordinary practices of self-purification taken by the mystics are based in a belief that evil in the world may be overcome.[39] For Thurman, the mystical experience, though it is encountered on an individual basis, cannot help but contain communal significance. In the mystical encounter with the Divine, the mystic is not only united with God, but also with all of creation, especially human life. Moreover, in order for the mystical experience to bear fruit in the life of the mystics, it must be realized in the community in which they live. He writes:

> The good which is given him must somehow be achieved in a framework of experiences native to his own life which his life 'for instances' in a rich variety of details. The ascetic impulse having as its purpose individual purification and living brings the realistic mystic face to face with the society in which he functions as a person. He discovers that he is a person, and a personality in a profound sense can only be achieved in a milieu of human relations.[40]

The implications of the social nature of the mystical experience described in the preceding quote are twofold for Thurman. First, individual mystics often come to the realization that those factors which inhibit relationship with the Divine are more than likely caused by social institutions or forces. Second, in the mystics' efforts to achieve the good received in the mystical experience, they must respond to human needs, for unmet needs diminish the life desired for humanity by God.[41]

Again, the situation in the United States at the beginning of the 21st century can be illustrative here. David R. Loy has made a case for the manner in which the market economy functions in the United States as a religion. It affects value systems by telling people that acquisition is good, and refusal to spend is not. It promises a type of salvation by announcing that we will be happy if only we buy enough goods, whether we need them or not.   In short, according to Loy, the market has become an idol worshipped by the people of the United States of America, and its following is growing through the process of globalization.[42] If the market holds the primary place in thier lives, are human persons not less able to love God with all their hearts, all their minds, and all their souls and their neighbor as themselves? Thurman's mystics, in seeking to encourage the development of relationship with God both in the life of the individuals mystics and in the lives of others, would seek to address this situation.

Although Underhill, Merton, and Thurman have brought to the fore the relevance of the mystical to the political, they have not provided an in-depth, systematic analysis of the manner in which the two are related. Though they have asserted that a connection exists and have made initial forays into the particulars of the relationship, more work needs to be done, as the persistence of the split soul mentality attests. The noted North American historian of mysticism, Bernard McGinn, French theologian and sociologist, Michel de Certeau, and German theologian, Johann Baptist Metz are three recent scholars who seek to address the relationship between mysticism and practical-political matters in their work. I will briefly summarize their contributions here.

By providing an impressive history of mysticism that includes a discussion of medieval mysticism in which he identifies a turn "from centering on inward-looking community to outward-looking encounter with the world," [43] Bernard McGinn does a great service for those attempting to formulate a mystical-political theology by historically documenting the fact that not all mystics removed themselves from the world. He buttresses his claim by citing examples of those mystics in history such as Bernard of Clairvaux and Joachim of Fiore who were not only advocates for institutional ecclesial reform, but also very concerned with the manner in which the church of their time was inhabiting the world. However, I must ask whether an historical approach to the matter at hand is sufficient. In his work, McGinn is not interested in a theology of mysticism that describes the manner in which the interior life and exterior behavior are connected. Rather, his historical approach tends toward that of Merton in that it cites examples of certain mystics as evidence of the connection between mysticism and the world without explaining the theology behind the relationship. People are to be inspired by the examples of the mystics, but McGinn does not provide a solution to the split soul mentality. How then are individuals concerned with the process of integrating the wisdom of the mystics into a mystical-political theology that is capable of speaking to the situation as it stands at the beginning of the 21st century to proceed?

Unlike McGinn, both Johann Baptist Metz and Michel de Certeau approach systematically the problem of the distinction between the mystical life and everyday life. For Metz, the following of Christ necessarily includes mystical and political components. The Christian message is such that the two are inextricably interconnected. One cannot exist without the other. The mystical element of Christianity, the encounter between Christ and believer, is such that it must inform and inspire the manner in which the believers inhabit and shape their communities. Without the mystical, the political is not given life by the transformation wrought by Christ. It becomes a matter of *living* together, not *loving* together. Conversely, without the political, the mystical bears no fruit, and the call of Christ to love one another goes unanswered. [44]

Certeau approaches the issue from another perspective. For him, the Christian is called to cross the boundaries encountered in life. The Christian is called to break with the comfortable life in which the ways of the world go unchallenged, engage those who live in the margins of society, and confront the practices that keep them there. In the same manner, the mystics cross the boundary of their experiences of union with the Divine to work for the will of God in the particular social context in which they are located. [45]

The list of scholars who have treated the relationship between mysticism and political theology could go on for some great length. It is a topic that has captured the attention of many theologians. I have chosen to offer Metz and Certeau as examples because they have dealt with the issue extensively. Scholars such as Howard Thurman, whose primary theological interest lies elsewhere, devote relatively little attention to the topic of mystical-political theology. However, despite the efforts of these thinkers, the split soul mentality persists in the world today, and its resistance to the efforts of these selected thinkers testifies to the fact that more work remains to be done on the issue.

I contend that the reason for this continued refusal to relinquish the split soul mentality is that emphasis has been too often placed on the nature of the experience and not enough attention has been paid to the subject who encounters the presence of the Divine in mystical union. I have already mentioned the role that the work of William James has played in systematizing the split soul. In his insistence on the passivity of the mystical experience,[46] he also contributes to this neglect of the subject. The result of an understanding of mysticism in which the subject passively receives mystical wisdom is that it reinforces the sense that the mystical experience is somehow separate from the rest of the world. Not only is the data of the experience qualitatively different, the person either operates differently or ceases to function at all. The wedge is driven further between the mystical experience and the affairs of the world.

When the work of the scholars mentioned in this introduction who have attempted to elucidate the connection between the mystical and everyday life is examined, the fact that they have all fallen into this mistake of concentrating on the experience to the neglect of the subject becomes apparent. For Thomas Merton, both the preparation for the mystical experience and the encounter itself are such that the contemplative must be removed from society to some extent. He does not, however, attend to the manner in which the contemplative appropriates the wisdom of the mystical encounter. Howard Thurman makes the claim that the mystic is compelled to effect the goodness received in the mystical encounter with God. However, he, like Merton, does not attend to the manner in which this goodness is received or how the mystics are to carry the received wisdom into the society in which they live. Evelyn Underhill is unable to completely resolve the issue of the split soul mentality because in her concentration on the experience she continues to speak in terms of the different levels or aspects of Reality without relating those planes to one another. In so doing, she risks perpetuating the split soul mentality because the world becomes separated into the sensible and the super-sensible.

Michel de Certeau and Johann Baptist Metz recognize that the mystical experience should not be cordoned off into a special category to which individuals should refer when faced with a given social concern, but their work also falls short, for both of these great thinkers fail to pay adequate attention to the manner in which the data, or lack thereof,[47] experienced in the mystical encounter with the Divine is appropriated by individual mystics. Certeau claims that the mystics must "carve out" space for the expression of their experience in the linguistic milieu of their given society,[48] but does not answer the question of how they know that for which they are attempting to make space. Metz speaks of the importance of the mystical and political elements of the Christian life, but he does not address the manner in which individuals appropriates the mystical in their lives. Can mystical experiences become an integral part of life if such moments of union with the Divine are not appropriated by subjects who know what they are doing when they are knowing? I do not believe so, for understanding how human subjects know is necessary if individuals are to do so authentically and bring the received wisdom of the mystical experience to bear on the political elements of human living.

In other words, the mystics of Metz and Certeau are attempting to express their mystical encounters in life and language before they know what it is they have learned from the experience. Metz and Certeau have put the proverbial cart before the horse, and their readers are left with the sense that these scholars have a great contribution to make regarding the relevance of mystical theology to political theology, but the manner in which this is done remains unclear. They are left with the question, "Yes, but what is it exactly that I am attempting to say in my life and language?" I believe that given this uncertainty, people have a propensity to revert to what is known and thus comfortable, namely the split soul mentality, and perhaps this is why the theologies of Metz and Certeau have failed to overcome the underutilization of mysticism as a resource for the amelioration of social ills.

Given the shortcomings of the previous attempts to express the relevance of mystical theology to political theology, I propose that the work of the Canadian scholar Bernard Lonergan (1904-1984) may be helpful. My first reason for doing so is that his cognitional theory provides the piece that is missing in the work of Metz, Certeau, and all others who have asserted a connection between mysticism and the political life, namely, the appropriation of what is learned in the mystical encounter with the Divine. According to Lonergan, the human subject first experiences the data of sense and consciousness. The former includes the information delivered by the five senses, seeing, smelling, tasting, touching, and hearing. The latter consists of the *"acts* of seeing, hearing, tasting, smelling, touching, perceiving, imagining, inquiring, understanding, formulating, reflecting, judging, and so forth."[49]   Human beings are not only able to experience the object of their operations, they can also reflect on the manner in which they do these things, and this concept is crucial to any attempt at understanding the work of Bernard Lonergan.   Thus, the data of sense and consciousness encompass all that Human subjects encounter in their lives.   They form the empirical basis for Lonergan's notion of the human subject and provide the object for the next level, that of understanding.

Once subjects experience the data of sense and/or consciousness, they move to the level of understanding what has been experienced.   Here persons seek to determine exactly what has been experienced by developing questions and hypotheses regarding the data.[50]   At this level of consciousness individuals raise possible explanations for the data that has been experienced. They are saying, "Perhaps this is why such and such happened, or how such and such happened," or "perhaps this is the identity of a certain object." Importantly, the goal of understanding is not to pronounce a judgment as to the identity of the occurrence.   Rather, at this level the subject is only investigating how or why the data are related to one another in order: 1) to ascertain the relationship between the experienced data and 2) to conceptualize explanatory possibilities.   Not until the third level, that of judgment, do human persons make a decision as to the correctness of the hypotheses formulated in the attempt to understand the data.

After possibilities have been raised, the next step is to marshal the evidence and pronounce judgment as to the verity or falsity of the insights that arose at the level of understanding.[51]   At the level of judgment then, the subject is saying either, "Yes, this is what is going on," "No, this is not what is going on," or "I am unable to pass judgment at this time and must return to my experiencing or understanding or leave the matter for another day."

After judgment has been reached, human subjects move to the level of decision in which they take action based on the judgment.   If, for instance, one affirms at the level of judgment that a certain societal practice is unacceptable, then that person must decide what to do about it.   Decision is the level where our experiencing, understanding, and judging come to expression in the actions human persons take in their lives.[52]

With such an explicit cognitional theory in place, Lonergan has provided a means by which mystics become better able to apply mystical wisdom to worldly matters.   Individuals experience the mystical union, understand what was communicated,[53] judge if this understanding is correct, and then decide to do something about it.   The vagueness regarding how their spiritual lives informs their political lives is addressed, and the horse is once again ahead of the cart.

The second contribution Lonergan makes to a mystical-political theology lies in his notion of foundational reality of the human subject, which is informed by intellectual, moral, and religious conversion. This issue of foundational reality will be treated in more detail later in this book, a sufficient summary of Lonergan's notion is a set of "logically first propositions," or "what is first in any ordered set."[54] Intellectual, religious, and moral conversion underlie all aspects of a person's operations. In other words, once individuals undergo religious conversion, not one element of their lives remains unaffected. Now, interactions with neighbors, the earth, or its nonhuman residents are colored by their relationship with the Divine. The horizon in which they operate has been radically altered, and their lives must change in accordance with the awareness of the presence of the Divine. The same goes for intellectual and moral conversion. Once human persons appropriate the manner in which human subjects know, then to operate authentically, they must attend to their knowing. Once human persons make the transition from a life based on value rather than satisfaction, their decisions must be made with this moral conversion in mind.

When these two elements of Lonergan's work are considered together, what Tad Dunne has named the "spiritually integrated subject" comes into consideration. The spiritually integrated subject, he claims, is able to move appropriately among five realms of meaning: 1) common sense, 2) theory, 3) method, 4) transcendence, and 5) historical and literary scholarship. With specific reference to the spiritually integrated mystic, then, the wisdom gained in the mystical encounter would become a part of all levels of meaning, and the wisdom of the mystical experience may be applied to the concerns of political theology.

Given the existence of the split soul mentality and the ability of the work of Bernard Lonergan to resist it, my working thesis in this book may be summarized as follows: *The reason for the inability of mystical-political theology to overcome the split soul mentality is that past attempts have failed to accord adequate attention to the operations of human subjects as they encounter loving union with the Divine, and I contend that Bernard Lonergan's work on the self-appropriating subject can answer this deficiency and enable mysticism to serve as an effective resource for political theology.* To work towards my goal of presenting and defending the above thesis, I will proceed in the following manner.

In any work based on the thought of Bernard Lonergan positioning oneself in his theological method is helpful.[55]   Lonergan's method divides the tasks of theology into two phases comprised of eight functional specialties which correspond to the operations of the human subject. The first is a mediated phase in which theologians undertake the tasks of research, interpretation, history, and dialectics. Research is a matter of gathering and attending to data, interpretation consists of seeking to understand the various positions that surface through research, and history entails judgment regarding the historical factors that contributed to and resulted from those movements and teachings that provide the data for research. Dialectics completes this first phase of theological method as these movements and teachings are clarified and set beside one another, exposing their differences and conflicts so that individuals may affirm or reject these options in the second phase.

The second, mediating, phase of Lonergan's method consists of the theological attempt to explain and communicate the relevance and meaning of the results of the first phase for the concrete historical context in which the theologian is located.   The first step in this phase is the specialty of foundations in which theologians objectify their conversion or lack thereof. Specifically, Lonergan writes of intellectual, moral, and religious conversion, topics which will receive more extensive treatment later in this book. Briefly put, intellectual conversion is a matter of becoming aware of the manner in which the human subject goes about the business of learning, moral conversion consists of a transition from a life based on satisfaction to one based on value, and religious conversion entails a falling in love with God in an unrestricted fashion. Conversion thus orients theologians as they work in the second phase and provides the basis for next functional specialty, that of doctrines.

In the specialty of doctrines, theologians affirm or reject those positions that have been clarified in dialectics. As they search for the formulation(s) of theological statements that adequately express their foundational reality, they are guided by those conversions that have been recognized in the work of foundations. Once these statements have been identified and affirmed, the functional specialty, systematics, seeks to clarify their meaning(s).   For example, what does it mean to believe in a Trinitarian God? What are the concrete implications of the doctrine of the Incarnation for a Christian living in the beginning of the 21st century? Communications, finally, completes the second phase as theologians working here share their findings so that others may share in the fruits of their labor.

The brief history of the split soul mentality may thus be seen as a brief venture into the specialties of research, interpretation, and history as I investigated the manner in which the divide between spirituality and everyday affairs came into being. Tad Dunne has named this rift the 'split soul' mentality,[56] and it is the result of religious and philosophical movements that have pushed Christianity far from the connection between the two loves of which Christ speaks in the Gospel. Although a treatment of the matter that takes into account every factor in the rise of the split soul mentality is far beyond the scope of this book, a picture has emerged of the path traveled by Western Christianity which resulted in the separation of the mysticism from political concerns[57] to a focus on mystical experience that neglects the human subject that encounters the immediate presence of the Divine.

Chapter One will present a dialectical option to the split soul mentality whose origin and persistence is presented in this introductory chapter. Through an examination of the work of the mystical theologians Evelyn Underhill and William Johnston, and political theologians Dorothee Sölle and Gustavo Gutiérrez, I will present a position regarding mystical and political theology that recognizes the connection between the two, and following the work of the specialty, doctrines, I affirm this understanding rather than the split soul mentality. The importance of this chapter thus lies not in the acceptance of a given theologian's position on mystical and political theology, but on their position as a dialectical option to the split soul mentality. Though the split soul mentality currently holds sway, it is not the only choice available to theologians and Christians outside the academy. The goal of the functional specialty, dialectics, is to clarify differing positions and find out why disagreement exists. In this case, I contend that the difference results from an inadequate position regarding the functioning of the human subject, and that the responsible choice is for an understanding of mysticism and political theology that recognizes and values their relationship to one another and results in a mystical-political theology.

The remaining chapters of the book will be dedicated to Lonergan's work regarding the human subject, for I believe that an adequate understanding of the human subject necessarily results in spirituality becoming part and parcel of involvement in socio-political affairs. Moreover, if persons are aware of the functions they perform as human subjects, they are better able to perform those functions. Lonergan names this awareness 'self-appropriation,' and the benefit of this process is that it provides the basis for the treatment of further questions.[58] As such, Chapters Three, Four, and Five are not a matter of theological investigation but a clarification of the manner in which Lonergan's notion of self-appropriation aids the theologian who affirms the doctrine that mystical and political theology do indeed bear directly on one another. If this effort is to be placed in Lonergan's functional specialties, it is most suited to the specialty of foundations, for this discipline is concerned with the foundational reality from which theologians proceed in the selection of doctrines, understanding thereof, and the attempt to communicate to others the fruits of their labor.

Chapter Two will take the first step in elucidating Lonergan's position regarding the self-appropriation of the human subject as it addresses the topic of his notion of patterns of experience. The patterns of experience, according to Lonergan, consist of the particularity of the experiences in which individuals encounter the data of sense and consciousness and try to make sense of that data.[59] The mystical pattern of experience differs from the passionless pursuit of scientific knowledge, which is unlike the encounter with a piece of great art, and so on. Because of the variety of patterns of experience in which individuals may find themselves, the ability to accurately discern the specifics of the given situation becomes very important indeed. Thus, the benefit of Lonergan's notion of patterns of experience lies in its ability to help people to clarify the nature of the experience in which they are located, the goal of their functioning and those elements of the human person relevant to the task at hand.

Although Lonergan may appear to be falling into the trap of the split soul mentality insofar as he asserts the presence of distinct patterns of experience which involve different aspects of the human subject, he is insulated from such a criticism by his insistence on the unity of human subjects even in their differentiation. It is the same subject who encounters the various patterns of experience, and though the data contained therein concerns such different matters as the intellectual search for truth or levels of meaning accessible only through one's feelings, the structure of the functioning of the human subject is invariant. Human subjects experience the data, seek to understand what has been experienced, pass judgment regarding the veracity of that understanding, and then make decisions based upon that judgment. Though the content of the structure may differ, the structure itself is consistent and provides a unity which resists the split soul mentality.

Additionally, what has been learned in one experience accompanies individuals as they move on to other experiences. As human persons learn new concepts, the nature of newly discovered objects, or new relationships between what has been previously learned, they are constructing a horizon. Once they have learned that the world is round, they proceed to other issues with this principle in place. With regard to mystical-political theology, then, once individuals have recognized the relevance of mysticism to political concerns, then they takes this conviction to consideration of more explicit issues such as the effects of the over-consumption of fossil fuels by industrialized nations on the concrete preparation for the realization of the Kingdom of God in history.

Chapter Three takes the next step in the clarification of Lonergan's position regarding the human subject by attending to the functioning of the human subject within the various patterns of experience, and to the differentiation of consciousness that allows the human subject to appropriately apply that functioning. The operations of the human subject consist of the person's ability to encounter reality and discover the meanings contained therein. A table is merely a flat surface to an infant, but to an adult, this object possesses a particular function and role in everyday living. Many are the schoolchildren corrected by the teacher for sitting on a table rather than using it as a work surface. As human persons go about this process of developing meaning in their lives, they perform the operations of experiencing the data, understanding the data, pronouncing judgment on that data, and making decisions based on that judgment.

As previously mentioned, however, the various patterns of experience involve different aspects of human persons as they perform the operations. Accurate understanding of the mystical experience requires attention to the affective element of the human person whereas the intellectual pattern rejects feelings as potentially misguiding the passionless pursuit of truth. Moreover, certain life experiences require more or less attention to one's knowing. The practical pattern is merely concerned with completing the particular task at hand and is not concerned with the deeper levels of meaning. Lonergan names the process of determining the pattern of experience in which the human subject finds him or herself and the goals germane thereto 'differentiation of consciousness,' and the benefit of the successful performance of this process lies in its ability to help individuals clarify the nature of the experience in which they are located, the goal of their functioning and those elements of the human person relevant to the task at hand. Am I in or reflecting upon a mystical, intellectual, or biological experience? Am I seeking general theoretical understanding or am I concerned only with the exigencies of the given moment? Are the feelings I am encountering at the given moment hindering my intellectual efforts, or are they necessary for understanding the meaning of the mystical or aesthetic experience in which I presently find myself? But throughout the different aspects of human living, the unity of the subject remains, and for the mystic living the mystical life, that element becomes present in all other patterns of experience.

Chapter Four will add a second piece to Lonergan's notion of self-appropriation in its discussion of the foundations from which the subject goes about the task of identifying the patterns of experience and the differentiation of consciousness that clarifies the subject's intentions in a given experience. Conversion, according to Lonergan, affects the individual's basic stance in the world. It is a decision for what a people stand, and about that against which they struggle.[60] The three conversions explicitly identified by Lonergan, namely intellectual, moral and religious, guide human subjects as they perform the operations of experiencing, understanding, judging, and deciding. The intellectually converted can not seek to know things without attention to the manner in which that task is undertaken, the morally converted must take into account the discernment of value when deciding between certain courses of action, and the life of the religiously converted is characterized by the state of being in love with God in an unrestricted fashion.

Therefore, when individuals try to make sense of the data present in a given experience, their conversions, or the lack thereof, play a decided role therein. When faced with the beauty of the Sistine Chapel, their religious conversion opens deeper levels of meaning that unreligious persons may miss. When deciding which automobile to purchase, morally converted individuals consider the choice to possess an ethical element. When pursuing scientific knowledge, the intellectually converted human subject seeks to know things as they truly exist, not merely as they seem to be from a given perspective. These conversions, moreover, are interrelated, for the scientific pursuit of knowledge may lead to a deeper appreciation of the Divine, or the conviction that certain methods of obtaining results must be rejected on moral grounds. If human persons are to appropriate their operations as human subjects, they must be conscious of and true to their conversion(s).

Chapter Five will consist of an application of the fruits of self-appropriation, namely, that it provides a basis for pursuing further questions.[61] In the case of this book, the further question is the manner in which self-appropriation functions in the task of mystical-political theology. Briefly put, self-appropriation guides the mystical-political theologian by clarifying the goals of the endeavor and the standpoint from which the theologian proceeds. Mystical theology may consist of understanding the content of the individual's mystical experience, the writings of previous mystics, or a combination of the two. If theologians are unclear as to the pattern of experience in which they are located, the results of the investigation may be mistaken or inadequate. If they are unaware of the manner in which the human subject functions, then their inquiry may be led astray by self-interest or emotional responses to the data. The relevance of self-appropriation to mystical-political theology thus consists of its ability to help theologians go about their task attentively with regard to the data, intelligently as they try to understand the data, reasonably as judgment is pronounced based on the sufficiency of the understanding, and responsibly as action is taken on the basis of that judgment. When theologians then turns their attention to political theology, the knowledge and wisdom gained in the task of mystical theology comes along, and through the clarity provided by self-appropriation, theologians may apply them to socio-political matters. With this strategy in mind, the discussion now turns to the presentation of a dialectical option to the split soul mentality in the work of the mystical and political theologians, Evelyn Underhill, William Johnston, Dorothee Sölle, and Gustavo Gutiérrez.

NOTES

[1] Tad Dunne, *Lonergan and Spirituality: Towards a Spiritual Integration* (Chicago: Loyola University Press, 1985), 3-6. Reinhold Niebuhr serves as a good example of a noted theologian who agrees with such a division between spirituality and the every day life as he writes, "In Catholic mysticism (particularly clearly in the mysticism of St. John of the Cross), the love of God is set in complete contradiction to the love of neighbor in such a way that the love of the creature is merely a stepladder to the love of God, which must be abandoned when the love of God (universal love) is reached." Reinhold Niebuhr, "Love and Law in Protestantism and Catholicism," in Robert MacAfee Brown, ed., *The Essential Reinhold Niebuhr: Selected Essays and Addresses* (New Haven: Yale University Press, 1986), 148. Elsewhere Niebuhr contends that the intensely personal nature of the religious experience hinders the ability of religious love to have a transformative effect on the societal level. Reinhold Niebuhr, *Moral Man and Immoral Society: A Study in Ethics and Politics* (New York: Charles Scribner's Sons, 1932), 81.

[2] John A.T. Robinson, *The Body: A Study in Pauline Theology* (Philadelphia: Westminster Press, 1952), 11-33.

[3] Walter Principe, "Toward Defining Spirituality," *Sciences religieuses/Studies in Religion*, 12:2 (1983): 130-31.

[4] Ibid., 131.

[5] Ibid., 131-32. For more on Madame Guyon, see Dorothy Gwayne Coslet, *Madame Jeanne Guyon, Child of Another World* (Fort Washington, PA: Christian Literature Crusade, 1984). For more on Fénélon, see Paul Janet, *Fénelon: His Life and Works*, trans. Victor Leuliette (Port Washington, N.Y., Kennikat Press, 1970); Katherine Day Little, *François de Fénelon: Study of a Personality* (New York: Harper, 1951).

[6] Bernard McGinn, *The Presence of God: A History of Western Christian Mysticism*, vol. III, *The Flowering of Mysticism: Men and Women of the New Mysticism – 1200-1350* (New York: Crossroad, 1998), 245. John McManners, "The Expansion of Christianity (1500-1800)," in John McManners, ed., *The Oxford History of Christianity* (New York: Oxford University Press, 1990), 299-300. Evelyn Underhill, *Mysticism: The Nature and Development of Spiritual Consciousness* (Oxford: Oneworld, 1999), 321-327. According to Underhill, the fundamental flaw in quietism lies in its mistaken notion that silence before God is the pinnacle of the spiritual life. Rather, silence is only the preparation taken by individuals to allow God to work in the entirety of their lives. Moreover, the accusations of quietism far exceed their actual presence in history. More often than not, Underhill claims, the appearance of quietism results from a looseness in language rather than a true embrace of the position.

[7] Principe notes as especially important the lecture given by Etienne Gilson at the inauguration of the chair in 'Histoire de la spiritualité' at the Institut Catholique de Paris in 1943. Ibid., 133. Although Gilson is primarily concerned with establishing the relationship between a history and theology of spirituality, he does speak of a purely spiritual world (monde des purs esprits) that transcends the order of the body (monde des choses sensibles et des corps). Etienne Gilson, *Théologie et histoire de la spiritualité*, Leçon inaugurale de la chaire

d'histoire de spiritualité prononcée à l'Institut Catholique de Paris, le 15 Novembre 1943 (Paris:Vrin, 1943), 12.

[8] Principe, 134. For this specific definition of spirituality Principe cites the *Oxford English Dictionary* (Vol.10, 624), though he mentions numerous other dictionaries that give similar definitions.

[9] Louis Dupré, *Passage to Modernity: An Essay in the Hermeneutics of Nature and Culture* (New Haven: Yale University Press, 1993).

[10] Ibid., 15-22.

[11] Ibid., 48-50.

[12] Ibid., 72-75. The issue of human persons as creators of meaning is not in and of itself problematic. As will be discussed in relation to the work of Bernard Lonergan, human beings do indeed discern and formulate meanings particular to their specific context. A problem arises, however, when we halt the process of developing meaning prematurely. Constructing an entirely instrumental view of the cosmos is possible, but this fails to take into consideration non-quantifiable aspects of human experience. The human person involves such matters as affectivity, religious experience, and the spiritual life which, although not measurable by the physical sciences, are no less a part of the person. Therefore, the discernment of meaning should not be brought to a close without taking into consideration such matters.

[13] Ibid., 72.

[14] Nominalism was a medieval philosophical/theological movement that drew a distinction between universal essences and their particular occurrences, and in some cases even denied the existence of the universal. In such a system, ideas have only a real rather than formal cause, and, "At that point the question how the world we know in our ideas relates to the real becomes a critical one." Ibid., 82. For the purposes of the present discussion, the problem of nominalism lies in the issue of the relationship between the understanding of God in our rationality and the manner in which God truly exists and acts. The nominalist position would hold that human beings cannot be certain that their ideas of God are accurate representations, and thus they can never truly know God. For a more in depth treatment of nominalism, see Justo L. Gonzalez, *A History of Christian Thought*, vol. II, *From Augustine to the Eve of the Reformation*, Rev. ed. (Nashville: Abingdon Press, 1987), 68-69, 317-324, and Armand A. Maurer, C.S.B., *Medieval Philosophy*, 2nd ed. The Etienne Gilson Series; 4 (Toronto: Pontifical Institute of Mediaeval Studies, 1982), 265-291.

[15] Dupré, 172-175.

[16] Ibid., 189.

[17] Ibid., 170-173.

[18] Ibid., 207-208.

[19] Ibid., 248.

[20] Jon Alexander, "What Do Recent Writers Mean by Spirituality," *Spirituality Today* 32 (1980): 248.

[21] Antinomianism was a theological movement that took the notion of salvation by faith alone to its extreme. It held that because salvation hinged solely on the dispensation of Grace, adherence to a moral law is of no use and individuals are not obliged to follow such an ethical guide. See, Justo L. González, *A History of Christian Thought*, vol. III, *From the Protestant Reformation to the Twentieth Century*, Rev. ed. (Nashville: Abingdon Press, 1987), 111-114, 147-148.

[22] Alexander specifically names A.A. Tanguerey's *The Spiritual Life* as representative of this perspective. Alexander, 249. Adolphe Tanquerey, *The Spiritual Life: A Treatise on Ascetical and Mystical Theology*, trans. Herman Brandeis (Tournai, Belgium: Desclée & Co., 1930).

[23] Alexander specifically names Reginald Garrigou-Lagrange as representative of this position. Ibid., 249-250. Reginald Garrigou-Lagrange, *The Three Ages of the Interior Life: Prelude of Eternal Life*, trans. M. Timothy Doyle (St. Louis: B. Herder Book Co., 1947-1948).

[24] Alexander, 251-252. Moreover, difficulty arises in the effort to discern between authentic and inauthentic spirituality. On a certain, perverse level, the actions of prejudiced individuals could be seen as an expression of their religious existence in a concrete situation. In light of this problem, a need remains for an understanding of spirituality that not only recognizes the experiential element of spirituality, but also provides a specific context for its expression and the means for discernment of spirits.

[25] William James, *Varieties of Religious Experience* (New York: Penguin Books, 1982), 381.

[26] Thomas Merton, *Contemplation in a World of Action* (Notre Dame, IN: University of Notre Dame Press, 1998), 8-11.

[27] Ibid., 135.

[28] Ibid., 128-140.

[29] Although this theme runs prominently in John of the Cross's work, consider the following example from *The Sayings of Light and Love*. "The Further you withdraw from earthly things the closer you approach heavenly things and the more you find in God." John of the Cross, *The Sayings of Light and Love*, 4:159, in *The Collected Works of John of the Cross*, Rev. ed. trans. Kieran Kavanaugh, O.C.D. and Otilio Rodriguez, O.C.D. (Washington, D.C.: ICS Publications, 1991), 97. In this book I will be using the following format to refer to classical works of spirituality. I will first provide the name of the work, followed by the chapter and verse (if numbered). Then I will provide the edition of the text I use, with the page of that work. Thus, the above quote may be found in Chapter Four, Verse 159 of *The Sayings of Light and Love*, which is on page 97 of Kavanaugh's and Rodriguez's edition of John of the Cross's collected works.

[30] Thérèse of Lisieux names her time before she entered the Carmelite monastery, the time "before I left the world." Thérèse of Lisieux, *The Story of a Soul: The Autobiography of St.*

Thérèse of Lisieux, 3rd ed. trans. John Clarke, O.C.D. (Washington, D.C.: ICS Publications, 1996), 112.

[31] Recall that the previously noted objection by Reinhold Niebuhr to mysticism (ftnt. 1) is based upon his reading of John of the Cross.

[32] Henry Suso's life was marked by practices as extreme as carrying on his back a cross into which he had driven nails that tore his flesh as he moved. Henry Suso, *The Exemplar*, 16, in *Henry Suso: The Exemplar with Two German Sermons*, ed. and trans. Frank Tobin The Classics of Western Spirituality: A Library of the Great Spiritual Masters (New York: Paulist Press, 1989), 89-91.

[33] For an in depth treatment of the life and writings of St. Francis see, *Francis of Assisi: Early Documents*, 3 vols., ed. Regis J. Armstrong, O.F.M. Cap., J.A. Wayne Hellmann, O.F.M. Conv., and William J. Short, O.F.M (New York, London, and Manila: New City Press, 1999) and, Arnaldo Fortini, *Francis of Assisi*, trans. Helen Moak (New York: Crossroad, 1981).

[34] Evelyn Underhill, *Practical Mysticism* (Columbus, OH: Ariel Press, 1986), 173-191.

[35] Underhill, *Mysticism*, 176-443.

[36] Underhill, *Practical Mysticism*, 38.

[37] Kieran Kavanaugh, O.C.D., "Introduction," in *Teresa of Avila: The Interior Castle*, trans. Kieran Kavanaugh, O.C.D. The Classics of Western Spirituality: A Library of the Great Spiritual Masters (New York: Paulist Press, 1979), 5.

[38] Underhill, *Mysticism*, 86.

[39] Howard Thurman, "Excerpt from 'Mysticism and Social Change,'" in *A Strange Freedom: The Best of Howard Thurman on Religious Experience and Public Life*, ed. Walter Earl Fluker and Catherine Tumber (Boston: Beacon Press, 1998), 111.

[40] Ibid., 116.

[41] Ibid., 117-120.

[42] David R. Loy, "The Religion of the Market," in *Visions of a New Earth: Religious Perspectives on Population, Consumption, and Ecology*, ed. Harold Coward and Daniel C. Maguire (Albany: State University of New York Press, 2000), 15-28.

[43] McGinn, 6.

[44] Johann Baptist Metz, *Followers of Christ: The Religious Life of the Church*, trans. Thomas Linton (New York: Paulist Press, 1978), 39-42.

[45] Michel de Certeau, "The Weakness of Believing: From the Body to Writing, a Christian Transit," in Graham Ward, ed., *The Certeau Reader* (Oxford: Blackwell Publishers, 2000),

226-236. See also, Philip Sheldrake, "Unending Desire: De Certeau's 'Mystics,'" *The Way: Supplements* 102 (2001): 44-45.

[46] James, 381-382.

[47] *Cloud of Unknowing*, ed. and trans., William Johnston (New York: Doubleday, 1973).

[48] Michel de Certeau, *La fable mystique: XVIe - XVIIe siècle* (France: Éditions Gallimard, 1982), 156-179.

[49] *Collected Works of Bernard Loneran*, vol. 3, *Insight: A Study of Human Understanding*, 5th rev. ed., eds. Frederick E. Crowe and Robert M. Doran (Toronto: University of Toronto Press, 1992), 299. Emphasis mine.

[50] *Collected Works of Bernard Lonergan*, vol. 5, *Understanding and Being: The Halifax Lectures on "Insight,"* eds. Frederick E. Crowe and Robert M. Doran (Toronto: University of Toronto Press, 1990), 36-38. For Lonergan's full treatment of the act of understanding, see chs. 1-8 of *Insight*.

[51] Lonergan, *Insight*, 296-303.

[52] Ibid., 636-639.

[53] To be faithful to the mystical tradition, I am not suggesting that human beings are capable of understanding the entirety of the mystical encounter with God. Rather, I am making the claim that as in other instances of theological understanding, human subjects are capable of understanding the content of the mystical experience in an "imperfect, analogous, obscure, and gradually developing" manner which is "nonetheless most profitable." Bernard Lonergan, *De Deo Trino II: Pars Systematica*, trans. John F. Brezovec (Rome: Gregorian University Press, 1964), 6.

[54] Bernard Lonergan, *Method in Theology*, 2nd ed. (New York: Herder and Herder, 1973; reprint, Toronto: University of Toronto Press, 1990, 1994, 1996), 269.

[55] Lonergan's full treatment of theological method is found in *Method*, especially chapters 5-14.

[56] Dunne, 3-6.

[57] In this dissertation I use the notions of political theology and political concerns, but this dissertation is not concerned with issues such as the relationship between church and state or the participation of the Christian in governmental policy, though these issues may arise as more work is done regarding the implications of the relevance of mysticism to everyday life. For this dissertation I am concerned with political theology and political concerns as they relate to the institutions and structures that guide human community, whether they are codified in law or governmental procedure or exist as societal norms. Matters such as racial or gender equality, for instance, are not necessarily guided by law but are concerns of political theology. Political theology, as will be demonstrated later, is concerned with examining the

extent to which human community is reflective of or participates in the biblical notion of the Kingdom of God.

[58] Lonergan, *Understanding and Being*, 35.

[59] Lonergan's use of this category will become clearer as the dissertation progresses. For now, describing the data of sense and consciousness as all the information available to human persons as they make their way in the world suffices. This may be a matter of paying attention to the five senses or to one's own functioning as a subject, both intellectually and affectively. Moreover, the data of consciousness importantly, is not limited to what the person knows, for much of human living consists of trying to make sense of the data.

[60] Lonergan, *Method*, 268.

[61] Lonergan, *Understanding and Being*, 35.

CHAPTER ONE
Mystical-Political Theology

Introduction

Having traced the problem of the split soul mentality, which has inhibited the application of mystical theology to political theology, and reasons for its predominance, the discussion now moves to the work of four theologians of the 20th century whose work helps to clarify the use of the term 'mystical-theology' in this book. The first pair of theologians, Evelyn Underhill and William Johnston, are scholars of mysticism whose work provides not only a descriptive account of the phenomenon of mystical experience in the Christian tradition, but also demonstrates that any attempt to separate the mystical life from the life of the community is mistaken. For Underhill, mystical union allows individuals to perceive clearly the true depths of Reality, and thus they become better able to act in accordance with God's loving will for the world. For Johnston, the mystical life of prayer both transforms the world by its very practice and in its inspiration of Christian persons to great action on behalf of the world. Taken together, the work of Underhill and Johnston presents a picture that clarifies how, by its very nature, mysticism is deeply involved in the affairs of human society. For Underhill and Johnston, any study of mysticism that fails to recognize this connection is unsatisfactory.

The second half of this chapter will be dedicated to the political theologies of Gustavo Gutiérrez and Dorothee Sölle. Gutiérrez argues persuasively for the political nature of any theological enterprise – either theologians support the existing establishment by failing to criticize current social structures or they resist the influence and impact of those structures by announcing the salvific message of the gospel. Sölle's political theology arises from her perception of the inadequacy of the existentialist theology that came to prominence in the 1960's and 70's. Such theology concentrates on individual believers to the neglect of the implications of the Christian faith for the community as a whole.

When the works of these theologians are considered collectively, the public dimension of the Christian faith becomes apparent, and thus mystical-political theology becomes a matter of elaborating the manner in which the spiritual life of the mystic is expressed in the larger arena of human society. The end result is an option for the theologian that stands in dialectical opposition to the split soul mentality, a choice, I contend, that is more faithful to the reality of the Western Christian tradition than the divorce between the interior and exterior lives.

Time and space constraints prevent a comprehensive treatment of the theologies of the four figures presented in this chapter. Therefore, I provide a select reading list of works on the issues of political and mystical theology in a footnote at the beginning of each section. Similarly, discussion of the theologians in this chapter will, for the most part, be limited to their major primary sources. Therefore, at the beginning of each discussion I provide an extended footnote for additional reading and secondary sources, with a more complete listing of primary works given in the bibliography.

Mysticism

The study of mysticism presents the contemporary student with complex problems.[1] Much of the difficulty comes from a lack of systematic study of mysticism until, roughly, the 16th and 17th centuries.[2] Prior to this time, theological reflection on mystical experience consisted largely of recording the particulars of the interior life from the perspective of individual mystics. Not surprisingly, this tactic led to great variety in the accounts of mystical experience and life as holy women and men sought to interpret the wisdom imparted by their experiences of the immediate presence of God. These interpretations could not help but be colored by individual concerns and socio-historical contexts.[3] Issues such as the authority of earlier spiritual guides and mystics or the importance of asceticism received greater or lesser attention depending upon the particular interests of individuals and the milieu in which they wrote. The concern of mystics prior to the 16th century, and to some extent after this, was not so much to develop a mystical theology that encompassed the experience of the entire Christian tradition, but to record the mystical life as each individual lived it.

Any attempt to present a mystical theology that attends to the wide scope of Western Christian mysticism runs the risk of neglecting certain aspects of that mystical tradition and overemphasizing others. The problem of the 'split soul' is the result of just such an oversight. Theologians have concentrated on the interior life of individual mystics to the neglect of the impact of mystical spirituality on exterior behavior. In an attempt to prevent such a mistake, I present here the work of two theologians who, though they largely agree with one another, bring their own particular lens to the study of mysticism. I hope that by providing their different perspectives on the topic of mystical theology any blind spots or overemphasized points in their theologies will be noted and compensated for.

Evelyn Underhill (1875-1941)

Evelyn Underhill was an Anglican theologian whose work focused on the manner in which the practical lives of the mystics and those who encountered them in life or through writings were affected by the mystical relationship with the Divine.[4] This, for Underhill, is far more important than any doctrine or specific teaching developed by mystics.[5] As such, her theological work is more concerned with the phenomenon of the mystical life as it is recorded by the mystics rather than with interpreting their wisdom regarding such issues as Christology, Trinitarian theology, or soteriology.[6] For example, Underhill utilizes the writings of Julian of Norwich to describe the mystical life to her readers,[7] but she does not deal with Julian's somewhat troubling assertion that all human beings were created at the same time,[8] which could lead to the accusation that Julian believed in the pre-existence of souls. A notable exception to this general avoidance of doctrine is Underhill's treatment of creation. This is not surprising, however, given her concern to communicate the manner in which the lives of the mystics are altered by their experience of union with the Divine. As such, her work is filled with descriptions of the mystics' perception of creation and the presence of the Divine in all aspects of Reality.[9]

Underhill's work demonstrates considerable development over her career. In the beginning of her theological endeavors, which may be marked with the publication of *Mysticism* in 1911, she advocated a "pure mysticism" in which the Divine is encountered as an impersonal infinite Reality. Hence, in this work she rarely mentions the role or identity of Christ in the mystical life. She does, however, make two concessions to a Christocentric mysticism. First, she acknowledges the role of Christ in the spiritual lives of many of the mystics she treats in this work, and secondly, she makes the claim that Christianity is the best path to the Divine because of its emphasis on historical expression, as emphasized in the doctrine of the Incarnation.[10] Despite these allowances, however, only much later under the direction of Baron Friedrich von Hügel, did Underhill herself ascribe to a distinctly Christian brand of mysticism.[11]

This transition to a Christocentric position was aided not only by her spiritual director, but also by her increasing awareness of the implications of the Incarnation for her distinctly practical brand of mysticism. Early on, Underhill recognized that mysticism was not solely a matter of an individual's relationship with the Divine. For her, mystical union was more than a matter of a quietist introversion. The mystical life gives energy to human activities in the world, and moreover, the truths received by the mystics enable them to become great sources of good in the world.[12] In the figure of Christ, Underhill finds the expression of the meeting between the divine and human elements of creation. Without this meeting place for the spiritual and the physical, what remains is either a theism that fails to accord adequate attention to the world and one's neighbors therein, or a situation in which individuals concentrate on societal issues to the neglect of the spiritual life. Only in the person and work of Christ do these two aspects become recognizable as constitutive parts of one Reality.[13]

In defining the characteristics of mysticism, Underhill sets herself in direct opposition to William James because of his concentration on the mystical experience as an incidence of profound spiritual awareness that is passive and somehow separated from the rest of human living.[14] For Underhill, mysticism is a matter of striving toward God, an "organic process which involves the perfect consummation of the love of God."[15] Mysticism is a continual growing toward God that becomes an element of every aspect of life.

In distinguishing her work from that of James, Underhill sets forth the following four distinguishing features. First, mysticism is not passive; it is an active and practical matter towards which individuals must travel a rigorous spiritual path in order to arrive at a life lived in union with the Divine. It is a matter of intuiting an absolute truth and seeking it out, akin to Plotinus's notion of "the flight of the Alone to the Alone."[16] For Underhill, individuals seek deeper relationship with the Divine; it is not merely given.[17]

Thinking of Underhill as holding to a Pelagian notion that the attainment of the mystical life is entirely within the power of human persons would be mistaken, however. Rather, a great deal of the mystical life is a matter of cleansing one's perceptions in order to be able to encounter both the world and God as they truly exist. In order to listen to the voice of God, people must first strive to hear it, and secondly, know how to do so.[18] As such, mysticism for Underhill involves both activity and passivity, but the latter cannot be effective without a great deal of preparation by the former.

Secondly, "the aims of mysticism are wholly transcendental and spiritual."[19] At first, this statement may be appear to be at odds with my claim that Underhill's mystics are actively engaged in the world and that her mystical theology helps to open the door for a mystical-political theology. This would be erroneous, however, for such a position assumes that a life focused on the spiritual does so to the neglect of the world. Indeed, Underhill is quick to point out that mystics do not neglect their duties to the community in which they are located.[20] Rather, Underhill's claim here may be read as a reaction to a dramatic rise of interest in magic or the occult in the early 20th century. In fact, Underhill at an early period in her life belonged to the occult group known as the Society of the Golden Dawn, "which was dedicated to a communal search for the world of spirits through ritual."[21] Authentic mysticism, unlike pursuits of the magical or occult, does not manipulate or rearrange the physical reality of the world or other persons for personal benefit. Rather, authentic mystical experience desires nothing other than the presence of the Divine. Temporary concerns such as the acquisition of wealth or power fall away, and because of the mystical encounter with Infinite Love, the mystic "will spend himself unceasingly for other men, [and] become an 'agent of Eternal Goodness.'"[22] This sentiment is echoed in Underhill's small work, *Concerning the Inner Life*, which she addressed to a school of clergy in the North of England. She writes, "We observe then that two of the three things for which our souls are made are matters of attitude of relation: adoration and awe. Unless those two are right, the last of the triad, service, won't be right."[23] For Underhill then, the spiritual life feeds and empowers a life of service to others.

Thirdly, Underhill describes the object of mysticism as "not merely the Reality of all that is, but also a living and personal object of love."[24] For the mystics, infinite love is the operative principle in their relationships with God, and infinite love separates the mystical life from other pursuits of the Divine which hold knowledge of God as their primary goal. This is not to say, however, that knowledge or wisdom is not gained from the mystical encounter. Rather, Underhill's point is that the mystical life cannot be attained by acts of reason. For her, love is the only path that reaches its culmination in mystical union with the Divine,[25] and "[w]e only know a thing by uniting with it; by assimilating it; by an interpretation of it and ourselves."[26] Moreover, the path of love that strives for union with God, who is love, enables the mystics to experience love more deeply, and this encounter with Infinite Love empowers the mystics to live in love in the world.[27]

Fourthly, Underhill describes mysticism as a definite psychological experience.[28] By this somewhat enigmatic phrase she attempts to convey the notion that the mystical life entails a complete alteration to the entirety of life. No aspect of living is untouched by an awareness of the loving presence of the Divine. All thoughts, desires, and actions are affected by this loving presence.   One's manner of inhabiting the world has been profoundly changed.[29]

To reach a psychological state in which the only motivation for all actions is love is a long process that Underhill terms the "mystic way."[30] Although her discussion of the mystic way may generally be summarized as consisting of purgation, illumination, and union, she includes the additional element of this path, conversion, which precedes purgation, and the dark night of the soul, which is a final interior purification of the self performed by God, rather than the mystic. I will now turn to a description of her work on the mystic way in an attempt to further clarify her theology of mysticism, which allows for a mystical-political theology.

Underhill's mystical path begins with the experience of a mystical conversion, which may be described as an awakening of the self to depths of Reality which were not previously realized. Certain life experiences, such as debilitating pain, exquisite beauty, or deep emotion are charged with such intensity that they disrupt the inner balance of the self, and individuals must readjust the manner in which they inhabit the world accordingly.[31]   For mystics, then, this adjustment involves embarking on the journey of purgation, illumination, and union which culminates in a life lived in profound awareness of the presence of God.

Such conversion experiences, according to Underhill, may be sudden, life-changing moments that jolt certain individuals to a larger world-consciousness and passion for God, or they may be a gradual process that opens them to wider and deeper awareness of Reality over an extended period of time.[32] As an example of the former, Underhill points to Francis of Assisi, whose mystical life began with his famous call from the crucifix in the church of San Damiano to "fix my church."[33]   Importantly, Underhill recognizes Francis's well-known and extended flight from God.   For approximately ten years, Francis had been hearing, but failing to respond thereto, the intimations of a call to a different way of spiritual life. However, only after that moment in the church did the presence of God so profoundly enter his life that he began to travel the mystic way.[34] The great Quaker mystic, George Fox, on the other hand, exhibits a mystical conversion of the more gradual type. Fox's spiritual life was marked by a gently progressive process that eventually moved Fox to the next stage of Underhill's mystic way, that of purgation.[35]

An important distinction should be drawn here.   Underhill defines mysticism as "the art of union with Reality" and the individual mystic as "the person who has attained this union in greater or less degree; or who aims at and believes in such attainment."[36] But, in the cases of the great mystics of the tradition, that is, those remarkable individuals whom the church (broadly speaking) has recognized as having experienced the unitive life, a conversion experience marks an awakening to deeper levels of Reality which had previously gone unnoticed. These persons then live life in a manner characterized by the seeking of union with this newly discovered Reality, and they are recognized as the spiritual giants of the Western Christian tradition. This is not to say that for Underhill the first mystical experience of a person's life necessarily leads to the next step on the mystic path. Some persons may encounter the Divine on the level of union, but do not feel called to pursue life lived in such intimate relation with the Divine.[37] Rather, such "ordinary mystics" continue to live a life whose ordinary flow may or may not be interrupted by experiences of union with God.

For the purposes of this discussion, a significant element of Underhill's description of the awakening of the self to the mystical life is that even though the mystical experience reveals aspects of Reality that were previously unknown, a certitude of the unity of Reality accompanies such an encounter. She writes, "The spiritual life we wish to study is *one life*, based on experience of one Reality."[38] Thus, though she wishes to reserve a special place for the mystics, Underhill does not wish to separate them from the world and persons encountered therein. Her work stands in direct opposition to the split soul.

The next stage in Underhill's mystic path is that of the purgation of the self. In the conversion experience, individuals awaken to the deeper levels of Reality that have previously gone unnoticed. However, understanding or unfettered access to these deeper elements does not necessarily follow awareness of them. Rather, the self, according to Underhill, must be reeducated in order to cast aside old concepts and manners of operating in the world in order to embrace Reality as it was encountered in the conversion experience.[39]

Such a process of purgation involves elimination from the self of anything not in congruence with the newfound awareness of Reality. It is a cleansing of the lens of perception through which the Divine and Reality are viewed.[40] For those called to the mystic life, the purgative stage of the mystic way is an almost automatic course following the conversion experience, for the awareness of the beauty and love of the Divine virtually compels mystics to rid themselves of the old manner of relating to the world, which is now understood to be inadequate.[41]

As the preceding paragraphs indicate, the process of purgation is, at its heart, a matter of training the self so as to focus on Reality in such a way that its infinite nature, infused as it is at all times and places with the presence of the Divine, becomes a fundamental aspect of the manner in which mystics inhabit the world. To accomplish this goal, they must leave behind all desires that either inhibit their approach to the Divine or actively pull them away. As such, many mystics have turned to sometimes extreme ascetic practices in an effort to deny themselves worldly pleasure so as to be better able to concentrate on spiritual growth.[42]

The above is not to say that Underhill understood the purgative stage to be solely a matter of self-denial. Rather, its goal is to gain a detachment from the manner in which the mystic formerly inhabited the world, and this may or not be accomplished through the ascetic life. The purgative stage concerns attitude rather than action, and once this detachment is reached, individuals are free to deepen their relationships with Reality unhindered by previous misconceptions or misplaced desires.[43]

The freedom conferred by purgation, then, opens new avenues of action which were previously unavailable. If individuals are centered on advancement in the workplace, then a great deal of their energy will be consumed by that goal. They may not be able to devote adequate attention to the moments of life in which glimpses of the true nature of Reality may be had or pursued, and courses of action that foster such moments may not be taken or even considered. Moreover, with such emphasis on success and advancement in the workplace people may act toward others in a decidedly unloving manner in an attempt to 'get a leg up' on the competition or receive greater compensation. With their center of life properly located through the detachment of purgation, however, individuals are free to devote time and energy to the transcendent aspects of life. Thus, although purgation involves a stripping away of certain aspects of the self that existed prior to the conversion experience, it also adds a profound sense of freedom, for false attachments are cast aside and no longer impede the pursuit of the infinite.

When those elements of life that hinder relationship with the Divine are removed through the process of purgation, and the self is refocused on the infinite, the mystic is ready to enter the phase of Underhill's mystic path known as illumination. At this point, individuals encounter the Divine in mystical union much more frequently because the hindrances to such experience have been eliminated through the process of purgation. This being the case, the sudden, unexpected inbreaking of mystical awareness of the presence of the Divine that characterized the time before and including mystical conversion is replaced by a life in which such encounters are quite frequent.[44]

This stage of illumination is distinguished from the final phase of Underhill's mystic path, union, in that the experience of mystical union appears to be intermittent rather than continual. This is not to say that the times spent outside of mystical union are not affected by the spiritual awareness fostered by mystical illumination. Rather, Underhill notes that individuals experience an increased perception of the presence of the Divine in the natural world, and their life is affected accordingly. The brilliant splendor of creation is no longer hidden, and the world is indeed a brighter place.[45]

The fourth stage of Underhill's mystical path, the dark night of the soul, enables mystics to live a life of union with God that is no longer interrupted by so-called ordinary experiences. Although this stage paves the way for such a life, it is a lonely and often frightening time because unlike the frequent experiences of union with the Divine in the stage of illumination, God can no longer be found anywhere. The point of this removal of the divine presence from the lives of the mystics is to effect a final purification in which individuals finally come to realize their utter dependence upon the Divine. Once this reality is known and accepted by the mystics, they emerge from the darkness into the light of the unitive life.[46]

The fifth stage of Underhill's mystic path is the unitive life, which is marked by the continual presence of union with the Divine. Such absorption into the Divine life entails the free participation in the Eternal because of the total surrender of false selfhood. The last remnants of that which maintained the separation between the mystics and the Divine have been eliminated. The will of God becomes their will, and thus they become agents of divine activity on earth.[47] Given the gospel's emphasis on love of neighbor and care for those in need, Underhill's mysticism takes on a social dimension that flies in the face of those arguments accusing mystics of forsaking the world. Such actions, moreover, are empowered by the conviction that they are acting in accordance with the divine will. The constraints of social expectations or limitations no longer apply as they go about their work. If an unjust social system is to fall, someone must push it, and with the removal of selfishness in purgation, mystics become better able to work for social orders that more closely reflect the will of the divine.

A second corporate dimension to Underhill's mysticism is that others are drawn to the spiritual vitality of the mystics. They become sources of inspiration and spiritual wisdom from which others may draw strength to challenge or correct injustice. The unitive life not only draws individuals into union with God, but also turns the attention of others toward the Divine.[48] Circles of union and unselfish behaviors centered on justice and peace radiate from the mystics, and great things can be done.[49] Underhill's mysticism is anything but a matter of cultivating the interior life to the exclusion of the exterior. The inner life bears fruit in the world, and mysticism becomes a great force for social change.

William Johnston (1925-)[50]

The mystical theology of William Johnston may be characterized as a response to a spiritual hunger in the Western hemishpere that has resulted from the domination of the scientific method in all aspects of human life. He writes the following in his, *Arise My Love; Mysticism for a New Era.*

> It is hardly surprising if the scientific mentality spread to the masses of the people, creating a new culture and a new consciousness that, abhorring abstract thinking, adopted a practical, empirical approach to life.[51]

As such, theology finds itself in a predicament; the reality of God is not a matter of empirical data in a scientific sense. Academics may study how individuals and cultures respond to the Divine, but they are faced with great difficulty when discussing the infinite reality that is God.[52] Theology becomes primarily a discussion not of God, but of previously formulated dogmas and doctrines. Thus, theologians tend to concentrate on elaborating upon sure and certain theological propositions rather than seeking to penetrate the divine mystery.[53] Such theology, Johnston contends, neglects another source for knowledge of the Divine, the knowledge born of love of God.[54]

The source of such knowledge is relationship with the Divine, which arises from prayer. Thus, Johnston's mystical theology may be summarized as a journey of prayer. The individual who ascends the mystical mountain moves from a dualistic sense of a God removed from the earthly world to a life of union with God and all of creation.[55] Although this upward sense of progress is present in Johnston's work, he differs from Underhill insofar as he understands spiritual growth as proceeding in a less linear fashion. Whereas Underhill views the mystical path as proceeding through the four stages of conversion, purgation, illumination, and union, Johnston's description entails only two identifiable stages, contemplation and the mystical life.[56]

In response to what he perceives to be the neglect of the knowledge of love in the Western world, Johnston's journey of prayer is profoundly influenced by the Eastern religions of Buddhism, Hinduism, and Islam, traditions whose history has been marked by contemplation rather than scientific discussion of the Divine.[57] The contribution of these religious traditions is that they emphasize an apophatic dimension, which, he claims, has been largely lost in recent times. For Johnston, then, the great contribution of Buddhism consists of the reminder to Christians not to become too attached to words and formulations, but to be more intensely aware of the reality to which they point.[58]

Christianity, on the other hand, with its tradition of prophetic mysticism and assertion of the indwelling of the Divine, emphasizes that any religious experience not grounded in the world with concrete implications for and actions in the world is ill-suited to confront socio-political structures that inhibit the flourishing of life.[59] The religions of the world thus have much to learn from one another. Though they differ in their doctrinal formulations and institutional structures, various religious traditions meet each other in the mystical experience. This awareness of the necessity of both the apophatic and the kataphatic fuels Johnston's mystical theology.[60]

Insistence on both aspects of mysticism sets the stage for Johnston's distinctly Trinitarian mystical theology. Christians are called to consider and imitate the life of Christ, the Word of God. Because human persons are able to look upon the example of Christ and form concepts applicable to their own lives, reflection upon the Word comprises the kataphatic element of Johnston's mystical theology. This results in the indwelling of Christ in the believer who becomes aware of and participates in the love that binds the Father and the Son. This love is beyond the conceptual awareness of the human person, and makes available the apophatic awareness and presence of God the Father.[61] This, Johnston claims, is the mysticism of Jesus Christ. At the point of his baptism, Jesus experienced with the 'inner eye of love,' which is the gift of the Spirit, his special relationship to the Father. Christian mystics are called to imitate the mystical life of Christ, and such a distinctly Christian mystical life is focused on the mystery of Christ in Scripture and sacrament.[62] The kataphatic and apophatic come together to form the spiritual life of Christian persons.

In a certain sense, Johnston perceives an objective element to Christian mysticism not present in the mysticism of other religions that stress the unity of all being. However, this objectivity is present in Johnston's theology only insofar as persons are committed to something that is greater than themselves. Christian mystics, though united with God, are not God, and thus in the Christian mystical experience individuals transcend themselves to focus on the ground of all being. Johnston writes:

I become my true self, hear myself called by name and cry out: 'Abba, Father!' This is the experience in which I become the other while remaining myself. Or, more correctly, I become the other and become myself. Paradoxical, you will say. Yes. Mysticism is full of paradox.[63]

The orientation to the mystery of Christ is simultaneously at the very core of the spiritual lives of Christian mystics and extends beyond the lives of these individuals to embrace all of creation.[64]

Johnston's journey of prayer centered on the mystery of Christ is primarily a matter of contemplative prayer.[65] This is not to say, however, that Johnston rejects the need for or efficacy of discursive prayer. Rather, his point is that the mystical ascent to God is marked by the recognition that resting in the knowledge *that* God exists is more important for the mystic than seeking to offer prayers of petition or trying to figure out *what* God is or *how* God works.[66] Discursive prayer has its place, but contemplative prayer marks the journey of the mystic.

Mystical contemplation, moreover, consists of different ways of being profoundly aware of God's presence. First, Johnston identifies 'acquired contemplation,' in which the prayer comes from the will of human persons, and he further subdivides this category into 'affective prayer' and 'prayer of simplicity.' In the former, mystics, having left behind reasoning and thinking in prayer, are so overcome by the presence of the Divine that reactions such as short outbursts or tears come forth unbidden. In the latter, individuals focus their minds and hearts on God through the repetition of a short phrase that serves to direct all of their energies toward the Divine.[67] Johnston's second category of mystical contemplation is that of 'infused contemplation.'[68] Such experiences are marked by the sense that God is so present to individuals that they cannot help but state that God approaches them, rather than they who draw near to the Divine.[69]

In these states of mystical contemplation, God is known not through the intellect, but through the interior life of the soul. Mystics encounter the Divine through love, and thus the knowledge gained is beyond all language, symbol, or concept. In agreement with the scholastics, Johnston holds that God communicates the Divine presence in a manner that bypasses the faculties of reason and the senses.[70] In other words, knowing that God exists and is love is one thing, but experiencing that existence and love at the very core of one's being is quite another.

As individuals move from the contemplative life to the mystical life, a profound and often painful stage takes place in their prayer life. Often described as the 'Dark Night,' this process, according to Johnston, is the result of the cleansing of the surface levels of the psyche accomplished through the relinquishing of the activities of reasoning about and forming images of God. When this takes place, the subconscious levels rise to the surface, and these too must be purified. Specifically, individuals come face to face with their 'shadow,' which Johnston describes in the following quotation.

> In the shadow lie all the parts of our personality that we have repressed or refused to face. Here lie the fears and anxieties, the frustrations and the traumas, the hurts and the resentments that we [have] accumulated... Here lies the terrible fear of death that we have never confronted. [71]

Moreover, the shadow of humanity as a whole rises to the consciousness of the individual, and when faced with these new perceptions of reality, God seems to be quite absent. [72]

Fortunately for the mystic, the sense of Divine absence is temporary, for in coming to terms with the shadow side of both the person and the human community, the final impediments to a life lived in union with God are removed. The anxieties and fears that lead to a rejection of the love of God are eliminated. Drawing again on John of the Cross, Johnston writes that the soul is like a wet log which when flame is first applied puts forth ugly, choking smoke. But when the log dries, it catches fire and is a light and source of comfort. Unlike the log, however, the soul is not consumed by the fire, but continues to exist in a purified state. [73]

Having emerged from the dark night, the mystic now lives a life of union with the Divine. Although this union is marked by detachment from material possessions, Johnston's mystical theology is far from dualistic. In fact, the overly dualistic interpretation of the mystical life in Western Christianity is what attracts Johnston to the religions of the East. Detachment, according to Johnston, is ultimately a question of freedom. If persons are not attached to certain possessions or a particular standard of living, they are free to act in accordance with the Divine will. [74] God is present in all things, and thus the world and the body may be vehicles for encountering the Divine, but the will and presence of God, which sustain creation, are more important than that which mediates them. In a mystical paradox, creation is good, but its goodness comes from its source, and as the basis of that goodness, God is the proper focus of the mystical life. Therefore, the mystic lives a life of detachment.

Johnston's mystical theology appears at first glance to fit precisely into the perception of mysticism that this book opposes, namely that mysticism is incapable of addressing the social issues that plague human society.

However, Johnston is indeed concerned about social issues and contends that mysticism is particularly well suited for taking up such matters. First, mystics are profoundly aware that existence is a unity. Although the constitutive elements of being possess their own particularity, the universe is bound together by the spirit of God, and the mystics, through the wisdom and knowledge received in their prayer lives, are profoundly aware of this. Such an awareness leads to a realization that human lives are intricately connected with the lives of others and the environment in which all human persons live. Dialogue on social issues, according to Johnston, will only bear fruit if the human community is united in mind and heart, and mysticism opens the way such unity.[75]

Secondly, the knowledge of the true self that is gained through the purification of the deeper levels of the psyche enables the mystic to make better decisions in the political and social realms because the affairs of everyday life enter the prayer life, and the prayer life enters everyday affairs.[76] Proper action thus arises spontaneously from the mystical life, and the wisdom gained in mystical union serves as a resource for discernment regarding such action.[77] The mystical life informs the actions of individuals as they seek to address the social ills of the community.

Thirdly, the mystics' growth in detachment and self-emptying invests them with extraordinary courage to confront the socio-political powers and structures that are destructive of life.[78] Because the mystic has been able to overcome attachment to material wealth and even physical well-being, such persons cannot be intimidated by the threat of personal loss, sickness or death. Even such activist figures as Mahatma Gandhi and Martin Luther King, Jr. were sunk deep in prayer – discursive, contemplative, perhaps even mystical. The spiritual lives of these individuals allowed them to face the destructive forces of the world with courage even at the cost of their lives, and this taproot of prayer continues to inspire people today to challenge oppressive social and political structures. Even after their tragic deaths, the social reforms and programs of Gandhi and Dr. King live on because their advocacy on behalf of the marginalized arose out of prayer rather than a drive for personal benefit.

Fourthly, and finally, mystical contemplatives have access to what Johnston terms 'the power of being.' Even when they sit in contemplation, which is void of any discursive element, the mystic is "radiating energy to the whole universe."[79] Although such an expression may be viewed with skepticism by those at the beginning of the 21st century, the notion possesses a precedent in *The Cloud of Unknowing*. The following is found therein.

For I tell you this, one loving blind desire for God alone is more valuable in itself, more pleasing to God and to the saints, more beneficial to your own growth, and more helpful to your friends, both living and dead, than anything else you could do.[80]

The fruits of contemplation are thus not limited to the life of individuals, but extend out to those around them. For Johnston, the mystical life necessarily involves a social dimension, whether through direct action or the mysterious benefits of contemplation.

Political Theology

In its most general sense, the notion of political theology refers to the recognition of the fact that the salvation proclaimed and wrought by Jesus Christ bears not only on the interior spirituality of individuals but also on the manner in which human society is organized and sustained.[81] As Paul Lakeland puts it, "At its simplest, it [political theology] believes that living the Christian life in the world *is* salvation."[82] The relationship between God and humanity is revealed and nourished in all aspects of human life, including the socio-political structures that govern human community. Political theology is the attempt to understand and explain this relationship in a manner that encourages the growth and flourishing of human community as the arena in which the relationship between God and humanity is expressed.[83] As such, political theology may be generically defined as reflection upon the working out and development of the relationship between God and humanity and acting for the advancement of this relationship in the socio-political context in which human persons go about their daily lives.

As with the previously discussed mystical theology, a comprehensive treatment of political theology far exceeds the scope of this work. Therefore, in the following pages I present the work of two noted political theologians, Gustavo Gutiérrez and Dorothee Sölle, in order to give a more concrete understanding of political theology. Stating the general, and rather obvious, principle that the Christian faith says much about the way Christian persons treat other human beings is one thing. Undertaking an explanation as to how and why the Christian faith bears directly on the political lives of believers is another. For both Gutiérrez and Sölle, the socio-political structures of the human community today fall short of the Kingdom of God whose coming is announced in the Gospel, and therefore the task of political theologians is to explicate this shortcoming and advocate action that cultivates a more just human society that bears greater resemblance to the Kingdom.[84]

Gustavo Gutiérrez (1928-)

In his most well known work, *A Theology of Liberation*, Gustavo Gutiérrez puts forth the idea that developing a theology of liberation is a matter of understanding the relationship between human liberation in the world and the salvific work of Christ.[85] This question, Gutiérrez claims, is integral to all Christian theology because the Christian faith has always been based on a notion of community, and thus all theology at least implicitly addresses the issue.[86] In other words, all theology is political for Gutiérrez because all theology bears upon and is affected by the "polis" in which human beings live with one another.[87]

In the twentieth century, theology renewed its awareness of its political nature in light of religious concerns regarding the Enlightenment. Prior to this renewal on the part of the so-called 'new political theology,'[88] theology was inattentive to or unable to resist the effects of the advent of modernity. Like Dupré, Gutiérrez sees an increased awareness in the 18th century of humanity's ability to affect the world in which persons live and create meanings.[89] Although such cognizance of humanity's ability to modify its historical situation would later be used by political theologians to present a notion of liberation and salvation in history, the people of the 18th century were dealing with the effects of the social movements of the time that emphasized individual liberty and the scientific revolution initiated by Galileo in the 16th century. These two factors, according to Gutiérrez, contributed to the widespread removal of religious belief and practice from the civil sphere and the breakup of Christendom.[90] Determining exactly how these two factors contribute to one another is difficult, and such a study would far exceed the purposes of the present work. For the current discussion, briefly discussing Gutiérrez's understanding of how they assisted in the de-politicization of religious belief in the modern age shall have to suffice.

Gutiérrez describes the social trend of the 18th century as demanding "individual liberties within the core of society, and this was the origin of the famous distinction between the citizen and the person, that is to say, between public and private worlds."[91] Religious freedom was included with these individual liberties, and religious freedom, and the expression thereof, became increasingly identified with the private world. Moreover, the scientific revolution initiated in the 16th century began to remove the necessity of God from the natural processes of the world. As a result, the 18th century became, to use Gutiérrez's terminology, "methodologically atheist."[92] Such a perspective began to affect political and philosophical thinking, and the outcome was a widely-held belief that the state was to be completely distinct from religiosity and accountable only to political criteria. This mindset of the separation of religious faith from socio-historical concerns is the perspective that Gutiérrez's political theology of liberation and salvation seeks to address.

Resistance to the removal of God from political matters, however, was limited by a lack of practical application of the rejection of modernity on the part of the church in doctrinal statements. Though not limited to the Roman Catholic Church, this rejection is most explicit in the papal documents that address the issues raised by modernity. These documents, according to Gutiérrez, are concerned primarily with three topics. First, the papacy was concerned that a secular society would potentially endanger the salvation of individuals.[93] With the religious liberty envisioned by the Enlightenment thinkers, people were no longer required to participate in a *specifically* Catholic society. Thus, by not applying the Catholic Church's rejection of modernity, people were free to choose which religion best suited them or even reject Christianity altogether while believing themselves not to be placing their souls at risk.

Secondly, the papal documents claimed that a Catholic social order was necessary in order to prevent humanity's natural tendency toward evil from leading individuals astray. Not only would the freedoms associated with modernity lead to the notion that salvation was possible outside the church, but the church would lose its ability to keep its flock on the right path. Many souls could be lost because the Church would no longer be able to oversee the religious lives of the people. Moreover, the unity fostered by such a normative role for the church would be lost.[94] Without such a unifying presence, society would be at a greater risk of disintegration, and its members would be forced to deal with all of the difficulties associated with social instability.

Thirdly, the popes were concerned that the Church would be threatened by the power of the state. To work for the salvation of souls, the Church needed to be absolutely free in its activity.[95] If the Church were to be required to be absent from certain elements of life, then its salvific mission would be compromised, and the fate of many souls would be negatively affected.

Although the Church at first rejected the social and philosophical changes of the Enlightenment, it gradually came to accept many of them. According to Gutiérrez, the first explicit step in this movement, though as a practical matter the Church had already begun to move toward granting its assent,[96] was an acknowledgment that although civil government was not the ideal situation, good could be accomplished through it. Such capitulation to the civil authorities was conditional, however, for a secular government was only to be accepted if the ideal of a Christian society was impossible to achieve.[97]

According to Gutiérrez, although this preliminary engagement with modernity was fraught with danger regarding the separation of the spiritual and the political, it opened the door for a theological renewal in the beginning of the 20th century. He writes the following of this "renovation of theology."

> Actually, it was a matter of a moderate and partial assimilation of certain aspects of the modern spirit: a critical attitude, a sense of history, a specific mentality, the value of subjectivity, a democratic spirit, appreciation of human progress, openness to contemporary philosophic currents, etc.[98]

This theological renovation paved the way for the Second Vatican Council, which, among many other things, embraced many of the scientific, philosophic, and political trends associated with the Enlightenment that had been previously rejected or given only lukewarm approval.[99] Moreover, the Council called for theological dialogue with the world as it exists in light of modernity in an effort to answer the question as to how the gospel may be preached to the nations in non-Christian social orders. Within this open dialogue Gutiérrez perceives the arrival of the aforementioned "new political theology."

The political theology that arose in response to the new dialogue with modernity and its issues is in large part a response to the Enlightenment's critique of religion and society. Gutiérrez's political theology is an attempt to respond to Enlightenment thinking and recover theology's role in the *polis* of human community by calling to mind the historical element of eschatology in light of the notion of personal freedom that is valued so highly by modernity.[100] Although Gutiérrez does not advocate a return to Christendom, he is insistent that the eschatological dimension of the Christian faith bears directly on human community. The Kingdom is coming, and Christians are to prepare and work for this coming reality through the exercise of their personal freedom in the construction of just societies. This, then, is the context of Gutiérrez's theological work as it seeks to establish the relationship between liberation and salvation.

Gutiérrez's understanding of liberation entails the release of the less powerful in society from the oppression and suffering that results from a socio-economic system that benefits the more powerful and works to keep those individuals in their position of power.[101] Such systems are in many ways the result of the unchecked pursuit of the ideals of freedom and democracy that arose in modernity, especially as manifested in the unrestrained pursuit of economic development.[102] In such situations, the freedom that is claimed to be present for all members of society is in actuality only an abstract reality for the great majority of the people. Practically speaking, the options available to individuals who are not in advantaged positions are greatly limited in comparison to the more powerful members of that society, and liberation would thus be a matter of enabling a practical freedom for all members of society.

Gutiérrez defines the other piece of his political theology, salvation, as the "communion of human beings with God and one another."[103] As such, salvation and liberation are inextricably linked because a true communion of human beings and God cannot be based upon a human community in which inequality and oppression are characteristic. Moreover, because such communion is realized in the salvific work of Christ, it becomes apparent that sin is not only an obstacle to participation in the world to come, but is also a socio-historical reality that resists the saving activity of Christ in the world.[104]

With regard to the eschatological dimension of salvation, Gutiérrez emphasizes that the eschatological promise of the Bible is an historical promise marked by the transformation of human society from being characterized by social, economic, and political iniquity to an exemplification of justice.[105] Although eschatology has traditionally been associated with the so-called "last things" or the end of the world, Gutiérrez reminds his readers that such an emphasis on the future saving activity of God gives meaning to the present human situation because the eschatological promise will be fulfilled through history.[106] Therefore, according to Gutiérrez, the eschatological issues of God's final judgment and saving activity require a commitment to the historical present that is already participating in the eschatological promise.

Gutiérrez's emphasis on salvation as a socio-historical reality underlines the notion that the Kingdom of God is to be reality here on earth. The presence of the Kingdom is marked by a society of peace and justice in which all persons are free from oppression and poverty.[107] For Gutiérrez, moreover, the coming of the Kingdom involves human participation.[108] Therefore, the use of Christianity to placate the poor and oppressed with a promise of reward in the afterlife runs counter to the message of the gospel.[109] Here is spelled out more clearly Gutiérrez's connection between salvation and liberation. The redemption associated with the coming of the Kingdom requires that Christians actively resist those social and political structures that currently bind human persons in situations of poverty and oppression. In order to participate in the coming of the Kingdom, followers of Christ must act in accordance with the ideals characteristic of such a socio-historical reality.

For Gutiérrez, acting in accordance with the ideals of the coming of the Kingdom of God entails what he names "conversion to the neighbor." This notion is based upon the understanding of every human person as a temple of God. The spirit of God is present and active in all people, and thus the Divine may be encountered in every human person.[110] Such an understanding of the presence of God in all persons, according to Gutiérrez, has implications for anyone who claims to know and love God. He writes, "If humanity, each person, is the living temple of God, we meet God in our encounter with others; we encounter God in the commitment to the historical process of humankind."[111] Thus, the conversion to the neighbor envisioned by Gutiérrez involves working for the justice of God in the temples of God, human beings.

A second element of working toward liberation in history involves a reexamination of history from the 'other' side, for gaining an appreciation of the conditions from which liberation is a necessary aspect of the Kingdom is impossible if attention is paid only to the history written by those who have benefited from those conditions.[112] If Christian persons are to stand in solidarity with their neighbors, they must be aware of those events that have led up to the present situation. He writes:

> Our approach to the past must be motivated not by nostalgia but by hope; not by a fixation upon former painful and traumatic occurrences, but by present suffering and the conviction that only a people which has a memory can transform the situation it is in and build a different world.[113]

By gaining an understanding of the historical and cultural factors that have given rise to the reality of sinful social structures, the church is better able to work for the liberation of the oppressed and participate in the coming of the Kingdom.

The role of a political theology, then, is not only to examine and explicate the connection between Christian salvation and liberation in human history, but it is also an effort to bring about more fully the Kingdom of God. Theology, according to Gutiérrez, serves as critical reflection on Christian praxis,[114] which involves living a life that is based upon faith. "Communion with the Lord inescapably means a Christian life centered around a concrete and creative commitment of service to others."[115] Theological reflection on an attempt to live according to such a Christian praxis thus involves the examination of the actions taken by individuals and societies in light of the Word of God in an effort to determine whether or not they foster the justice-based community that is characteristic of the Kingdom.[116]

Political theology and praxis, however, do not involve the colonization of the social sciences, whose analyses have provided a great deal of material upon which political theology has reflected. Theologians should not take upon themselves to do the work of economists or political scientists. To do so would be to risk becoming irrelevant because of a confusion of methods and categories. Rather, the political theologian is to reflect upon the issues identified by the social sciences in light of the need for salvation and liberation.[117] In other words, the task of the theologian is not to develop strategies for maximum economic development, but to assess the extent to which such policies work toward the liberation of the oppressed and thus work for the coming of the Kingdom.

Finally, Gutiérrez importantly does not advocate a complete split with the tradition in order to start anew in an increased awareness of the political nature of theology. Rather, he claims that to undertake a liberating praxis, revisitation and reinterpretation of one's faith and understanding of history in light of the Gospel's message of liberation and salvation are necessary. Through the hermeneutic of Christ's action on behalf of the marginalized in society, the human community must come to terms with its failure to live up to Christ's message of the coming of the Kingdom and confront those forces and institutions that continue to fall short today.[118] To do so is to enable activity on behalf of the poor and oppressed, action based on the belief in a Christ who liberates in history.

Dorothee Sölle (1929-2003)

For Dorothee Sölle,[119] no experience of God is the sole possession of any given person.[120] This conviction arises out of what she calls a "politicization of conscience" that had its origins in the evensong gatherings in Köln in the late 1960's, which were comprised of an ecumenical collection of individuals who were convinced of the inherent connection between politics and faith.[121] By means of its exploration of this conviction through biblical readings, liturgy, and prayer, the group developed the notion that theological reflection without political action amounted to hypocrisy.[122]

Unsurprisingly for someone concerned with the connection between theology and politics in the late 60's, Dorothee Sölle spent a considerable amount of time reflecting upon the theological implications of the war in Vietnam. In so doing, she became convinced that the phrase, 'theology after

Auschwitz' was an inappropriate line of theological investigation. In the bombing of Vietnam, she claimed, the horrors which entered the human consciousness so profoundly at Auschwitz continued, and thus theological reflection must be done in the awareness that such staggering evil did not end with the defeat of Hitler, but remained through the political actions of other governments.[123] The goal of theology then, is not simply to come to terms with what has taken place in the past, but to develop ways of addressing the socio-political ills that are occurring in the present.

Early in her career, Sölle identifies the existential problem of humanity as a tension between the experiences of uniqueness and the technological notion of interchangeable parts. Her answer is that although individual human persons are irreplaceable, they may be represented, and this is done by Christ, who is also the representative of God on earth. Because the life and ontological identity of Jesus presents the fullness of both God and humanity, human persons achieve their full identity only with and in God.[124] This is where she differs from the 'Death of God' movement that was prominent at the time and against which she was working. Whereas theologians in this group propose that the experience of humanity tells individuals that God does not intervene in the affairs of the world and thus may be pronounced dead, Sölle maintains that it is not God who is dead, but classical theism.[125] Thus, she is able to maintain that God continues to be present in the world through the representative work of Christ.

This conviction regarding the presence of God in history allows Sölle to undertake her political theology. For her, such a theology begins with the issue of authentic life for all human persons.[126] She writes,

> We understand the gospel in its seriousness only when we consider the political horizon of life, only when we become aware that the failure or attainment of life is governed by social presuppositions and belongs to the political dimension of experience.[127]

From such a perspective, salvation does not involve being saved *from* history, but occurs *in* history, for sin, like the encounter with God, is encountered in the concrete socio-historical structures that human persons erect as they go about their lives.[128] The new life preached by the gospel is inhibited by social structures that, for example, inhibit mother-child relationships or organize society on a Darwinian model wherein the strong prey upon the weak.[129] Moreover, such structures not only inhibit authentic human existence, but also hinder the ability of human persons to foster the very relationship with God that provides the means to such a life. Believing in the loving presence of the Divine is harder for individuals to believe they have suffered injustices that result from sinful social structures.[130] Therefore, if theology is to be true to the gospel upon which it is based, it will challenge those aspects of society which prevent the attainment of authentic life.

Thus, for Sölle, political theology must not remain a purely academic exercise, for the fruits of theological endeavors must be lived in a life of Christian praxis. Too often, she claims, theologians have performed their work from the perspective of scientific neutrality in which they have distanced themselves from their concrete historical reality.[131] For Sölle, Christian praxis is centered on a notion of resistance to a world of social structures that function as a prison in which human persons have fallen asleep spiritually, and for theologians to resist such structures they must realize that their prison is formed by a specific context.[132]

The social structures with which Sölle is most concerned are those of globalization and individualization. She understands the former to be an economic system based on ever-increasing levels of production, consumption and growth. As the technology on which this system is based has improved, this socio-economic order has expanded beyond national borders to include countries and people that do not share in its benefits, resulting in the presence of an elite, comprised of twenty percent of the world's population, whose economic success comes at the expense of the other eighty percent.[133]

The second focus of Sölle's concern, individualization, is connected with the rise of globalization. The more the global market economy grows, she claims, the more disconnected human persons become as the former social and ecological webs that structured human society disappear. The person required by globalization is one who is willing to ignore or remain unaware of the implications of acting in the global market economy. Such persons do not ask about the ethical implications of the products they buy or the practices of the businesses from which goods or services are procured. Meaning and enjoyment are no longer to be found in human community or religious faith, but through consumption of the products of the market.[134] Without a perceived need for spiritual fulfillment or community, human persons become more isolated from one another, and the only tool for addressing the resulting alienation is the consumption advocated by the global economy, which results in increasing isolation.

Human beings have become accustomed to operating within such a world; they are numb to the effects of globalization and individualization. Moreover, they are no longer able to find their way back to sources that once provided meaning and fulfillment for their forebears. They have 'fallen asleep' in a prison whose bars are made of the market economy and its deleterious effect on human society.[135] For Sölle, the only appropriate response for Christians to the prison in which humanity lives is resistance, but before this can be done, they must escape the prison guards of the ego, possession, and violence.

According to Sölle, the ego is, at its most basic level, a concern for oneself that prevents human beings from living in authentic community with other persons and God. It does so by drawing people's attention away from the needs and interests of others to the meeting of their own. The great irony of the ego, however, is that it is unable to deliver on its promises to resolve such selfish issues, for humanity is only fully human when in community, and the ego keeps human beings in the prison in which the presence of God and the fulfillment of human life cannot be found.[136]

In order to escape from the prison formed by globalization and individualization, overcoming the ego is necessary, and this endeavor, according to Sölle, lies at the heart of the Christian message and is most strongly present in the tradition among the mystics. The inward journey of the mystics is a process of immersing oneself in God rather than the self.[137] With their concentration on God rather than the selfish desires of the ego, they become involved in the concerns of the Divine which encompass all of creation. Thus, the desire for the thriving of all replaces the drive for personal success,[138] which in the globalized free market economy comes at the expense of others,[139] and they are able to escape the prison guard of the ego.

The second factor that functions to keep persons in a state of inactivity regarding the numbing effects of globalization and individualization is the notion of possession. She writes, "Possessions are often regarded as a kind of life-threatening drug, impeding the power of judgment."[140] Possessions negatively affect our judgment insofar as individuals come to view the world in which they live as a vast array of things to have and to own. Moreover, Sölle claims, the desire to have is not only marked by an insatiable appetite to acquire more material possessions, but it also transforms the manner in which relationships are viewed.

> Like objects that one wants to have available, partners, relatives, and friends come to be seen as having to be possessed. The ownership relation that develops and prevails assumes a natural right to dispose [of] a person like an object. Enjoyment and pleasure obscure clear judgment because, as John of the Cross put it, there is no conscious enjoying of a creature without simultaneously wanting to own it.[141]

Thus, as a result of this hunger for acquisition, not only are persons endlessly seeking to attain more wealth and property, but they do so with the mindset that other human beings are disposable if they get in the way of this drive for personal gain or other desires of the ego. Children and parents disown each other, and powerful nations and international corporations disregard the well-being of those in less economically empowered areas of the world.

The alternative to a worldview based on possession is a manner of inhabiting the world in which goods are procured with their function in mind rather than acquiring them in an effort to satisfy a voracious hunger for material possessions or to further one's place in society.[142] Sölle is realistic here in her acknowledgment of the fact that human beings require certain material goods in order to survive, and though she discusses and admires those remarkable individuals such as Francis of Assisi, John Woolman, and Dorothy Day who entered into voluntary poverty,[143] she advocates a middle path in which persons are conscious of those who are negatively affected by the investments made, products purchased, and the businesses patronized. Men and women who embrace radical poverty remind the rest of humanity that they do not have to be enslaved by the market that tells them to acquire as much as they can. They remind others that, ultimately, attention is rightly placed on God and those whom God loves, and in so doing they help to set persons free from the prison guard of possession.[144]

The third prison guard named by Sölle is violence, both in such overt actions as physical violence and in more subtle applications as economic or judiciary violence. The primary function of violence is to threaten and deny the fundamental unity of all creation. "To exist free of violence means much more than that: it means to think and act with other living beings in a common life."[145] For persons to be held in the prison of globalization and individualization, structures must exist that, on the one hand, bolster this reality while threatening the unity Sölle perceives in creation on the other. Such social and political structures do violence by exploiting those perceived as other for personal or national gain. Moreover, if those oppressed others refuse to accept such abuse, powerful nations and individuals retaliate with further violence, and the unity of creation is further destroyed.[146]

Sölle's metaphor of the prison of globalization and individualization and its guards, ego, possession, and violence, forms a political interpretation of sin. A politically interpreted notion of sin recognizes the fact that sin is not only an interior matter. When a single person sins, other aspects of creation are affected negatively.[147] Because of the unity of creation and the reach of sin beyond the actual act of commission, theological reflection on sin and redemption and praxis coming from such thought[148] must contain a political element.

A political interpretation of sin, however, is not limited to recognition of the far-reaching effects of personal sin. The prison of globalization has created socio-political structures that are inherently sinful insofar as they compel members of society to sin and thus function to keep the oppressed in subjection to the more powerful elements of society.[149]   As concrete examples of such a sinful social structure, Sölle offers the consuming of bananas grown in South America and the acceptance of periodic rent increases. The former involves exploited workers who often earn less than a living wage. The latter helps to keep rental prices at a level that maintains or increases the number of homeless in America.[150]   Although many well-intentioned people are opposed to such exploitation, the market functions in such a manner that goods produced in a more ethical manner cannot compete.   Thus, even the option of responsible consumer decisions is removed from those who live in the global market economy. The system itself functions in a violent manner that offends the fundamental union of creation.   Moreover, even when a thirst for justice arises, the practical implications are such that many are discouraged from effective action. The system makes change hard to come by, and reluctant collaboration with the sinful social structures is encouraged.[151]

The appropriate theological and practical reaction to a politically interpreted notion of sin and the prison of globalization and individualization, for Sölle, is resistance. Resistance comes in many forms, and its impetus lies in the recognition that the gospel message sets humanity free from the prison guards of the ego, possessions, and violence.   That which sets human beings free from these factors is an active struggle against self-definition in terms of social or economic status rather than in light of one's relationships with God and others.[152]   A life lived without the recognition of the presence of the Divine at all times and in all places is a life lived on the terms of the wholly secular. It sets up relationships between human persons in terms of the 'other' and views 'others' as sources of competition which must be bested or eliminated rather than a celebration of the life offered by the gospel.[153]   Resistance against the prison guards, on the other hand, is a matter of human persons turning their attention to God and seeking to lose themselves in the infinite reality of the Divine.[154]   In this way, life ceases to be a conglomeration of isolated particularities, and the fundamental unity of all creation is recognized.[155]

Conclusion

In this chapter I have presented the work of four noted theologians on the topics of mystical and political theology, and I will now draw some of their insights together to form a working description of mystical-political theology that stands in opposition to the split soul mentality. First, although mysticism entails the awareness of the immediate presence of God, Christian mysticism is, by its very nature, corporate, and therefore the mystical life bears directly on humanity's common life. Either, as with both Underhill and Johnston, the interior life inspires people to action in the exterior life, or, particular to Johnston, the very act of contemplation is beneficial for the world. The love of God and the love of neighbor are so intertwined that the act of loving God is an act of loving neighbor and has an impact on the world around the mystic.

Secondly, the mystical life is always historically conditioned.[156] The historical context in which the mystics live cannot help but affect their spiritual lives. The concerns of the world consistently appear in the spiritual legacy of these remarkable individuals. If the riches left behind by the mystics are to be mined, or if people today are to make sense of their own mystical encounters with the Divine and apply the wisdom gained therein, account must be taken of their historical context. In light of the insights gained from these theologians, it becomes evident that a view of mysticism that cordons the interior life off from the social and political affairs of the human community is misinformed. Mystical wisdom has a great deal to say about the manner in which human persons live with one another, and it has served as the inspiration for heroic actions on behalf of justice in the past.

Thirdly, as Gutiérrez asserts, all theology either supports or resists the structures and institutions that create and maintain human community. Therefore, the role of political theology is to elaborate upon the connection between liberation and the salvation wrought by Christ and challenge those societal principles that resist this bond and work against the coming of the Kingdom. Moreover, according to Dorothee Sölle, the role of a political theology is to resist those societal forces that try to isolate individuals from one another and the rest of creation. The Kingdom of God is a historical reality in which the unity of creation comes to expression in human community.

A mystical-political theology based upon the principles developed by the theologians in this chapter would therefore entail the investigation of the manner in which mysticism becomes a factor in believers' working for the Kingdom of God in history. Such a theology recognizes that the immediate presence of God characteristic of mysticism imparts an intimate knowledge of the will of God for the flourishing of creation. With this wisdom, mystics are better able to work for the Divine plan in the world. Moreover, mysticism's concentration on the life of prayer liberates the mystic from societal messages such as consumerism or the inevitability of violence that isolates human persons from another. Without these constraints, mystics are free to work for a human community more representative of the Kingdom of God. The direct encounter with divine love also informs the mystic about the nature of love and the manner in which human beings should treat one another. Finally, a political approach to the writings of the mystics by later Christians allows these spiritual leaders to speak to believers today with their relevance to the Kingdom in mind. Although mystical texts may not appear at first to possess such societal implications, political theology reminds us that all theology is political in nature, even the mystical theology of past ages.

With this understanding of mystical-political theology that stands in opposition to the split soul in place, the task now becomes the explication of a framework in which the political implications of the mystical life can be appropriated by the mystics and implemented in everyday life. This is the relevance of Bernard Lonergan's notion of self-appropriation to mystical-political theology, and the following chapters are dedicated to this pursuit.

NOTES

[1] For those readers who wish to consult a work devoted solely to mystical theology I offer the following selected suggestions: Louis Bouyer, *Introduction à la vie spirituale: Précis de théologie ascétique et mystique* (Paris: Desclée, 1960); Walter Holden Capps and Wendy M. Wright, eds., *An Invitation to Western Mysticism*, Harper Forum Books (San Francisco: Harper & Row, 1978); Louis K. Dupré, *The Deeper Life: An Introduction to Christian Mysticism* (New York: Crossroad, 1981); Harvey D. Egan, *Christian Mysticism: The Future of a Tradition* (New York: Pueblo, 1984); Margaret Lewis Furse, *Mysticism: Window on a World View* (Nashville: Abingdon Press, 1977); Alban Goodier, *The Life That Is Light*, 3 vols. (London: Burns, Oates, & Washbourne, 1935); David Granfield, *Heightened Consciousness: The Mystical Difference* (New York: Paulist Press, 1991); Patrick Grant, *Literature of Mysticism in Western Tradition* (New York: St. Martin's Press, 1983); Georgia Harkness, *Mysticism: Its Meaning and Message* (Nashville: Abingdon Press, 1973); Arthur W. Hopkinson, *Mysticism: Old and New* (Port Washington, NY: Kennikat Press, 1971); Friedrich von Hügel, *The Mystical Element of Religion as Studied in Saint Catherine of Genoa and Her Friends*, 2 vols., 2nd ed. (London: J.M. Dent & Sons, 1961); Maria Jaoudi, *Christian Mysticism East and West: What the Masters Teach Us* (New York: Paulist Press, 1998); Beverly Lanzetta, *The Other Side of Nothingness: Toward a Theology of Radical Openness* (Albany: State University of New York Press, 2001); George A. Maloney, *The Breath of the Mystic* (Denville, NJ: Dimension Books, 1974); Mark Allen McIntosh, *Mystical Theology: The Integrity of Spirituality and Theology*, Challenges in Contemporary Theology (Malden, MA: Blackwell, 1998); William McNamara, *Christian Mysticism: A Psychotherapy* (Chicago: Franciscan Herald Press, 1981); Hubertus Mynarek, *Mystik und Vernunft: Zwei Pole einer Wirklichkeit* (Olten: Walter-Verlag, 1991); Frederick Sontag, *Love Beyond Pain: Mysticism within Christianity* (New York: Paulist Press, 1977); Arthur A. Vogel, *The Power of His Resurrection: The Mystical Life of Christians* (New York: Seabury Press, 1976); Alan Watts, *Behold the Spirit: A Study in the Necessity of Mystical Religion* (New York: Pantheon Books, 1971).

[2] Michel de Certeau argues this point in Michel de Certeau, *La fable mystique: XVIᵉ - XVIIᵉ siècle* (Paris: Gallimard, 1982).

[3] This is not to say that mystics did not refer to the texts of previous spiritual leaders. As examples, consider that the author of *The Cloud of Unknowing* relied heavily upon the writings of Pseudo-Dionysius, and the rise of a distinctly Franciscan mysticism modeled after the life of Francis of Assisi similarly testifies to the fact that mystics often relied on the experiences of others to pursue and understand their own spirituality. Bernard McGinn treats Franciscan mysticism in Bernard McGinn, *The Presence of God: A History of Western Christian Mysticism*, vol. 3, *The Flowering of Mysticism: Men and Women of the New Mysticism – 1200-1350* (New York: Crossroad, 1998), 70-152.

[4] For those readers interested in pursuing secondary reading on Evelyn Underhill, the following will prove helpful: Christopher J.R. Armstrong, *Evelyn Underhill: An Introduction to Her Life and Writings* (Grand Rapids: Eerdmans, 1976); Grace Adolphsen Brame, "The Extraordinary within the Ordinary: The Life and Message of Evelyn Underhill (1875-1941)," in *Feminist Voices in Spirituality*, ed. Pierre Hegy, Studies in Women and Religion; 38 (Lewiston, NY: Edwin Mellen, 1996), 101-124; Annice Callahan, *Spiritual Guides for Today:*

Evelyn Underhill, Dorothy Day, Karl Rahner, Simone Weil, Thomas Merton, Henri Nouwen (New York: Crossroad, 1992); Annice Callahan, *Evelyn Underhill: Spirituality for Daily Living* (Lanham, MD: University Press of America, 1997); Margaret Cropper, *Evelyn Underhill* (New York: Longmans, Green, 1958); Dana Green, *Evelyn Underhill: Artist of the Infinite Life* (New York: Crossroad, 1990); Kevin Hogan, "The Experience of Reality: Evelyn Underhill and Religious Pluralism," *Anglican Theological Review* 74 (1992): 334-347; Grace M. Jantzen, "The Legacy of Evelyn Underhill," *Feminist Theology* 4 (1993): 79-100; Géza von Molnár, "Mysticism and a Romantic Concept of Art: Observations on Evelyn Underhill's Practical Mysticism and Novalis' Heinrich von Ofterdingen," *Studia Mystica* 6 (1983): 66-75; Delroy Oberg, "Head v. Heart: Mysticism and Theology in the Life of Evelyn Underhill," *St. Mark's Review* 149 (1992): 7-14; Michael Ramsey and A.M. Allchin, *Evelyn Underhill: Two Centenary Essays* (Oxford: S.L.G. Press, 1977); Susan J. Smalley, "Evelyn Underhill and the Mystical Tradition," in *Scripture, Tradition and Reason*, ed. Richard Bouckham and Benjamin Drewery (Edinburgh: T&T Clark, 1998), 266-287; Terry Tastard, "Divine Presence and Human Freedom: The Spirituality of Evelyn Underhill Reconsidered," *Theology* 94 (1991): 426-432.

[5] Annice Callahan, *Evelyn Underhill: Spirituality for Daily Living* (Lanham, MD: University Press of America, 1997), 4.

[6] This is not to say that Underhill entirely neglected the teachings of the mystics. Producing such works as *Mysticism* and *Mystics of the Church* would be very difficult without presenting the reader with at least a thumbnail sketch of what certain mystics of the tradition have to teach their readers. My point here is that Underhill is much less of an interpreter of the doctrines developed by the mystics than she is a commentator on the spiritual lives of these individuals.

[7] Evelyn Underhill, *Mysticism: The Nature and Development of Spiritual Consciousness* (Oxford: Oneworld, 1999), 68, 90.

[8] Julian of Norwich, *Showings (Long Text)*, 58:1-10, in *Julian of Norwich: Showings*, The Classics of Western Spirituality: A Library of the Great Masters, trans. Edmund Colledge, O.S.A. (New York: Paulist Press, 1978), 293. This issue finds resonance in the Beguine mystical movement of the 13th century. These women mystics were individuals who lived free forms of the religious life a without a monastic rule. These women spoke regularly about the preexistence of the human soul in the consciousness of God. Since God knows all at all times, human souls, and even bodies, can be said to have existed eternally. This appears to be a matter of the scholastic distinction between actual and essential existence. However, these women did not have wide access to the work of the scholastic theologians and thus did not have the tools to elaborate a comprehensive doctrine of the preexistence of human souls. Nor should these women be expected to have the same philosophical and theological interests as the scholastics. Moreover, as a result of their emphasis on love over reason, mystics have seldom been accused of terminological accuracy. Demanding of the Beguines the rigorous theological standards of other times and places would be mistaken. For a discussion of the Beguines, see Bernard McGinn, *The Flowering of Mysticism*, 199-265.

[9] Underhill, *Mysticism*, 100-103, *Practical Mysticism*, 35-48, to name a couple of instances.

[10] Underhill, *Mysticism*, 105-107.

[11] The role of von Hügel in this transition has been ably documented by Christopher J.R. Armstrong. Although the theme of Underhill's development as a theologian runs throughout his book, particular emphasis on the role of von Hügel may be found in his chapter entitled, "Help in a Time of Need." Christopher J.R. Armstrong, *Evelyn Underhill: An Introduction to her Life and Writings* (Grand Rapids, MI: Eerdmans, 1975).

[12] Underhill, *Practical Mysticism*, 172-191.

[13] Margaret Cropper, *Evelyn Underhill* (New York: Longmans, Green and Co., 1958), 101-103.

[14] The four characteristics of the mystical experience for James are passivity, transient nature, noetic quality, and ineffability. William James, *Varieties of Religious Experience* (New York: Penguin Books, 1982), 380-382.

[15] Underhill, *Mysticism*, 81.

[16] *Plotinus*, 7 vols. trans A.H. Armstrong, LC (Cambridge, MA: Harvard University Press, 1966-1988). Underhill, *Mysticism*, 234.

[17] Ibid., 82-83.

[18] Underhill, *Practical Mysticism*, 35-48.

[19] Underhill, *Mysticism*, 81.

[20] Ibid.

[21] Callahan, *Evelyn Underhill*, 1-2.

[22] Underhill, *Mysticism*, 84.

[23] Evelyn Underhill, *Concerning the Inner Life* (Oxford: Oneworld, 1999), 23.

[24] Underhill, *Mysticism*, 81.

[25] Ibid., 85-86.

[26] Underhill, *Practical Mysticism*, 23-24.

[27] Underhill, *Mysticism*, 84, Callahan, *Evelyn Underhill*, 36.

[28] Underhill, *Mysticism*, 81, 90.

[29] Ibid., 90-92.

[30] Armstrong contends that later in her career Evelyn Underhill did not emphasize the mystic way as it is elaborated in *Mysticism*. He contends that Underhill came to emphasize a non-

evolutionary scheme for the mystical life involving the elements of adoration, communion, and cooperation. He is, however, the only commentator I have found who claims that Underhill left behind the mystic way described by *Mysticism*, and his treatment of the issue can only be described as cursory as it is limited to three sentences of his introduction. Armstrong, *xx*. This bears on one of the difficulties associated with any discussion of the work of Evelyn Underhill insofar as she draws no distinction between the mystical and the spiritual life. Generally speaking, mysticism is often understood as the highest level of the spiritual life, its intensity being so much greater than other spiritual experiences that it becomes a different type of experience entirely. This is not so for Underhill. As Dana Greene puts it, "The mystic way is the spiritual way, open to all, participated in by the many, fully realized by the few." Dana Green, *Evelyn Underhill: Artist of the Infinite Life* (New York: Crossroad, 1990), 5. This being the case, I would disagree with any contention that her later work, in which the term "mysticism" rarely occurs specifically, is not appropriate to a discussion of mystical theology. A distinction between the spiritual and the mystical is not appropriate when dealing with the work of Evelyn Underhill, and any of her discussions concerning the spiritual life are relevant to a treatment of mystical theology.

[31] Underhill, *Practical Mysticism*, 34.

[32] Underhill, *Mysticism*, 176-177.

[33] Ibid., 180.

[34] For a comprehensive treatment of the life of Francis of Assisi, see Arnoldo Fortini, *Francis of Assisi*, 2 vols., trans. Helen Moak (New York: Crossroad, 1981).

[35] Underhill, *Mysticism*, 177. For the spiritual life of George Fox, see George Fox, *The Journal of George Fox*, ed. Rufus M. Jones (Richmond, IN: Friends United Press, 1976).

[36] Underhill, *Practical Mysticism*, 23.

[37] Underhill, *Mysticism*, 178-179.

[38] Evelyn Underhill, *The Life of the Spirit and the Life of Today* (San Francisco: Harper & Row, 1986), 5.

[39] Ibid., 68.

[40] Underhill, *Mysticism*, 198-199.

[41] Ibid., 200, 381.

[42] Henry Suso was especially famous for his ascetic zeal. His purgative stage lasted about seventeen years and included such practices as sleeping in a hair shirt whose inside was adorned with nails. When he realized that he may subconsciously try to relieve himself of his discomfort by scratching his skin in his sleep, Suso bound his hands with a leather strap that wrapped around his neck. While Suso stands decidedly at the far end of the spectrum of examples of purgation, he serves as an illustration of the fervor with which mystics have pursued their relationship with God. For his life story, see *Henry Suso: The Exemplar with*

Two German Sermons, The Classics of Western Spirituality: A Library of the Great Spiritual Masters, ed. and trans. Frank Tobin (New York: Paulist Press, 1989). Some scholars contend that the self-inflicted pain of the ascetics was not solely a matter of self-purification. Caroline Walker Bynum, for instance, claims that in the Middle Ages, the body was becoming increasingly acknowledged as a vehicle for relationship with the Divine. Moreover, for the women mystics of the time, the body was one of the few aspects of their lives over which they could exercise control. Thus, these women were seizing control of their spirituality through their bodies. Caroline Walker Bynum, "The Female Body and Religious Practice," in Caroline Walker Bynum, *Fragmentation and Redemption: Essays on Gender and the Human Body in Medieval Religion* (New York: Zone Books, 1991), 183.

[43] Underhill, *Mysticism*, 210-212., *Practical Mysticism*, 95-102.

[44] Underhill, *Mysticism*, 240-242.

[45] Ibid., 249.

[46] Underhill, *Mysticism*, 399-400.

[47] Ibid., 416.

[48] Ibid., 416, 432; Callahan, *Evelyn Underhill*, 3, 16, 38-39.

[49] According to Callahan, this teaching and inspiration of others is Underhill's greatest contribution to today. Callahan, *Evelyn Underhill*, 3.

[50] Although Johnston is a Catholic theologian, he concentrates heavily on the relationship between Western Christian mystical theology and Asian mystical traditions. As such, his theology is informed a great deal by the wisdom of Asian religion, especially as it pertains to contemplation and meditation.

[51] William Johnston, *Arise My Love: Mysticism for a New Era* (Maryknoll: Orbis, 2000), 13.

[52] Ibid.

[53] Ibid., 31-33.

[54] Johnston, *Arise My Love*, 13-14. Johnston does not wish for theologians to cease their valuable work of elaborating upon the teachings of the church in a language that suits the culture of the times. His point is only that such theology is unable to address the knowledge of God that is gained through love rather than the intellect. William Johnston, *The Inner Eye of Love: Mysticism and Religion* (San Francisco: Harper & Row, 1978), 82.

[55] Johnston, *Arise My Love*, 88-91.

[56] Ibid., 102. However, although she is more linear in her mystical theology, Underhill does allow for the ups and downs of the mystical life. This is most evident in her treatment of the dark night of the soul, which, she claims, may be gradual in both its onset and departure, involving times of both consolation and desolation. Underhill, *Mysticism*, 383, 402. My point

here is only that Underhill's mystical theology proceeds upon a much more regular and predictable path than does Johnston's.

[57] Although the influence of eastern religion runs throughout Johnston's work, he devotes special attention to this topic in William Johnston, *Mystical Theology: The Science of Love* (Maryknoll: Orbis, 1998), 88-99, 113-125; *The Inner Eye of Love*, 72-86; *Arise My Love*, 40-66; *The Mirror Mind: Spirituality and Transformation* (San Francisco: Harper & Row, 1981), 33-41, 88-102; *Christian Zen* (San Francisco: Harper & Row, 1979); *The Still Point: Reflections on Zen and Christian Mysticism* (New York: Fordham University Press, 1970).

[58] Johnston, *The Inner Eye of Love*, 82.

[59] Johnston, *Arise My Love*, 116-119.

[60] In the present work, I am relying upon the traditional distinction between kataphatic and apophatic mysticism.   The former is characterized by actual content in the mystical experience, often in the form of Divine voices or images. In these cases, the mystic comes to learn something of God and is able to say what God is, although the knowledge remains imperfect and incomplete. Apophatic mysticism, on the other hand, involves experiences of union with God void of all images and concepts. Here the individual can only say what God is not. For more on this important distinction see Johnston, *Arise My Love*, 116-119, 162-163; Andrew Louth, *The Origins of Christian Mysticism: From Plato to Denys* (Oxford: Clarendon, 1981), 164-183.

[61] Johnston, *Arise My Love*, 112-113; *Mystical Theology*, 40-42.

[62] William Johnston, *The Wounded Stag: Christian Mysticism Today* (New York: Harper & Row, 1984; reprint, New York: Fordham University Press, 1998), 20.

[63] Johnston, *The Inner Eye of Love*, 46-47.

[64] Ibid., 12-14.

[65] Johnston, *Mystical Theology*, 16, 66; *Arise My* Love, 88-90; *Being in Love: The Practice of Christian Prayer*, 2nd ed. (New York: Fordham University Press, 1999), 47.

[66] Interestingly, Johnston links this awareness of the reality of God to Lonergan's fifth transcendental precept, "Be in Love." Johnston, *The Inner Eye of Love*, 62-63.

[67] William Johnston, *Being in Love: The Practice of Christian Prayer* (New York: Fordham University Press, 1999), 45; *The Inner Eye of Love*, 30.

[68] Johnston did not originally wholeheartedly endorse the categories of 'acquired' and 'infused' contemplation. In *Being in Love*, which first appeared in 1984, Johnston indicates the inadequacy of these terms because Christian mysticism is not a matter of technique, but of love, and, in accordance with the First Letter of John, "We love because he first loved us" (1 Jo 4:19; NRSV). Johnston, *Being in Love*, 47-48. In *Arise My Love*, which was published in 2000, however, he writes, "I have come to see that it is useful to distinguish between

contemplation that is the fruit of human effort aided by ordinary grace and contemplation experienced as undeserved and gratuitous gift." Johnston, *Arise My Love*, 247 n. 5.

[69] Johnston, *Being in Love*, 45-46; *Arise My Love*, 92-93; *Mystical Theology*, 52; *The Inner Eye of Love*, 30-31; *The Wounded Stag*, 42-43. This distinction drawn by Johnston with regard to discursive and mystical prayer may be further illustrated by the notions of essential and existential prayer. The former, which seems to fit with discursive prayer, is prayer that is focused on *what* God and the individual are. Here, the person focuses on the attributes of God, the individual, and the relationship between the two. Existential prayer, on the other hand, corresponds to mystical contemplation and is concerned with *that* God and the person are. This opens the way for Divine Wisdom to enter the deeper levels of the psyche. Johnston, *Being in Love*, 56-62.

[70] Johnston, *The Inner Eye of Love*, 33.

[71] Johnston, *Arise My Love*, 103-104.

[72] Ibid., 104.

[73] Ibid., 104, 109. John of the Cross develops his analogy of the log through *The Dark Night* and *The Living Flame of Love*. *The Collected Works of St. John of the Cross*, trans. Kieran Kavanaugh, OCD and Otilio Rodriguez, OCD (Washington DC: ICS Publications, 1991), 353-457, 633-715.

[74] Johnston, *Mystical Theology*, 261.

[75] Johnston, *Arise My Love*, 224-229; *Mystical Theology*, 206-207, 219.

[76] Johnston, *The Wounded Stag*, 123-126.

[77] Johnston, *Arise My Love*, 241-243.

[78] Johnston, *Mystical Theology*, 258.

[79] Ibid., 261.

[80] *The Cloud* of Unknowing, 9, in *The Cloud of Unknowing and The Book of Privy Counseling*, ed. William Johnston (New York: Doubleday, 1973), 60.

[81] For additional reading on the topic of political theology I offer the following: Don S. Browning, "Practical Theology and Political Theology," *Theology Today* 42 (1985): 15-33; Lester L. Field, *Liberty, Dominion and the Two Swords: On the Origins of Western Political Theology* (Notre Dame, IN: Univeristy of Notre Dame Press, 1998); Howard P. Kainz, *Democracy and the "Kingdom of God,"* Marquette Studies in Philosophy, no. 6 (Milwaukee, WI: Marquette Univeristy Press, 1995); Alistair Kee, *A Reader in Political Theology* (Philadelphia: Westminster Press, 1975); Robert Kress, "Theological Method: Praxis and Liberation," *Communio* 6 (1979): 113-134; Paul Lakeland, *Freedom in Christ: An Introduction to Political Theology* (New York: Fordham University Press, 1986); Gerrit Manenshijn, "'Jesus Is the Christ': The Political Theology of Leviathan," trans. John Vriend,

Journal of Religious Ethics 25 (1997): 35-64; Reinhart Maurer, "Thesen zur politischen Theologie: Augustinsche Tradition und heutige Probleme," *Zeitschrift fur Theologie und Kirche* 79:3 (1982): 349-373; Bruce T. Morrill, *Anamnesis as Dangerous Memory: Political and Liturgical Theology in Dialogue* (Collegeville, MN: Liturgical Press, 2000); Francis Oakley, *Politics and Eternity: Studies in the History of Medieval and Early-Modern Political Thought*, Studies in the History of Christian Thought, vol. 92 (Leiden; Boston: Brill, 1999); Oliver O'Donovan, *The Desire of the Nations: Rediscovering the Roots of Political Theology* (Cambridge, England; New York: Cambridge University Press, 1996); Leroy S. Rouner, ed., *Civil Religion and Political Theology*, Boston University Studies in Philosophy and Religion, vol. 8 (Notre Dame, IN: University of Notre Dame Press, 1986); Stephen B. Scharper, *Redeeming the Time: A Political Theology of the Environment* (New York: Continuum, 1997); Rudolf J. Siebert, *From Critical Theory to Communicative Political Theology: Universal Solidarity*, American University Studies VII, Theology and Religion, vol. 52 (New York: Peter Lang, 1989); Douglas Sturm, "Praxis and Promise: On the Ethics of Political Theology," *Ethics* 92 (1982): 733-750; John J. Vincent, "Doing Political Theology," *Drew Gateway* 50:2 (1979): 32-43.

[82] Paul Lakeland, *Freedom in Christ: An Introduction to Political Theology* (New York: Fordham University Press, 1986), 4.

[83] Ibid., 5-7.

[84] The Kingdom of God whose coming is announced by Christ in the gospel consists of a reality characterized by justice, peace, and the flourishing of human persons under the dominion of Christ. No longer will the poor and oppressed be dominated by the powerful. (Lk 4:16-21, 6:20-26, 7:22, 12:21; Mt 11:5, 25:31-46). The transformation of the human community wrought by the coming of the Kingdom will therefore involve a radical change in the structures and institutions that govern human living. Instead of many people living in poverty, the needs of all will be met. Rather than oppression, liberation and peace will replace violence and oppression. Importantly, however, although Jesus announces the arrival of the Kingdom (Mk 1:15, 9:1; Lk 11:20, 17:21) it still has not come in its fullness (Mt 4:17; 6:10). Therefore, one of the tasks of political theology is to analyze human societies today in an effort to identify and rectify those situations that are insufficient in light of the announcement of the Kingdom and inhibit its coming. As Guttiérrez notes, the Kingdom is both a spiritual and earthly reality. It is a gift from God, but it also involves human cooperation in its coming as Christians take the message of the Kingdom and apply it in the political realm by constructing just and peaceful communities. Therefore, when the terms "Kingdom of God" or "Kingdom of God on earth" are used in this book, I am referring to the ongoing transformation of the world into a reality more in consonance with Christ's announcement of both the arrival of the Kingdom and its future coming in fullness. Gustavo Gutiérrez, *A Theology of Liberation: History, Politics, and Salvation*, rev. ed. (Maryknoll, NY: Orbis Books, 1988), 131-132.

[85] For those readers interested in pursuing further secondary reading on Gutiérrez, I offer the following selected list. Leandre Boisvert, "Les images bibliques de dieu dans l'oeuvre de Gustavo Gutiérrez," *Église et theologie* 19:3 (1988): 307-321; Robert McAfee Brown, *Gustavo Gutiérrez*, Makers of Contemporary Theology (Atlanta: John Knox Press, 1980); Robert McAfee Brown, *Gustavo Gutiérrez: An Introduction to Liberation Theology* (MaryKnoll, NY: Orbis Books, 1990); Robert McAfee Brown, "Spirituality and Liberation:

The Case for Gustavo Gutiérrez," *Worship* 58 (1984): 395-404; Curt Cadorette, *From the Heart of the People: The Theology of Gustavo Gutiérrez* (Oak Park, IL: Meyer Stone Books, 1988); Marc H. Ellis and Otto Maduro, eds., *Expanding the View: Gustavo Gutiérrez and the Future of Liberation Theology* (Maryknoll, NY: Orbis Books, 1990); Marc H. Ellis and Otto Maduro, eds., *The Future of Liberation Theology: Essays in Honor of Gustavo Gutiérrez* (Maryknoll, NY: Orbis Books, 1989); Francis Guibal, "The Force subversive de l'evangile: Sur la pensee theologique de Gustavo Gutiérrez," *Recherches de science religieuse* 77:4 (1989): 483-508; Gaspar Martinez, *Confronting the Mystery of God: Political, Liberation, and Public Theologies* (New York: Continuum, 2001); Joyce Murray, "Liberation for Communion in the Soteriology of Gustavo Gutiérrez," *Theological Studies* 59 (1998): 51-59; James B. Nickoloff, "The Ecclesiology of Gustavo Gutiérrez," *Theological Studies* 54 (1993): 512-535; Jeffrey S. Siker, "Uses of the Bible in the Theology of Gustavo Gutiérrez: Liberating Scriptures of the Poor," *Biblical Interpretation* 4 (1996): 40-71

[86] Gutiérrez, *Theology of Liberation*, 29.

[87] Ibid., 30. A distinction is in order here regarding the relationship between liberation theology and political theology, namely that liberation theology is a subdivision of the broader category of political theology. Political theology is concerned with theological examination of social structures and institutions, but liberation theology undertakes this task from the particular perspective of the plight of the poor and the liberation of people from the oppressive forces that push certain persons or groups to the margins of society.

[88] Gutiérrez explicitly identifies Johann Baptist Metz and Jürgen Moltmann. Gustavo Gutiérrez, "Freedom and Salvation: A Political Problem," in Gustavo Gutiérrez and Richard Schaull, *Liberation and Change* (Atlanta: John Knox Press, 1977), 57-58.

[89] Gustavo Gutiérrez, *The Power of the Poor in History*, trans. Robert R. Barr (Maryknoll: Orbis Books, 1983), 171.

[90] Ibid., 27-28.

[91] Ibid., 28, 175-176.

[92] Gutiérrez, "Freedom and Salvation," 29.

[93] Gutiérrez, "Freedom and Salvation," 34-35.

[94] Ibid., 35.

[95] Ibid., 36.

[96] Ibid., 36-37.

[97] Ibid., 46-47.

[98] Ibid., 49.

[99] Ibid., 53.

[100] Ibid., 58.

[101] Gutiérrez, *Theology of Liberation*, 16-22. Although release from oppressive socio-political structures is the most easily visible aspect of liberation, Gutiérrez identifies two additional aspects. An anthropological transformation is also necessary in which human beings recognize their inherent freedom in any situation, no matter how stifling it may be. Gutiérrez's third dimension of liberation is spiritual, by which persons are reconciled to God and one another. Ibid., *xxxviii*.

[102] Ibid., 14-16. Gutiérrez, "Freedom and Salvation," 60.

[103] Gutiéirrez, *A Theology of Liberation*, 85.

[104] Ibid.

[105] Ibid., 95-97.

[106] Ibid., 95.

[107] Ibid., 97.

[108] Ibid., 132.

[109] Gutiérrez, *The Power of the Poor in History*, 39.

[110] Gutiérrez, *A Theology of Liberation*, 106-110.

[111] Ibid., 110.

[112] Gustavo Gutiérrez, "Toward the Fifth Centenary," trans. Dinah Livingstone, in *The Density of the Present: Selected Writings* (Maryknoll, Orbis Books, 1999), 103-106.

[113] Ibid., 106.

[114] Gustavo Gutiérrez, "Theology: A Critical Reflection," in *Gustavo Gutiérrez: Essential Writings*, ed. James B. Nickoloff (Maryknoll: Orbis, 1996), 31-34.

[115] Gutiérrez, *A Theology of Liberation*, 9.

[116] Gutiérrez, *The Power of the Poor in History*, 58-60.

[117] Gustavo Gutiérrez, "Liberation and Development: A Challenge to Theology," trans. Margaret Wilde, in *The Density of the Present: Selected Writings* (Maryknoll: Orbis, 1999), 134.

[118] Gutiérrez, "Freedom and Salvation," 80-83.

[119] For those readers interested in pursuing further secondary reading on Sölle, I offer the following selected list. Friedrich Delekat, "Zur Theologie von Dorothee Sölle," *Kerygma und*

Dogma 16:2 (1970): 130-143; Jacques Gurber, "La 'Representation' de Dorothee Sölle," 2 parts, *Revue d'histoire et de philosophie religieuses* 66 (2 Ap, 1986): 179-210; Jacques Gurber, "La 'Representation' de Dorothee Sölle," 2 parts, *Revue d'histoire et de philosophie religieuses* 66 (3 Jl, 1986): 287-318; Susi Hausammann, "Atheistisch zu Gott beten: Eine Auseinandersetzung mit D. Sölle," *Evangelische Theologie* 31 (1971): 414-436; Richard Higginson, "From Carl Schmitt to Dorothee Sölle: Has Political Theology Turned Full Circle?" *Churchman* 97:2 (1983): 132-140; Heidemarie Lämmerman-Kuhn, *Sensibilität für den Menschen: Theologie und Anthropologie bei Dorothee Sölle*, Würzburger Studien zur Fundamentaltheologie, Bd. 4 (Frankfurt am Main; New York: Lang, 1988); Beyers Naudé, *Hope for Faith: A Conversation*, Risk Book Series, no. 31 (Geneva: WCC Publications; Grand Rabids, MI: Eerdmans, 1986); Ernst Saxer, *Vorsehung und Verheissung Gottes: Vier theologische Modelle (Calvin, Scleiermacher, Barth, Sölle) une ein systematischer Versuch*, Studien zur Dogmengeschichte und systematischen Theologie, Bd. 34 (Zürich: Theologischer Verlag, 1980).

[120] Dorothee Sölle, *The Silent Cry: Mysticism and Resistance*, trans. Barbara and Martin Rumscheidt (Minneapolis: Fortress Press, 2001), 3.

[121] Dorothee Sölle, *Gegenwind: Erinnerungen* (Hamburg: Hoffmann und Campe, 1995), 70. See also, Dorothee Sölle and Fulbert Seffensky, ed., *Politisches Nachtgebet in Köln*, 2 vols. (Stuttgart/Mainz: Kreuz/Grünewald, 1971).

[122] Sölle, *Gegenwind*, 71.

[123] Ibid., 43; Dorothee Sölle, "Eine Erinnerung um der Zukunft willen," in Edward Schillebeeckx, hrsg., *Mystik und Politik: Theologie im Ringen um Geschichte und Gesellschaft; Johann Baptist Metz zu Ehren zum 60. Geburtstag* (Mainz: Matthias-Grünewald-Verlag, 1988), 14.

[124] Dorothee Sölle, *Stellvertretung: Ein Kapitel Theologie nach dem "Tode Gottes"* (Stuttgart: Kreuz-Verlag, 1965), 171-174.

[125] John Shelley, "Introduction," in Dorothee Sölle, *Political Theology*, trans. John Shelley (Philadelphia: Fortress Press, 1974), x-xi.

[126] *Political Theology*, 60-61. Sölle is not working here with a Lonerganian notion of authenticity. Rather, her sense of the term is a matter of living a life that is truly human, as opposed to the perversion of human life through sin.

[127] Ibid., 59.

[128] Ibid., 83-84.

[129] Ibid., 61.

[130] Ibid.

[131] Shelley, 16-17.

[132] Sölle, *The Silent Cry*, 191.

[133] Ibid., 191; Dorothee Sölle and Fulbert Steffensky, *Not Just Yes and Amen: Christians with a Cause*, trans. Rowohlt Taschenbuch Verlag (Philadelphia: Fortress Press, 1985), 15-16.

[134] Ibid., 191-192. John F. Kavanaugh argues this point extensively and effectively in John F. Kavanaugh, *Following Christ in a Consumer Society* (Maryknoll, NY: Orbis Books, 2006).

[135] Ibid., 191. For the notion of falling asleep in prison Sölle relies upon the work of the Muslim mystic Rumi who writes, "Why, when God's world is so big / did you fall asleep in a prison / of all places."

[136] Sölle, *The Silent Cry*, 209-214.

[137] Ibid., 211-212.

[138] Ibid., 230.

[139] Sölle, *Not Just Yes and Amen*, 15.

[140] Sölle, *The Silent Cry*, 233.

[141] Ibid., 234.

[142] Ibid., 234-235.

[143] Ibid., 236-252.

[144] Ibid., 252-257.

[145] Ibid., 260.

[146] Ibid., 260-261. The extent of this spiral of the violent destruction of creation's unity becomes profoundly apparent insofar as even the notion of peace cannot be separated from the issue of security, militarily interpreted. Sölle, *Gegenwind*, 221-222. Because of such perversion of language, Sölle asserts that new religious language must be developed if humanity is to address violent social structures. "When a word like *love* is applied to the car, or a word like *purity* to a special detergent; these words have no meaning anymore but are destroyed." Dorothee Sölle, *On Earth as in Heaven: A Liberation Spirituality of Sharing*, trans. Marc Batko (Louisville, KY: Westminster/John Knox Press, 1993), 87. Her suggestion is that an effort should be made to incorporate the more affective language of myth and poetry into discussions of the transformation of reality into one more representative of the coming of the Kingdom of God. Ibid., 87-89. I will return to this issue later in this work in the context of opening the wisdom of the mystical life to political theology and action.

[147] Sölle, *Political Theology*, 85.

[148] The difference between Gutiérrez and Sölle on the order of theory and praxis is interesting. For Gutiérrez, as previously noted, theory is the result of theological reflection on the action

of the oppressed in history, whereas for Sölle praxis puts into action the theories that arise from a politically interpreted theology. This is due to the fact that Sölle is concerned with the development of a 'First World' theology of liberation. Sölle, "Erinerung," 17-18. Importantly, however, Sölle's theological reflection starts with the condition of the poor. Reflecting upon the circumstances and actions of the poor, the theologian analyzes the situation and develops a theology that encourages further action on behalf of the poor. Dorothee Sölle, *On Earth as in Heaven*, x-xi. Thus, the fundamental difference between Sölle and Gutiérrez lies in the one doing the theology. For Gutiérrez it is the poor, and for Sölle, it is the 'First World' acting on behalf of and in solidarity with the poor.

[149] Sölle, *Political Theology*, 83-84.

[150] Ibid., 84.

[151] Sölle, *The Silent Cry*, 266.

[152] Ibid., 212-213.

[153] Dorothee Sölle, *Death by Bread Alone: Texts and Reflections on Religious Experience*, trans. David L. Scheidt (Philadelphia: Fortress Press, 1978), 4-9.

[154] Sölle, *The Silent Cry*, 227-229.

[155] Like Gutiérrez, resistance, for Sölle, does not entail a complete break with the Christian tradition. Rather, her contention is that to do so would be to fall into the fundamental mistake made by secular social reform movements, specifically state socialism, namely, the attempt to establish a new social reality from scratch. Sölle, *The Silent Cry*, 197; Sölle, "Erinnerung," 15. These movements claim that human history is so distorted and inhibiting of human life as to be useless for the establishment of a just social order. Sölle claims, on the other hand, that the Christian tradition provides the resource of a "good beginning" which serves as a model for the ideals that the world is supposed to embody. Sölle, *The Silent Cry*, 197. Without such an underpinning, secular movements must create their own ideals and meanings, and one must ask whether these are affected by the same deficient history that they reject. Moreover, the Christian tradition also possesses the idea of worldly renewal or renovation that better embodies God's original designs for creation. She writes, "Whoever desires the new needs the memory and the feast that, even now, celebrate the renewing." Sölle, *The Silent Cry*, 197. Sölle's political theology is thus not a rejection of the tradition, but a transformation of the present reality in light of the liberating message of the gospel.

[156] For a more detailed description of the historically conditioned nature of mysticism, I recommend Bernard McGinn's multivolume set, *The Presence of God: A History of Western Christian Mysticism*, which is scheduled to contain five volumes, four of which have been published at the time of this book. Bernard McGinn, *The Presence of God: A History of Western Christian Mysticism*, 5 vols. (New York: Crossroad, 1991--).

CHAPTER TWO

Self-Appropriation I: Patterns of Experience

Introduction

Whereas the introduction and first chapter of this book focused on the state of affairs in the realms of mystical and political theology, the current chapter will take the first step in clarifying the relevance of Bernard Lonergan's notion of self-appropriation to mystical-political theology. Broadly speaking, self-appropriation is a matter of attending to the operations of the human subject with regard to the situation in which individuals are located and the goals pursued therein. This process bears fruit insofar as it provides a basis from which individuals may pursue further questions. If people do not attend to their operations as they go about daily life, they will find that discovering adequate solutions to the various problems life presents is difficult. Certain data may be overlooked, and the data that is noticed may be improperly understood. These issues subsequently affect judgment; premature judgment or judgment made on incomplete data, in turn, may yield irresponsible decisions. This process of experiencing, understanding, and judging comprises Lonergan's cognitional theory, and it leads to the subsequent issue of deciding what to do with what has been learned. If persons are to perform these operations properly, they must attend to the manner which they execute them and the particularities of the moment.

Before human subjects can go about the business of attending to their operations, they must first become aware of the situation in which they are functioning. Although human intellectual activity follows the same recurrent pattern regardless of the issue under investigation, the human subject performs these operations under different circumstances, according to the vagaries of life. The goal may be a general theory, or solely the concrete particularity of the given situation. The concern may be the aesthetic elements of the moment, or exclusively intelligent inquiry. The investigation may possess religious implications, or it may be a purely humanistic matter.

Lonergan addresses the great variety in human experience with his notion of patterns of experience, and he explicitly identifies "the biological, aesthetic, intellectual, dramatic, practical, or worshipful patterns of experience within which the operations [of the human subject] occur."[1] Although the data of sense and consciousness differs according to the specific type of experience within each of these patterns, human persons must be cognizant of the fact that the subject who is experiencing the data remains a unity.[2] Thus, although the mystic's life of prayer may fit into a specific pattern of experience, the wisdom and knowledge gained through experiencing, understanding, and judging the data of the experience accompanies the mystics as they encounter new life situations.[3] Unlike the mentality of the split soul, which seeks to splinter the subject into opposites, the spiritual and the practical self, Lonergan's insistence on the unity of the subject enables an integration of the subject which allows the data gleaned from each pattern of experience to be involved in other aspects of life. Moreover, the consistency of the operations performed by the human subject challenges the notion that mystical knowing is qualitatively different from other instances of knowing. Although the data of the mystical experience is particular to that pattern, the operations remain the same, and mystical knowing is therefore not restricted to a select few fortunate enough to gain entrance into an esoteric group of individuals who have experienced union with the Divine.

In a second contribution, Lonergan posits that although human cognition follows a uniform set of operations, the concerns of the persons may vary from individual to individual and group to group. Although scholars devote their professional energy to the development of theoretical formulations that apply generally, the vast majority of individuals are concerned only with the particular concrete instance in which they find themselves at any given moment. According to Lonergan, this is the difference between the realm of theory and the realm of common sense, and if human subjects are to attend to their operations, they must be aware of this distinction. A common sense solution to a wide-ranging and complex problem will prove to be unsatisfactory in the long term because it is only concerned with the present situation. Although it may be well-intentioned, common sense fails to take into consideration the broader context and further implications of the issue, which are the domain of theoretical knowing. Therefore, as human persons perform the cognitional operations they must take account of this differentiation of consciousness if they are to carry out those operations in a self-appropriated manner. Otherwise, individuals run the risk of applying common sense solutions to larger, theoretical lines of investigation.

Biological Pattern of Experience

The first pattern of experience to be described here is the biological pattern, which consists of the purely physiological functions of the human person. Although persons become aware of the data delivered by their senses and subsequently develop the meaning of the data, the actual functioning of their eyes, ears, nose, etc., which does not require intellectual activity on their part, comes first. Nor does the normal operating of the organs, tissues, and systems necessary for the sustaining of life require attention at all times. Individuals become aware of the biological pattern of experience, according to Lonergan, only when some factor interrupts the functioning of their organs. Only then do they ask what is wrong and attend to the actual workings of the organs themselves. People do not perceive the vibrations of the eardrum, but when their hearing is impaired as the result of a nearby loud sound, not only is the normal experience of hearing absent, but pain or numbness are often associated with the trauma to the eardrum. Without such an interruption, the biological pattern of experience functions on its own, delivering to human consciousness the data for the operations of the human subject in a non-reflective stimulus-response pattern.[4]

Aesthetic Pattern of Experience

Secondly, Lonergan identifies the aesthetic pattern of experience, which consists, broadly speaking, of the joys and pains of life that go beyond the pleasure or hardship associated with the biological pattern of experience. Although the consumption of the food required for life is operative in the biological pattern, individuals may also feel a certain level of enjoyment when sitting down to a fine meal. Exercise keeps the body in shape, but some also take great joy in that endeavor while others perceive it as a chore only to be done because of its health benefits. On a more intellectual level, even mathematicians who deal with sterile calculations may experience a sense of wonder as they make sense of the problems or proofs at hand. An important aspect of the aesthetic pattern of experience is that it testifies to the freedom of humanity, for people are free to do as they please; human persons are not restricted to the mere satisfaction of biological necessity.[5]

According to Lonergan, however, feelings are not always a positive factor, for they can derail the authentic functioning of human subjects. Specifically, he identifies individual and group biases which place the feelings or concerns of an individual or a particular group above the authentic performance of human living. The egoistic tendencies of individual bias are the result of "an incomplete development of intelligence"[6] and may be the result of either intentional concentration on selfish interests or of a lack of willingness to apply the knowledge or solution relevant to one's own life on a more general level.[7] Perhaps someone has discovered a way to maximize the profits of a given business, but refrains from communicating the strategy out of a fear of competition. The newly found procedure may have a detrimental effect on others, but individuals fail to take this into consideration either consciously or subconsciously, and the result of such instances of individual biases is that certain individuals benefit, but the effects on others are not taken into consideration.

Whereas individual bias is self-centered with regard to one person, group bias involves selfishness with regard to the particular social group to which persons belong. This is most easily seen at the national level where more powerful countries inflict their economic and military will on other nations with little or no regard for the effects of a policy on the people of the other nations.[8] In either case, the feelings associated with a certain manner of existing derail the project of human authenticity,[9] and the effects may be more or less disastrous depending on the given situation.

The preceding paragraphs represent, albeit briefly, Lonergan's treatment of feelings in *Insight*, but his understanding of human affectivity underwent considerable development throughout the course of his career. Whereas in *Insight* feelings are primarily viewed as contributing to bias, which threatens the authenticity of the performance of the cognitional operations,[10] *Method* allows for their entrance into the discernment of value with regard to matters of moral decision-making. Here, Lonergan asserts that feelings are indeed capable of playing a positive role in the functioning of the human subject rather than only serving as a threat to the endeavor of authentic living.[11] Moreover, as Robert Doran notes, the affective dimension of the human person is always present in the psychic undercurrent of the personality, which is comprised of "the sensitively experienced movement of life."[12] Even in the supposedly purely intellectual task of reading a text and appropriating its material the reader undergoes affective responses which may either help or hinder the undertaking. If individuals are excited about a book, they may read it with great enthusiasm and make connections with other readings. If, on the other hand, the book is written poorly, the goal may become less one of understanding the author's meaning and more a matter of just getting through the book to satisfy the demands of a college professor.

Given the potential for feelings to affect the human subject either positively or negatively, those who wish to operate authentically must be vigilant as to the effects of feeling on such an attempt. Robert Doran seeks to provide such a measure of control over the appropriation of the meanings contained within the aesthetic pattern of experience with his notion of psychic conversion. Although I will explore Doran's notion in greater detail in the following chapter with regard to the highly affective and symbolic nature of the mystical experience, I presently describe psychic conversion as a means by which the human subject may come to some level of critical control over the meanings associated with symbols and feelings. Psychic conversion thus allows individuals to recognize and understand the affective dimension of human existence as it is represented symbolically, and feelings are able to aid rather than hinder authentic human existence.

Intellectual Pattern of Experience

The intellectual pattern of experience is a matter of intelligent investigation into a question that stands before the human subject. Not only do human beings seek to know what they have encountered in the other patterns, they can also seek to know their knowing. Despite the excitement that may take possession of scholars as they pursue a certain issue, the intellectual pattern of experience is not swayed by capricious moods or emotions. Rather, the human subject in the intellectual pattern of experience operates within the 'passionless calm' of inquiry where the only concern is the solution to the problem or the answer to the question. The extent to which each individual person truly operates in this ideal manner may vary, but the purely intellectual pattern of experience is not concerned with external factors involved in the other patterns of experience except to identify them and keep them from interfering with the inquiry.[13]

Dramatic Pattern of Experience

The dramatic pattern of experience is concerned with the ordinary, everyday living of human life. As human persons go about their daily business, they do not operate solely within the biological pattern of experience. Likes and dislikes, preferences and disinclinations enter into human consciousness as responses to stimuli. Nor do persons operate exclusively inside the aesthetic pattern. Everyday life presents concrete problems and obstacles that must be addressed by intelligent inquiry. This intelligent inquiry, however, is of a different order than the intellectual pattern of experience insofar as the strategies persons employ in the dramatic pattern are concerned not so much with the acquisition of knowledge, but with the role they play in a given social reality, namely, the specific concrete situation in which they live. Moreover, this concern with the concrete is not a purely practical or instrumental means of going about their lives. Rather, the social milieu imbues the biological, aesthetic and intellectual aspects of human living with meaning and significance. Thus human living becomes dramatic in the artistic sense, and ordinary living becomes a matter of "learning a role and developing in oneself the feelings appropriate to its performance."[14] Human participation in society involves more than fulfilling an instrumental need. People are more than their jobs, and thus their place in society become more of a role than a function.

In order for individuals to play their artistic role in given concrete situations, some level of freedom must be present in their lives. If human persons are without choice regarding the shape of their lives life, they remain in the biological pattern of stimulus and response. Human freedom, however, is a limited reality, because, according to Lonergan, a tension exists in the functioning of the human subject between neural processes and psychic determination.[15] Psychic determination, that is, acknowledgment and recognition of the affective element of human living, must gain some control over neural processes, which is to say bodily movement and process, if human beings are to exercise dramatic freedom in life. With affectivity guiding neural processes, eating is not merely eating, and wearing clothing is not merely striving to maintain body heat because these activities take on an added dimension of significance. Human beings enjoy certain foods and develop mealtime rituals, and clothing becomes an expression of likes and dislikes or roles in society.

The limitation placed on human freedom by the tension between psychic determination and neural processes therefore arises from the biological need for food, clothing, and shelter, and affective responses to those needs. Individuals may desire a certain food, but if they fail to recognize the biological necessity of a balanced diet they will run into health difficulties. Human beings are not free to do whatever they please because pleasure may lead to physical harm. With regard to the roles individuals play in society in the dramatic pattern of experience, they may prefer a given role, but that role may not provide for their physical needs. Many parents have sacrificed joy in the workplace in order to provide for their family.

Psychic determination, moreover, enables the subconscious neural processes of the human person to organize and thematize the data encountered in such processes through symbolic representation.[16] Even human knowing, according to Lonergan, involves activity on the part of the subconscious in the formulation of insight, and human persons may only proceed to the levels of understanding and judgment through the representation of what they encounter in neural process.[17]

Unfortunately, because the dramatic pattern of experience brings with it a preceding set of circumstances regarding individuals' roles in society and the potential for discord between their neural demands and their psychic representation, it carries also the prospect to derail the cognitive process of human subjects. Lonergan names this going astray 'dramatic bias,' and he writes the following of this disruption of human knowing.

> If prepossessions and prejudices notoriously vitiate theoretical investigations, much more easily can elementary passions bias understanding in practical and personal matters. Nor has such a bias merely some single and isolated effect. To exclude an insight is also to exclude the further questions that would arise from it, and the complementary insights that would carry it toward a rounded and balanced viewpoint.[18]

The social milieu that informs the dramatic pattern of experience thus may serve as a hindrance to the pursuit of knowing as it provides the base material from which human subjects proceed. Perhaps a given society encourages the notion that certain of its constitutive groups are inferior or that military might is the only answer to global issues. In such cases, the accepted dramatic roles for certain individuals and groups of persons prevent the consideration of some of the data or courses of action. Moreover, if affectivity runs roughshod over the aspect of human inquiry that is neural process, emotion interferes with the investigation of the matter at hand. Instead of inspirational dramatic artistry, it becomes the twisted artistry of the demonic ruled by prejudice and malice.[19]

Practical Pattern of Experience

The practical pattern of experience is the realm of common sense. Human knowing, according to Lonergan, is not restricted to the intellectual pattern of experience in which academics reside. Rather, human knowing is present in virtually every moment of human living, for human beings are always experiencing data, understanding that data, and making judgments as to the veracity of their understanding. The practical pattern of experience, however, is not concerned with general, theoretical knowledge of a matter. Rather, in the practical pattern of experience, individuals are concerned only with achieving a certain task. Making breakfast or planning a vacation involves human intelligence, but they do not require comprehensive knowledge of the reasons why certain foods taste good together or the reasons behind the design of the freeway system in the United States.

Unlike the dramatic pattern of experience, persons in the practical pattern are not concerned with the role they play in a given society, but only with completing the task at hand. Consider the previous example of making breakfast. For those doing so only for themselves, the task may take on a very practical purpose, namely, to get out the door and go to work. If, on the other hand, a parent is making breakfast for a child, then the task takes on more of the characteristics of the dramatic pattern because the adult is taking on the role of the parent, which comes with its particularities according to cultural or personal expectations and responsibilities.

Worshipful Pattern of Experience[20]

The worshipful pattern of experience occurs under the impact of religious conversion within a specific religious context. As Denise Lardner Carmody notes, Lonergan's treatment of religious conversion bears a decidedly intellectualist cast. Although Lonergan's thoughts demonstrate considerable growth in the time between *Insight* and *Method*, this focus on the intellect in connection with religious conversion is never lost entirely. Briefly put, the development of Lonergan's thought lies in a transition wherein the question of God becomes more important than the answer.[21] The question of God lies at the very heart of human intentionality, for the existence of God is an issue implicit in every line of questioning. At the very core of humanity's encounter with the universe is the question of the origin and ground of all being, the question of God.[22]

The fulfillment of this intentionality toward God is, according to Lonergan, the act of falling in love with God, an experience that brings with it a sense of purpose and peace to life, and its absence opens the way for the trivialization of human life as people encounter a universe which lacks an ultimate ground.[23] Falling in love with God, moreover, is a matter of loving in an unrestricted fashion. "Just as unrestricted questioning is our capacity for self-transcendence, so being in love in an unrestricted fashion is the proper fulfillment of that capacity."[24] The unrestricted act of falling in love with God establishes a new foundational reality in which human persons operate. All knowing, valuing, and acting are transformed in light of this love, and this act is thus the basic formulation of Lonergan's use of the term, 'religious conversion.'

To speak of religious conversion as the act of falling in love with God may appear at first to run the risk of losing the traditional Christian assertion that individuals receive rather than achieve religious conversion. Lonergan avoids this danger by claiming that religious conversion is the result of the prior reality of God's love flooding human hearts through the Holy Spirit.[25] The love of God is the experience of being grasped by ultimate concern, a total surrender to the will of the Divine, which leads to a deep sense of joy, purpose, and meaning in life.[26] It is a matter of God approaching human beings in love and the response, or lack thereof, on the part of human persons.

Although Lonergan's work contains many glowing passages regarding the transformative effect of falling in love with God, his most explicit treatment of love comes in his article, "Finality, Love, Marriage," which appeared some 30 years prior to *Method*.[27] Here, Lonergan asserts that the concept of love is one of great complexity, for it is at the same time an act of a faculty and the act of a subject. As an act of a faculty, love is a response to the natural desire for the good. Because it is a response to the aspiration for the good, love is the first principle of the process aimed toward the end that is loved. In other words, love as act of a faculty is that which drives human persons to express love toward others in words or actions. In this expression, human beings desire and encourage good for their beloved.

As an act of a subject, according to Lonergan, love "is the principle of union between different subjects."[28] Here, love is that which binds two persons together, forming the basis from which love as an act of faculty may proceed. This union of subjects, moreover, may be of two kinds, that of the union that exists between two persons pursuing a common goal and that of two persons when that goal has been reached.[29] For example, two loving individuals working together to provide more adequately for those members of society who are pushed to the margins are bound by the common goal of furthering justice in the community. When they reach their goal, the connection between the two takes on a different character as they acknowledge in one another a job well done.

In the functioning of the human person, moreover, reflection upon the functioning and object of love occurs, and this leads in turn to the production of further instances of the good.[30] As the two good Samaritans of the preceding paragraph reflect upon the positive changes in society effected by their efforts, they may decide to take another step in the overcoming of social ills. Love, then, is capable of becoming a transformative force insofar as human beings reflect and act upon their loving and the beneficence they feel for their beloved. Human beings operate within a radically altered reality when they act according to love of God and neighbor.

Unfortunately, Lonergan does not provide his reader with a detailed analysis of the reflection undertaken by the rational loving subject. He writes throughout the article of the perfection of the process of loving, but surprisingly for a thinker so interested in the operations of the human person, he provides very little in the way of concrete analysis. A more comprehensive treatment of the act of loving from a Lonerganian framework may be found in the work of Tad Dunne. Dunne presents his work on the nature of loving in the fourth chapter of his *Lonergan and Spirituality*, and his efforts provide a more concrete expression of what Lonergan means by defining religious conversion as falling in love with God. He writes:

> We want to grasp which of the many movements in our consciousness is love, and we want to understand how that love functions. No doubt, we will not understand everything about love, but at least we can understand where understanding leaves off, and at that point we can gaze in reverence at the mystery... In our chapter on Knowing, we saw that to understand anything, we need to understand the processes that condition its existences. That is, we grasp things not by an imaginative reconstruction, ... but by a grasp of the recurring processes that keep the 'thing' functioning as it does.[31]

In other words, just as human persons can know their knowing, they can also know how they love. The implications of intellectual conversion, that is, knowing one's knowing, are far-reaching and enable a more authentic human existence. Likewise, if human persons know their falling in love with God, they are better able to go about their lives authentically. Religious conversion becomes a part of their foundational reality, and for that reality to come to expression they must advert to it.

According to Dunne, the act of loving consists of two elements. First, the persons who love feel benevolent towards those who are the objects of their love. They want good things to happen to those they love, and they take actions to encourage those things. Secondly, they appreciate the other person. Whereas benevolence focuses on a desired future that is beneficial, when human beings appreciate those whom they love, they are recognizing the good that is already present. These two aspects of loving interact with one another, for as the good desired for one's beloved is achieved, the lover appreciates the new state of wellness. But, as Dunne notes, lovers are always looking forward to an even greater good. Thus, benevolence and appreciation exist in a dynamic state, each leading to the other.[32]

Benevolence and appreciation do not arise spontaneously, however, for they have their source in transcendent love. Transcendent love, Dunne claims, may be manifest at certain times or places and in certain individuals or objects, but no particular instance is exhaustive of it. It may be evident in the love a friend has for another, but always goes beyond the given situation. When people envision good things for their beloved, they are transcending the given situation, and without such transcendence, the love they have for one another faces a limit. But for love, no bounds exist to the good desired for one another.[33]

In addition to knowing human loving, knowing that one is loved is also possible, and this is a trickier matter than it first appears. According to Dunne, advertence to being loved is largely a matter of coming to the decision that one is indeed loved. Much like the operations performed in other matters of knowing, there comes a time when persons must decide whether or not to believe the words and actions of another who professes love. It is, in essence, a decision to let oneself be loved.[34] In the case of transcendent love, being loved is a matter of recognizing the deeper source from which particular instances of loving arise. Thus, for Dunne, the basis for loving the source of transcendent love is the very fact that human persons love and are loved in their everyday lives, and the object of the response to transcendent love is God.[35]

At this point, the Christian particularity of Lonergan's work on religious conversion needs clarification. Lonergan himself, after all, relies upon Heiler's assertion of infinite Divine love as a point of contact among the world religions.[36] What is the role of Christ, Scripture, and tradition in the experience of falling in love with God?[37] These factors play a role in the decision to accept the gift of God's transcendent love for Christian persons.

The issue at hand here is the expression of religious conversion within the specific context of the Christian religion. On the topic of religion, Lonergan writes, "Before it enters the world mediated by meaning, religion is the prior word God speaks to us by flooding our hearts with his love."[38] The life of Christ and the church, as they have been handed down through Scripture and tradition, may thus be understood as the mediation of the encounter with God in which human beings fall in love with God in an unrestricted fashion. When the prior word of God is expressed outwardly in the concrete reality of a human historical situation, this outward expression plays a constitutive role for individual believers and the community formed as these persons express the Word of God received in the state of being in love with God in an unrestricted fashion. The expression of the religious love shared by the members of the community helps the community to take shape and become a presence in the world.[39]

Moreover, the community that is constituted by the outward expression of the word, in turn, shapes subsequent manifestations of the word in the lives of persons and the community as a whole.

> For however personal and intimate is religious experience, still it is not solitary. The same gift can be given to many, and the many can recognize in one another a common orientation in their living and feeling, in their criteria and their goals. From a common communion with God there springs a religious community.[40]

Therefore, Christian mystics recount their experiences as visions of Christ or the Triune God, Muslim mystics do so in a decidedly Muslim manner, Buddhists as Buddhists, etc.

The particular concrete manifestation of the Word spoken to human hearts illustrates the distinction between faith and belief.   Faith, for Lonergan, is the knowledge born of religious love.[41] Faith is not, however, the same type of knowledge that is gained through the performance of the cognitional operations.   Rather, it is "the prior act of appreciation or evaluation that discerns and welcomes God as the transcendent Thou in both nature and history."[42]   Beliefs, on the other hand, are the historically conditioned outward expressions of the inner word that demarcate religious communities and shape the experiences and accounts of individuals.[43]

Within the historical situation of communities of belief the worshipful pattern of experience is located. Although Lonergan's description of this pattern of experience is limited to a gathering of persons in the development of holiness,[44] he does treat extensively the nature of prayer, and prayer is the foundational element in the vocation to holiness effected by religious conversion.[45]   In his 1963 lecture entitled, "The Mediation of Christ in Prayer," Lonergan writes of the specifically Christian notion that the Triune God becomes present to believers as they approach the Divine through prayer, and the mediation of this presence is of two kinds. First, Lonergan describes the objective notion of mediation in which Christ mediates to human persons something of the nature of the Divine and the makeup of the life lived according to God's will.[46] In worship, human beings recognize something of the glory of God, and this realization bears fruit in the concrete living of their lives. In a secondary, subjective, sense, Christ mediates those aspects of the human person that are of a supernatural order. Christians are not their own, but belong to God, and as Lonergan puts it, "[They] are adoptive children of the Father,"[47] and this identity is located in the subjective level of the human person. Christians, regardless of the pattern of experience in which they are located, are always aware of the presence of God at all times and in all things. Before Christ mediates the awareness of the Christian identity as adopted children of God, it exists in human persons subconsciously, but when they become aware of it, their lives are transformed insofar as their new awareness leads to development in holiness. Thus, the subjective mediation of Christ, is not a matter of the mediation of the Divine, but of the nature of the human person in loving relationship with the Divine.[48] When Christians approach God in worship, they receive from Christ a deeper grasp of themselves in the state of being in love with God, and the awakening to a more profound awareness of themselves and God forms the worshipful pattern of experience.

Mystical Pattern of Experience

The preceding paragraphs have provided an account of the patterns of experience listed by Lonergan in the earlier quotation from *Method*: "the biological, aesthetic, intellectual, dramatic, practical, or worshipful patterns of experience within with the operations [of the human subject] occur."[49] Lonergan did not intend, however, for this list of six patterns of experience to be a comprehensive catalog of the particularities of human experience. The fact that the list of patterns of experience has grown from four to six in the time between *Insight* and *Method* testifies to the open-ended nature of the patterns of experience. Moreover, Lonergan himself states that his treatment of the patterns in *Insight* was not meant to be an exhaustive list.[50] As such, Lonergan's specific mention of mystical experience of the transcendent in *Philosophy of God and Theology* and *Insight* is not surprising.[51] With the room left by Lonergan for the expansion of the patterns of consciousness in mind, the following is a treatment of the mystical pattern of experience drawn from the few mentions of mysticism by Lonergan himself and later commentators.

Although the relation of Lonergan's theological proposals to mysticism has received relatively little attention until recently, mysticism appears to be an integral element of Lonergan's theological endeavors.[52] On the few occasions that he treats the subject of mysticism directly, Lonergan usually refers the reader to the work of William Johnston or Karl Rahner. Gordon Rixon notes that a precise determination of Lonergan's position on the topic of mysticism remains difficult to ascertain. Given the centrality of mysticism to this book, the description of the mystical pattern of experience will be of greater depth than the previous patterns, and what follows is my attempt to develop an understanding of mysticism that is consistent with Lonergan's notion of self-appropriation and is of use in resisting the split soul mentality.

As a Jesuit priest, Lonergan's grasp of mysticism was deeply affected by the *Spiritual Exercises* of St. Ignatius of Loyola.[53] According to Rixon, Lonergan understood the *Spiritual Exercises* as a guide to assist persons in their cooperation with the Grace of God. This experience of cooperative

Grace directs Christians as they seek to grow in their identity as living members of Jesus Christ. The unitive effect produced by this cooperation strengthens their desire for God in all aspects of life, a consequence described by Ignatius as transforming union. In his appropriation of this Ignatian idea of transforming union, Lonergan does not write of the individual's entire life as characterized by union with God, but rather maintains that the mystical experience entails a break in the normal consciousness of human persons. After such an experience they return to functioning in other patterns of experience. Their functioning as human subjects, however, is now informed by the mystical encounter with God, but the mystical experience itself has a definite starting and ending point, just as the other patterns of experience do. Ignatius's transformative union, by serving as a source from which inspiration and guidance for a life of service may flow,[54] enables the mystical experience to bear directly on the everyday functioning of individual persons.

Although Rixon's analysis of Lonergan's understanding of mysticism is helpful in its identification of the sources that affected Lonergan's thinking on the subject, Rixon does not undertake the task of explicating the manner in which mysticism fits into Lonergan's understanding of the human subject. This task is taken up by James Robertson Price III, who claims that in order to comprehend Lonergan's work on mysticism a distinction must be drawn between mystical and religious consciousness.[55] Religious conversion, as previously discussed, consists of the act of falling in love with God, an act which entails two distinct elements. First, the gift of God's love floods human hearts, and secondly, there is the human response to this gift. According to Price, religious consciousness is comprised of the response to the gift of God's love, and mystical consciousness, on the other hand, is a particular awareness of the gift itself.[56]

The key to understanding the particular awareness of the gift of God's love present in mystical consciousness lies in the intersubjectivity present in the human-Divine relationship in the mystical pattern of experience. On the topic of intersubjectivity, Lonergan follows the work of Max Scheler, who identifies a relationship of 'emotional identification,' wherein either an awareness of a distinction between persons has not yet developed, or the persons involved withdraw from such distinction into a sense of unity. An example of the former would be the attitude of a baby toward its mother, and instances of the latter may be found in hypnosis or sexuality wherein people lapse into a common stream of consciousness.[57] According to Price, Lonergan's understanding of mystical consciousness falls into the category of a withdrawal from differentiation into a sense of unity wherein the mystic leaves behind objective knowledge of God and moves to an immediate awareness of God's love.[58]

Within this framework of mystical consciousness two issues must be clarified. First, Lonergan's use of the notion of 'immediacy' is used to refer to experience before the human subject discerns the meanings contained in the experience through later acts of understanding. Thus, Lonergan's use of the term 'immediacy' is different than the Scholastic usage of the term, which is the denial of an object that exists between the act and the object.[59] Only by reflecting upon the data of sense and consciousness do people move from the world of immediacy inhabited by the infant to the world mediated by meaning wherein the subject ascertains the intelligibility of the surrounding world. In the case of the emotional identification that characterizes the mystical experience, however, the immediacy of the experience is mediated by the prayer life of individuals. Hence, Lonergan is able to speak of mystical consciousness as 'mediated immediacy.'[60]

Secondly, the intersubjective relationship that exists in the mystical encounter with God differs from the objective nature of religious consciousness.[61] The term 'objective' does not mean the objectivity that is associated with the veracity of one's knowing. Rather, the sense of objectivity operative here intends the principal notion of objectivity that, according to Lonergan, consists of three separate judgments: "I am." "You are." "I am not you." By virtue of these three affirmations, a relationship is established between subject and object that recognizes the connection between the two, yet maintains the difference.[62] In other words, even though a relationship comprised of two persons is a relationship between two subjects, an objective element exists insofar as the distinction between the two is real. As such, the objectivity of religious consciousness consists of the judgments: "I am." "God is." "I am not God."[63]

However, if, as Price asserts, Lonergan's understanding of mystical experience involves withdrawal from differentiation into a sense of unity, how can an account for a unitive state that does not blur the distinction between the mystic and God be developed? Christian mysticism holds that mystics do not become God, but rather that they participate in the Divine life without losing their individuality. Price contends that in the case of mystical consciousness, the intersubjective nature of the relationship may best be described as the series of affirmations: "I am, you are, I am you." He writes:

> In this pattern, the first two judgments, "I am" and "you are," are the same as in the attainment of the "objective" distinction. [It is] with the third judgment that the difference emerges, for in a state of vital unity the subject does not make the judgment "I am not you," a judgment which would affirm an objective distinction

between discrete subjects. Instead, the subject makes the judgment "I <u>am</u> you," (or perhaps better, "I am we"), and by so doing affirms the vital unity of itself with the other.[64]

In this series of judgments, the subject with whom mystics are in relationship, namely God, is not encountered as something "out there," but as an interior reality that floods the entirety of their being. The union is not, however, one of total dissolution, for the first two judgments assert the differentiation that continues to exist between the mystic and God, but the third judgment affirms the relationship of emotional identification.

Given this description, the discussion can now turn to an examination of the emergence of the intersubjective relationship in the mystical pattern of experience. According to Price, the mystical life, as with all religious experience, begins with the gift of God's love which floods human hearts through the power of the Holy Spirit. The human response to this gift is religious conversion wherein individual fall in love with God in return. The cultivation of prayer life as an aspect of the dynamic state of loving God, in some individuals, may lead to "an explicit awareness of mystical encounter with the divine, an awareness which culminates in the withdrawal into the cloud of unknowing."[65] In other words, the mystic experiences the immediacy of the gift of God's love, which is mediated through the development of the mystic's spiritual life.[66]

The preceding paragraphs provide a summary of Price's work on mystical consciousness from within a Lonerganian perspective, but the issue of the content of the mystical experience remains, for consciousness and knowledge are two different things. According to Lonergan, the content of the mystical experience consists of a love with God that is so deep that individuals are content to rest in the presence of Divine love without needing images or concepts to define the experience. They are comfortable with saying only what God is not. The mystical experience is a 'cloud of unkowing,' accessible through a 'cloud of forgetting.' Through the appropriation of these experiences, mystics deepen their appreciation of the Divine in all of creation and participate more authentically therein. As Rixon puts it, "the mystic's withdrawal into apophatic prayer returns to find its authentic expression in the expansive freedom of a kataphatic spirituality."[67] Though the experience of union contains no images or concepts, when mystics seek to express their encounter with God they must do so through language.

A Lonerganian position regarding mysticism is thus one in which comprehension of the mystical encounter only comes later as mystics reflect upon their experiences.[68] However, as I indicated in Chapter One, a strand of mysticism also exists that is characterized by the presence of such phenomena as visions or auditions. Even Ignatius of Loyola, whose spirituality informed Lonergan's work on the subject, received numerous visions as a part of his prayer life. For instance, the following is found in Ignatius's third person *Autobiography*.

> During all this time, our Lord appeared to him often, giving him great consolation and determination; but what he seemed to see was something round and large, as though it were of gold: and this was what presented itself to him.[69]

Ignatius's account of this experience is of a decidedly different nature than the cloud of unknowing that characterizes much of Lonergan's work on mysticism. Rather than an utter lack of content, the experience consisted of the presence of Christ and the appearance of the mysterious golden object. Julian of Norwich and Hildegard of Bingen[70] similarly recount visionary experiences. Mysticism entailing the reception of visions or Divine words abounds in the Western Christian tradition, and any satisfactory account of the mystical experience must take this into account.

Although Lonergan does not specifically address the issue of such a kataphatic mysticism, he is certainly open to the notion of God speaking to the hearts of God's people. He writes that treatment of "questions regarding revelation and inspiration, scripture and tradition, development and authority, schisms and heresies" are to be left to other theologians.[71] Moreover, "before it enters into the world mediated by meaning, religion is the prior word God speaks to us by flooding our hearts with his love."[72] This word, he claims, reveals both something of the nature of God and of the relationship with the Divine into which converted persons enter. When individuals reflect upon the word spoken to their hearts, they are able to communicate what has been learned to others. Taken collectively, I believe these statements indicate a willingness on Lonergan's part to acknowledge the existence of mystical experiences and knowledge other than the cloud of unknowing that characterizes his description of mysticism. In such cases, as with all human functioning, expression of the mystical life is a matter of attending to the data of the revelatory mystical experience, seeking to understand that data, pronouncing judgment on that understanding, and making decisions based upon that judgment.

Conclusion

In this chapter I have presented Lonergan's notion of the patterns of experience and how the particularities of those patterns may demand attention to different aspects of the human person. Despite the fact that human consciousness encounters a great variety and combinations of these patterns, however, the human subject remains a unity and carries the knowledge and awareness gained from one pattern to subsequent patterns. With specific regard to mysticism, the mystical pattern of experience consists of a profound unity with the Divine wherein the persons find a level of intersubjectivity unique to this pattern which consists of the three affirmations, "I am, You are, and I am You (or I am We)." The split soul mentality tries to leave behind the third affirmation and the wisdom gained in the mystical pattern of experience. Therefore, as individuals operating under the influence of the split soul mentality address matters in the other patterns of experience they not only are in danger of bracketing from consideration the gift of mystical wisdom, but also run the further risk of confusing the relevance of this wisdom to other matters. In the case of the former, mysticism is understood as extraneous to socio-political matters, and in the latter, the operating of the subject is hindered so that persons are more prone to make erroneous judgments or take misguided actions on the basis of the mystical experience. The aforementioned Henry Suso, for instance, perhaps allowed his spirituality to interfere with the practical and biological matters of his life through his extreme asceticism. Bernard of Clairvaux, moreover, was an ardent supporter of the Crusades, though he later changed his position in light of their failure.[73] I suggest that for both of these individuals, a lack of self-appropriation led to a mistaken application of their understanding of the content of their spiritual lives. Neither was able to apply authentically the wisdom of the mystical experience to their concrete living, a shortcoming that recognition of the particularities of the various patterns of experience may be able to address.

NOTES

[1] Bernard Lonergan, *Method in Theology*, 2nd ed. (New York: Herder and Herder, 1973; reprint, Toronto: University of Toronto Press, 1990, 1994, 1996), 286. See also, *Collected Works of Bernard Loneran*, vol. 3, *Insight: A Study of Human Understanding*, 5th rev. ed., eds. Frederick E. Crowe and Robert M. Doran (Toronto: University of Toronto Press, 1992), 204-212. This chapter will take the additional step of investigating a specifically mystical pattern of experience, which Lonergan identifies, but does not clarify in Chapter 14 of *Insight*.

[2] Tad Dunne names this unity of the subject, 'spiritual integration,' which he describes as enabling "a person to ground all the workings of the mind and all the practical decisions of a responsible life in the love of divine Mystery." Tad Dunne, *Lonergan and Spirituality: Toward a Spiritual Integration* (Chicago: Loyola University Press, 1985), 183. Thus, as will be described in the coming chapters, the self-appropriated subject is able to identify the particularities of a given experience and bring the insights and knowledge from that experience to others and do so *appropriately*. Self-appropriated persons are therefore not only aware of their functioning as subjects but are also able to recognize when the data from previous functioning is relevant to later efforts.

[3] For Lonergan, the principles affirmed in the act of judgment form a horizon in which human subjects operate. Thus, once individuals verify the relevance of mysticism to political affairs, they go on to treat subsequent issues with this notion in mind. Lonergan, *Method*, 235-237. If this were not the case, people would have to relearn every previous bit of knowledge every time they sought to appropriate a new experience. I will return to this topic later in this book in a discussion regarding Lonergan's notion of the horizon in which human persons operate.

[4] Lonergan, *Insight*, 204-207. The biological pattern of experience may at first appear to possess little relevance for this book, but the example of the ascetic mystics helps illustrates its bearing on the study of mysticism. For example, many women mystics of the Middle Ages began to view the body as a means to facilitate the encounter with the Divine. Caroline Walker Bynum, "The Female Body and Religious Practice," in Caroline Walker Bynum, *Fragmentation and Redemption: Essays on Gender and the Human Body in Medieval Religion* (New York: Zone Books, 1991), 183. St. Paul's experience on the way to Damascus further demonstrates the impact on one's religious sensibilities of having the biological pattern of experience interrupted (Acts 9:8-9).

[5] Lonergan, *Insight*, 207-209.

[6] Ibid,, 245.

[7] Ibid., 244-247.

[8] Ibid., 247-250.

[9] Lonergan uses the term, 'authenticity' in a specific context. Human persons may be said to be operating authentically when they attend to the data, understand that data as it exists independently of the subject, make judgments according to the understanding of the data, and make responsible decisions on the basis of that judgment. In doing so, individuals come to

know a thing and take action based on that knowledge, not from the perspective of the individual knower, but on the basis of what a thing truly is. Therefore, according to Lonergan, human knowing intends being. Lonergan, *Insight*, 387. Authenticity, moreover, also involves matters of moral decision-making and religious living. Just as human persons can know things as they truly are, they can also discern the truly good, and this discernment provides the foundation for moral living. Religiously speaking, when human beings fall in love with God in an unrestricted fashion, they are seeking not just being, but the ground of all being. Individuals transcend their particular situation, and thus Lonergan makes the statement, "Man achieves authenticity in self-transcendence." Lonergan, *Method*, 104.

[10] Lonergan, *Insight*, 629.

[11] Lonergan treats feelings in pages 30-34 of *Method* and the notion of judgments of value on pages 34-41. For a more in-depth examination of the progression of Lonergan's thought on value and the good, see M. Shawn Copeland, *A Genetic Study of the Idea of the Human Good in the Thought of Bernard Lonergan* (Ph.D. diss., Boston College1991), 150-253. For a discussion of Lonergan's transition and its impact especially on matters of moral decision-making, see Frederick E. Crowe, SJ, "An Exploration of Lonergan's New Notion of Value," in *Appropriating the Lonergan Idea*, ed. Michael Vertin (Washington D.C.: The Catholic University Press of America, 1989), 52-54; and Walter E. Conn, "Bernard Lonergan on Value," *The Thomist* 40 (1976): 243.

[12] Robert Doran, *Theology and the Dialectics of History* (Toronto: University of Toronto Press), 46.

[13] Ibid., 209-210.

[14] Lonergan, *Insight*, 212.

[15] Although Lonergan does not include such factors in his discussion of the dramatic pattern of experience, the exercise of freedom may also be influenced by the role played by individuals in society. Their financial situation or social role may prevent them from taking certain courses of action or even considering certain issues. If they are poor, living where they most desire may be difficult. Likewise, those who have never left the city may find envisioning a life in the country difficult.

[16] Lonergan, *Insight*, 212-214. See also, Frank Paul Braio, *Lonergan's Retrieval of the Notion of Human Being: Clarifications of and Reflections on the Argument of "Insight," Chapters I-XVIII* (Lanham, MD: University Press of America, 1988), 109-111. Robert Doran names this tension between neural demands and psychic representation the 'basic dialectic of the subject,' and proposes his notion of psychic conversion as a means to encourage the symbolic representation of subconscious neural demands. Doran, *Theology and the Dialectics of History*, 71-72.

[17] At first glance the notion of subconscious activity in human inquiry may seem to run counter to Lonergan's insistence on the willful dedication necessary to perform the cognitional operations authentically. He is insistent, however, that insights spring unbidden to the fore of human consciousness as individuals seek to understand the data examined at the level of experience. He writes, "What we have to grasp is that insight (1) comes as a release

to the tension of inquiry, (2) *comes suddenly and unexpectedly*, (3) is a function not of outer circumstances but of inner conditions, (4) pivots between the concrete and the abstract, and (5) passes into the habitual texture of one's mind." Emphasis mine. Lonergan, *Insight*, 38. His favorite example of this phenomenon is Archimedes's famous "Eureka" moment in the bath whereby he discovered that weighing the king's crown in water was the best way to ensure the king's crown was indeed made of gold. Ibid., 27-31. The solution to Archimedes's problem burst suddenly and unexpectedly into consciousness as a function of the subconscious.

[18] Ibid., 214.

[19] Lonergan, *Method*, 111.

[20] In the time since this book originally appeared as my doctoral dissertation, I have developed the work presented in the following section more fully with regard to the worshipful pattern of experience in Ian Bell, "An Elaboration of the Worshipful Pattern of Experience in the Work of Bernard Lonergan," *Worship* 81:6 (Nov 2007): 521-540. Much of the following was originally published in this article and appears here with some editing with the generous permission of *Worship*.

[21] Denise Lardner Carmody, "The Desire for Transcendence: Religious Conversion," in Vernon Gregson, ed., *The Desires of the Human Heart: An Introduction to the Theology of Bernard Lonergan* (Mahwah, NJ: Paulist Press, 1988), 57. For a more detailed treatment of Lonergan's development with regard to religious conversion see Michael L. Rende, *Lonergan on Conversion: The Development of a Notion* (Lanham, MD: University Press of America, 1991).

[22] Lonergan, *Method*, 102-103.

[23] Ibid., 105.

[24] Ibid., 106.

[25] As a Jesuit priest and Christian theologian, Lonergan's primary concern with regard to religious conversion is a specifically Christian understanding of that notion. This is not to say, however, that Lonergan was completely unconcerned with the relevance of his work for religious conversion as it is found in other religious traditions. In this regard Lonergan refers his readers to the work of Friedrich Heiler on the commonalities of world religions. Lonergan, *Method*, 109. Friedrich Heiler, "The History of Religions as a Preparation for the Cooperation of Religions," in Mircea Eliade and J. Kitagawa, eds., *The History of Religions* (Chicago: University of Chicago Press, 1959), 142-153. Inter-religious dialogue in a Lonerganian framework is also the focus of Vernon Gregson in his *Lonergan, Spirituality, and the Meeting of Religions*. Here, Gregson argues that foundational theology, understood as reflection upon one's religious conversion, enables theologians from any religious tradition to better understand their own encounters with the Divine and thus be better able to enter into dialogue with others. Vernon Gregson, *Lonergan, Spirituality, and the Meeting of Religions*, College Theology Society Studies in Religion, vol. 2 (Lanham, MD: University Press of America, 1985).

[26] Lonergan, *Method*, 240-241.

[27] This article was first published as, Bernard Lonergan, "Finality, Love, Marriage," *Theological Studies* 4 (1943): 477-510. I will refer to this article as it appears in *Collection*. Bernard Lonergan, "Finality, Love, Marriage," in *Collection: Papers by Bernard Lonergan, S.J.*, ed. F.E. Crowe, S.J. (Montreal: Palm Publishers, 1967), 16-53.

[28] Lonergan, "Finality, Love, Marriage," 23.

[29] Ibid.

[30] Ibid., 29.

[31] Dunne, 105.

[32] Ibid., 107.

[33] Ibid.

[34] Ibid., 110.

[35] Ibid., 111.

[36] Lonergan, *Method*, 109.

[37] Lonergan's work on the role of Scripture and tradition and Christology are beyond the scope of this study. For Lonergan's treatment of these issues, see the following. Bernard Lonergan, "Christ as Subject: A Reply," in *Collection: Papers by Bernard Lonergan, S.J.*, ed. F.E. Crowe, S.J. (Montreal: Palm Publishers, 1967), 164-197; Bernard Lonergan, "The Dehellenization of Dogma," in *A Second Collection*, ed., William F.J. Ryan, S.J. and Bernard J. Tyrrell, S.J. (Philadelphia: The Westminster Press, 1974), 11-32.

[38] Lonergan, *Method*, 112.

[39] Ibid., 112-113.

[40] Ibid., 118.

[41] Ibid., 115.

[42] Dunne, 119.

[43] Gregson, *Lonergan, Spririruality, and the Meeting of Religions*, 99-100.

[44] Lonergan, *Method*, 116.

[45] Ibid., 240-241.

[46] Bernard Lonergan, "The Mediation of Christ in Prayer," in *Collected Works of Bernard Loneran*, vol. 6, *Philosophical and Theological Papers 1958-1964*, eds. Robert C. Croken, Frederick E. Crowe, and Robert M. Doran (Toronto: University of Toronto Press, 1996), 177.

[47] Ibid., 179.

[48] Ibid., 178-182.

[49] Lonergan, *Method*, 286.

[50] *Collected Works of Lonergan*, vol. 5, *Understanding and Being: The Halifax Lectures on "Insight,"* eds., Elizabeth A. Morelli and Mark D. Morelli (Toronto: University of Toronto Press, 1990), 320. Compare also Lonergan's handling of patterns of experience in *Insight*, where he describes only dramatic, aesthetic, intellectual, and biological (though he mentions the mystical pattern without explanation), with the more extensive treatment in *Method*.

[51] Bernard Lonergan, "The Functional Specialty, Systematics," in *Philosophy of God, and Theology: The Relationship between Philosophy of God and the Functional Specialty, Systematics*, St. Michael's Lectures, Gonzaga University, Spokane, WA (London: Darton, Longman & Todd, 1972), 38-39; *Insight*, 410.

[52] William Johnston, for instance, provides the following anecdote. [He] "met Bernard Lonergan in Boston a few years before his death in 1984 and told him that his method culminates in mystical experience. Lonergan smiled and said, 'Yes, yes...!'" William Johnston, *Mystical Theology: The Science of Love* (Maryknoll, NY: Orbis Books, 1998), 7 nt. 14. Contrast this with Richard M. Liddy's contention that early in his career Lonergan was not particularly interested in mysticism. Richard M. Liddy, *Transforming Light: Intellectual Conversion in the Early Lonergan* (Collegville, MN: The Liturgical Press, 1993), 7. This discrepancy lends credence to Gordon Rixon's account that Lonergan did not fully understand the Ignatian notion of consolation without a cause, which came to inform Lonergan's understanding of mysticism, until the years 1975-1976. Gordon Rixon, "Lonergan and Mysticism." *Theological Studies* 62 (2001): 481.

[53] For the text of the *Spiritual Exercises*, see *Ignatius of Loyola: Spiritual Exercises and Selected Works*, ed. George E. Ganss, S.J., trans. Parmananda R. Divarkar, S.J., Edward J. Malatesta, S.J., Martin E. Palmer, S.J., The Classics of Western Spirituality: A Library of the Great Spiritual Masters (Mahwah: Paulist Press, 1991), 113-214.

[54] Rixon, 484-487.

[55] Price uses the term 'religious consciousness' interchangeably with 'religious experience.' He writes, "since Lonergan locates religious experience among the data of consciousness, it may therefore also, and with accuracy, be referred to as religious consciousness." James Robertson Price III, "Lonergan and the Foundation of a Contemporary Mystical Theology," in Fred Lawrence, ed., *Lonergan Workshop*, vol. 5 (Chico, CA: Scholars Press, 1985), 168.

[56] Ibid., 167.

[57] Lonergan, *Method*, 58-59.

[58] Ibid., 77.

[59] Rixon, 492, nt. 48. For the scholastics, an example of a mediated object would be something that is known only through the pedagogy of another person. Here, something stands between the act of knowing and the object being investigated. Immediacy, on the other hand involves only the knower and the object or principle under consideration.

[60] Lonergan, *Method*, 77.

[61] Price, 171.

[62] Lonergan, *Insight*, 399-402; Price, 171.

[63] Price, 171.

[64] Price, 171.

[65] Ibid., 175.

[66] This is not to say that the cultivation of the spiritual life is the only manner by which Divine love is mediated to the mystic. The mystical tradition contains the presence of individuals who encounter God's loving presence through such avenues as interaction with other persons or nature. Consider, for example, the tradition of the spiritual mentor who serves as a guide and resource for those who sought to deepen their relationship with God, or the role played by animals in the life of Francis of Assisi. For the former, see Lavinia Byrne, ed., *Traditions of Spiritual Guidance* (Collegeville, MN: The Liturgical Press, 1990); Edward C. Sellner, *Mentoring: The Ministry of Spiritual Kinship* (Notre Dame, IN: Ave Maria Press, 1990). For the life of Francis, see *Francis of Assisi: Early Documents*, 3 vols., ed. Regis J. Armstrong, O.F.M. Cap., J.A. Wayne Hellmann, O.F.M. Conv., and William J. Short, O.F.M (New York, London, and Manila: New City Press, 1999); Arnaldo Fortini, *Francis of Assisi*, trans. Helen Moak (New York: Crossroak, 1981).

[67] Rixon, 491-492. Lonergan, *Method*, 29, 77, 273

[68] Lonergan, "The Functional Specialty, Systematics," 39.

[69] Ignatius of Loyola, *Spiritual Exercises and Selected Works*, 86.

[70] For an account of Hildegard's mystical experiences, see Sabina Flanagan, *Hildegard of Bingen, 1098-1179: A Visionary Life* (New York: Routledge, 1989); Matthew Fox, ed., *Hildegard of Bingen's Book of Divine Works with Letters and Songs*, trans. Robert Cunningham, Ronald Miller, Jerry Dybdal, and Matthew Fox (Santa Fe, NM: Bear & Co., 1987); Kathryn Kerby-Fulton, "Prophet and Reformer 'Smoke in the Vineyard,'" in Barbara Newman, ed., *Voice of the Living Light: Hildegard of Bingen and Her World* (Berkely: University of California Press, 1998); *Hildegard of Bingen: Scivias*, The Classics of Western Spirituality: A Library of the Great Spiritual Masters, trans. Mother Columba Hart and Jane Bishop (Mahwah: Paulist Press, 1990); Constant J. Mews, "From *Scivias* to the *Liber Divinorum Operum*: Hildegard's Apocalyptic Imagination and the Call to Reform," *Journal of Religious History* 24/1 (Feb 2000): 44-56; Monks Gottfried and Theodoric, *The Life of Holy*

Hildegard. Translated from Latin to German with Commentary by Adelgundis Führkötter, OSB. Translated from German to English by James McGrath (Collegeville: The Liturgical Press, 1995). For an account of Julian of Norwich's mystical experiences, see *Julian of Norwich: Showings*, trans. Edmund Colledge, O.S.A and James Walsh, S.J. The Classics of Western Spirituality: A Library of the Great Spiritual Masters (Mahwah: Paulist Press, 1978).

[71] Lonergan, *Method*, 119.

[72] Ibid., 112.

[73] For the spirituality of Bernard of Clairvaux, I suggest the following. G.R. Evans, *Bernard of Clairvaux* (New York: Oxford University Press, 2000); Etienne Gilson, *The Mystical Theology of Bernard of Clairvaux*, trans. A.H.C. Gilson (Kalamazoo: Cistercian Publications, 1990); Brian Patrick McGuire, *The Difficult Saint: Bernard of Clairvaux and His Tradition*, Cistercian Studies Series, no. 126 (Kalamazoo: Cistercian Publications, 1991); John R. Sommerfeldt, *The Spiritual Teachings of Bernard of Clairvaux: An Intellectual History of the Early Cistercian Order*, The Cistercian Fathers Series, no. 125 (Kalamazoo: Cistercian Publications, 1991).

CHAPTER THREE

Self-Appropriation II: Operations
of the Human Subject

Introduction

The previous chapter was dedicated to a presentation of Lonergan's position regarding the patterns of experience in which human persons find themselves in the living of their lives. The present chapter is concerned with the performance of the operations of human subjects as they encounter those patterns and seek to ascertain the meanings contained therein.

According to Lonergan, meaning is not a simple matter, for several levels of meaning may exist in any given experience. Individuals may be concerned only with the identification of a single meaning, purely intellectual meanings, affective meanings, or any combination of the meanings present in a given experience. Failure to recognize this plurality of meanings is characteristic of the split soul mentality, which acknowledges only one level of meaning. Therefore, Lonergan proposes his notion of 'differentiation of consciousness,' which consists of the ability of human persons to identify properly the meaning(s) sought in a given experience. Such a determination enables individuals to perform the operations of the subject in a manner appropriate to the situation. Certain meanings may be neglected or left for later reflection, concern for different levels of meaning may require a more or less complete investigation, and attention may be paid differently to the various sources, acts, and terms of meaning.

Sources of meaning consist of the performance of the operations of the human subject and the data of consciousness intended by those operations. Acts of meaning are a matter of examining these operations, considering the data, and formulating the meaning(s) of the experience in language. A term of meaning, finally, is what is meant by the sources of meaning. A distinction exists, however, according to Lonergan between 'meaning' and 'meant' insofar as individuals may conceive of a meaning that is not necessarily intended by the source of meaning.[1] To illustrate this difference, consider the example of individuals from Central or South America who speak of the sport of *futbol*. They are most likely referring to the sport known to many in North America as soccer. On the other hand, someone from the United States hears this term and probably thinks of *football* as it is played in the NFL. In this case, the meaning of the word as formulated by the North American differs from the term of meaning intended by the Central or South American.

Differentiation of consciousness is thus a matter of sorting through the various levels of meaning and appropriately attending to operations of the human subject that lead to discernment of meaning in a given experience. This attention to the various depths of meaning results in the ability to apply the operations of the human subject in a manner appropriate to a given situation. According to Lonergan, no less than four realms of meaning exist for the human subject, and if individuals are to discern accurately the meaning(s) contained within a given experience, they do well to be aware of the realm of meaning in which they are operating.[2]

Operations of the Human Subject

Once individual persons clarify for themselves the pattern of experience in which they find themselves and the goals of the situation, they are better able to attend to their functioning as human subjects within the given pattern. Not only are human beings able to experience the concrete reality in which they find themselves, but they are also able to experience their experiencing and subsequent reflection as they try to understand the data of consciousness and pass judgment on the results of their understanding. As stated in the introduction, Lonergan identifies four basic operations of the human subject, namely: experiencing, understanding, judging, and deciding. Briefly put, experiencing involves attention to the entirety of the data present in a given situation. Understanding is the attempt to make sense of that data, and judging is the affirmation or rejection of the explanatory proposals raised in the effort to understand the data. Decision, finally, entails the question of what to do with that which has been affirmed or rejected in judgment.

Although these operations describe the process of human knowing, Lonergan also names them as levels of consciousness, for human biengs encounter very few, if any, moments that are void of human knowing. If persons are conscious, they experience data. Upon waking, they encounter the surrounding environment, and questions emerge almost immediately. Moreover, human beings cannot help but continue on to the levels of understanding, judging, and deciding. Humanity is, by its very nature, intelligent, and even the decision to live life in defiance of this rational nature is an act of experiencing, understanding, judging, deciding, albeit foolishly. "One cannot renounce one's intelligence, and the greater the effort one makes to do so, the more one betrays that one is by nature intelligent."[3] From the mundane tasks of making coffee in the morning to the intellectual rigors of the academy, individuals perform the activities of experiencing, understanding, and judging, which are completed by the fourth step, decision. Even in so mundane a task as making coffee, if people refrain from attending to their knowing, they run the risk of poorly brewed coffee.[4] As such, becoming aware of the operations of the human subject is a change not in the manner in which human persons know, but a greater awareness of that process and the resulting ability to do so better. As Frederick Crowe notes, "Method then is not essential to obtaining results, but it accelerates the process, eliminates misconceptions."[5] If human beings attend to their knowing, then they are better equipped to become better knowers.

Experiencing

For Lonergan, the operation of experiencing is a matter of attending to the data of sense and consciousness. The former consists of the information delivered by the five senses, and the latter includes the acts of sensing and the cognitional activities performed in human knowing.[6] Human subjects are not only able to encounter the world around them, but are also able to reflect upon the manner in which it is experienced. The data of sense and consciousness thus encompass the entire spectrum of that which comprises human existence.

The patterns of human experience described in the previous chapter thus serve as categories to guide the act of attending to the data of sense and consciousness. If individuals are attempting to discern the meaning of a piece of art, they would be mistaken to treat the endeavor as a purely intellectual exercise, for art appreciation is not a passionless affair. Similarly, if they are concerned with the performance of their role in society, both intellectual and affective elements are involved, and to ignore one or the other is to play the role in an inferior fashion.

The concern of the subject on the level of experience is therefore to pay attention to the data. What is the nature of the thing under consideration? If it is an object, what are its physical and functional characteristics? If it is a principle or a text, what is it trying to communicate? If persons wish to know authentically, only when they attend to all of the available data do they move beyond this phase, and Lonergan summarizes this demand in the first transcendental precept, "Be attentive."[7]

Understanding

Lonergan's second cognitional level, that of understanding, is characterized by intelligent investigation into spontaneously arising insights into the data gathered on the level of experience. Insights are glimmers of enlightenment as to the nature of the thing or concept under consideration and are the result of the innate human desire to know.[8] Remaining content with such a flicker of understanding is not sufficient, however, for any insight is only one of many that could explain the focus of investigation. The possibility glimpsed in the moment of insight must be examined, and alternatives must be considered. Thus, the level of understanding is a matter of formulating explanatory hypotheses regarding the relationship or workings of the experienced data. Perhaps x is the nature of the thing in question, or perhaps y is the relationship of two or more things. The level of understanding, then, is intelligent inquiry, for it tries to grasp the intelligibility of the object or concept and is guided by the second transcendental precept, "Be intelligent."[9]

Here, too, individuals must take care to recognize the pattern of experience in which they are performing the task of understanding. Because the data arises from different aspects of human experience, they must undertake the effort to understand the data appropriately. In the purely intellectual pattern of experience, feelings are viewed with suspicion. For the mystic, however, quite the opposite is the case. In the mystical life, the intellect takes a back seat to affectivity, and if mystics and their readers are to operate authentically, they must take this into account.

Judging

The third level of human consciousness is that of judgment. Here, human subjects reflect upon the hypotheses formulated in the level of understanding and evaluate them, determining whether they are true or false.[10] If individuals determine that the data is sufficient to affirm a certain theory as true, then they may be said to know something. If, on the other hand, the theory is deemed to be inadequate, authentically operating individuals must consider one or more alternative proposals in order to reach the truth of the matter. Thus, the operative transcendental precept in the level of judgment is, "Be reasonable."[11] When the evidence demands assent, authentically operating individuals are obliged to judge in the affirmative. If, on the other hand, the evidence is insufficient to affirm the truth of the possibility raised in understanding, judgment must be in the negative. The theory is then to be rejected or deemed to be merely probable rather than certain.

The crucial point here regards the moment at which the process of proposing theories and pronouncing judgments comes to an end. When has understanding of the matter been achieved, and when can someone truly say that this is so or is not so? Lonergan's answer to this issue lies in his notion of the 'unconditioned.' Unconditioneds, according to Lonergan, exist in two forms: the 'virtually unconditioned' and the 'formally unconditioned.'[12] Whereas the former consists of something whose conditions are met, the latter consists of something that has no conditions whatsoever, namely God. The formally unconditioned must be bracketed for the moment because judgment on the presence of the Divine is a matter reserved in this book for discussion of religious rather than intellectual conversion.[13]   Virtually unconditioneds, on the other hand, entail something that has conditions, but whose conditions are met.[14]   As a rather mundane example, consider the mental activity of determining the identity of something that is spherical. In order to arrive at the judgment that the item under consideration is a baseball, individuals must ask certain questions.   What size is it?   How are its constitutive components attached to one another, etc.?   Once all of the conditions of a baseball have been met, then a judgment may be made that the object truly is a baseball.   If, however, the answer to one of the conditions is contrary to what a baseball is, an alternative theory must be proposed and examined in light of the new set of conditions.

Objectivity of Knowing

The question that arises here concerns the objectivity of the judgments made by the person in the intellectual pattern of experience. To affirm or renounce a thing in its relation to the individual is one thing, but to be able to pass judgment on a thing as it exists independently of the knower and as it stands in relation to other things or human persons is quite another. To address the problem of the objectivity of truth claims on the level of judgment Lonergan proposes the 'principal notion of objectivity,' which consists of the acknowledgement of the fact that any number of things exist which are distinct from one another. As human subjects in their desire to know seek the reality of these individual things, a distinction becomes apparent between subject and the object.[15]   Generally speaking, then, objectivity is the knowledge of a thing as it exists, and Lonergan identifies three aspects of this idea.

Working backwards, from the level of judgment to experience, he names three corresponding facets of objectivity: absolute, normative, and experiential. Absolute objectivity resides in the fact that the content of judgment is absolute.[16] The only possible answers to the question, "Is it so?" are either "yes" or "no." If persons are unable to pronounce a verdict in the affirmative or negative, then they have not yet come to the level of judgment and must return to a review of the data of experience or the performance of the act of understanding in an effort to come to a point where a judgment can be made. Absolute objectivity is not, however, a matter solely of the individual knower, for advertence to the operations of the human subject enables persons to go beyond themselves, and in so doing they achieve authenticity. As such, absolute objectivity is an affirmation of the reality of the thing as it truly exists independently of the knower. The thing in question is open to investigation by other persons, and if they also adhere to the method, they should come to the same judgment, barring their posing of further pertinent questions that did not occur to the first person.[17]

The second element of objectivity is 'normative objectivity,' which corresponds to the level of understanding. Normative objectivity is the giving of free rein to the cognitional process in its attempt to understand the data gathered at the level of experience. It is thus the conscious attempt to avoid the entrance of such factors as personal emotions and desires that would skew the results of the investigation.[18] If, for example, individuals are investigating the plight of the poor in America, the fear of somehow being implicated in the structures that allow poverty to persist may very well taint the investigation.

Thirdly, Lonergan describes 'experiential objectivity,' which is attention to the data as it is given to the subject.[19] This is the objectivity that arises from attention to the first transcendental precept, "Be attentive." When human persons are exploring a matter, they may project into the data factors that simply are not there. In the excitement of the investigation certain preconceptions or desires to achieve a certain result may lead them to ignore certain data or mistakenly identify what is present.

The Role of Definitions in Judging

At first glance Lonergan may appear to be rejecting any claim of certain knowledge of a thing because the point at which absolute objectivity is reached is difficult to determine. Importantly, however, all realities other than God fall into the category of virtually unconditioneds, whose conditions must be established and met before the identity of a thing can be determined, and this is the role played by definitions. First, Lonergan identifies nominal definitions, which convey the correct usage of names, such as may be found in a dictionary.[20] Secondly, explanatory definitions add a level of understanding to the definition. In drawing this distinction, Lonergan refers to the example of a circle. A nominal definition of a circle would be "a perfectly round plane curve."[21] An explanatory definition is exemplified by the further statement that in any given circle, all radii are equal. The third type of definition is an implicit definition which consists of an explanatory definition without the nominal. To clarify the notion of an implicit definition, Lonergan presents the example of the relationship between points and lines. "Two points determine a straight line; a straight line is determined by two points."[22] The implicit definition, however, does not rely upon the nominal definition of points and lines, and thus the definition may be expanded to two of any something that determines another. The significance of the implicit definition is that it allows for abstract consideration insofar as it allows people to move beyond the specific instance under consideration.[23]

With regard to the notion of a virtually unconditioned, a nominal definition contains the conditions that must be met in order to pronounce judgment regarding the identity of the thing in question and helps people as they seek to classify what they encounter in their lives. Once individuals determine that a given object is "a piece of furniture consisting of a smooth flat slab fixed on legs," they may appropriately use the term, 'table' to refer to the object.[24] Although the table may be put to different uses, such as a sitting surface, it remains a table, and thus nominal definitions have a permanency about them that allows for definite knowledge of a thing and the insight into the identity of the object is therefore invulnerable. The unqualified nature of this assertion must be noted. An insight is not invulnerable when no more questions arise in the mind of the subject, but rather when no more pertinent questions exist.

Explanatory definitions, rather than allowing judgment as to the identity of the thing in question, add to the understanding of the matter. Moreover, they are not the finished products that nominal definitions are, for human persons can never fully understand a thing.

> As answers accumulate, as they correct, complete, qualify one another, knowledge advances. But answers only give rise to still further questions. Objects are never completely, exhaustively known, for our intending always goes beyond present achievements.[25]

Even with regard to the earlier, mundane example of the baseball, an infinite number of questions can be asked. Of what material is the cover of the ball?

Why does it have its particular properties?   Why will it only go so far? Individuals can pursue the matter to the extreme of the electrons, neutrons, and protons of the ball's constituent atoms, though the practical usefulness of such inquiry may be questionable.   Additionally, as scientific knowledge progresses, new questions which have not been yet conceived may be asked, and the explanatory definitions of a baseball may become more and more complex.

Implicit definitions allow for generality in the knowledge of the object. At the risk of running the example of the baseball into the ground, whether people envision its stitching as a zipper or the interlocking teeth of animal makes no difference.   The human person is still able to examine a thing and reach judgment regarding the matter. Despite the cultural particularity of the examples used to understand the object under consideration, an implicit definition enables human persons to know an object.

The Role of Probability in Judging

In addition to the role played by definitions in the act of judging, Lonergan also relies upon the mathematical principle of probability with regard to the limit approached in the task of pronouncing judgment.   Lonergan writes the following.

> The probable judgment results from rational procedures.   Though it rests on incomplete knowledge, still there has to be some approximations toward completeness.   Though it fails to reach the virtually unconditioned, still it has to be closing in upon that exigent norm.[26]

Thus, the more individuals learn about a thing, the more they are able to pronounce judgment regarding its nature. Though they will never be able to exhaust their understanding of it, they are still able to approach that limit, and as they draw near, a point comes when indecision or stubbornness become the only basis for not declaring a verdict.[27]

Therefore, the operations of the human subject proceed upwards to the set of conditions that must be met in order for a given object to be known. Lonergan describes this process as the scissors-like action of a heuristic structure. Just as human persons proceed from the data to the conditions, they also utilize the conditions to guide their questioning.[28] If they are to determine whether a given piece of furniture is indeed a table, they must first have a working definition of a table in order to authentically pronounce judgment regarding the object's identity.

When pronouncing judgment on principles and ideas, the conditions that must be met are of a different nature. Instead of definitions, persons work here with notions such as truth and logic that vary according to the discipline in which they are working. Scientifically speaking, people in the 21st century know that Copernicus was right regarding the heliocentric nature of the solar system and that force equals mass times acceleration because of the verification of these ideas through repeated tests. Historians, on the other hand, do not have the luxury of being able to repeat the matter under investigation, but they do have the concrete instance and various accounts thereof. Theologians likewise, have the wealth of Scripture and tradition against which to measure the validity of their work. In all of these cases, the heuristic structure is a procedure that moves both upwards from the data to conditions that must be met and downwards from these conditions as they guide lines of questioning.

Self-Correcting Nature of Human Knowing

As the previous discussion of the act of understanding indicates, Lonergan holds that nothing may be understood in its entirety. The basis for this claim lies first in the fact that all questioning leads to God, and the human mind cannot fully comprehend the infinite.[29] Secondly, the human situation is one of continual movement. As the human condition changes, so does human questioning, and therefore, human knowledge progresses over time. New questions arise, and the resolution of these matters leads to the rejection of certain positions and the refinement of others.[30]

The process of revising and improving that is contained within human knowing leads Lonergan to assert that human cognition is a self-correcting process. "[I]nsights not only arise in answer to questions but also are followed by further questions."[31] Authentically operating human persons must always allow for the possibility of revision with regard to their knowing. Humanity continues to move forward, and as new data is encountered, humanity must account for it and, when necessary, adjust or refine previous judgments in accordance with the new data. If amendment is not necessary, moreover, that judgment can serve as the springboard for further investigation.[32]

The process of human knowing is not only marked by revision of previous judgments and hypotheses, but also by a verification of correct positions, which is reached both directly and indirectly. It is direct as students recreate the experiments of the past in an effort to gain a basic knowledge of a topic in order to proceed to further investigation or as the efforts of previous individuals are reexamined in an attempt to determine if any data was previously missed. Verification is indirect insofar as a given principle is presupposed in later research. [33]   Galileo's work on falling bodies, for instance, has been indirectly verified a great many times over the centuries as scientists sought to develop strategies for such projects as returning astronauts safely from space or improving parachutes. The success of their efforts verified Galileo's work insofar as they did not have to establish new laws that govern the rate of an object's descent. On the other hand, Galileo's work has been verified directly every time students have measured the rate at which objects fall as part of their scientific education.

Common Sense

The preceding pages were concerned with the intellectual operations of the human subject in seeking to know the world in which persons live. Lonergan describes this process as the transition from the world of immediacy of the infant to the world of meaning, for the objects, persons, and principles with which individuals come into contact are no longer mysterious entities that condition their existence, but things which they come to understand and whose reality they affirm in the act of judgment.[34] Although infants may enjoy the shelter of a house, only with the operations of the subject do they recognize it as a home.

The drive to know and to discern meaning in life, however, is not limited to the realm of theory.   Generally, human beings are not necessarily concerned with the conditions that any shelter must meet if it is to be a home. Often, they are concerned only with their particular home. Such moments of practical concern, according to Lonergan, are not outside the human subject's functioning as an intelligent being. Because the desire to know is fundamental to being human, intelligence is demonstrated in all aspects of human life, from purchasing goods to the performance of one's chosen profession. In everyday life, however, a lack of refinement exists in human knowing, for individuals are concerned with particular and concrete issues rather than general principles or unifying theories.[35]

> Common sense... never aspires to universally valid knowledge, and it never attempts exhaustive communication. Its concern is the concrete and particular. Its function is to master each situation as it arises. Its procedure is to reach an incomplete set of insights that is to be completed only be adding on each occasion the further insights that scrutiny of the occasion reveals.[36]

For example, to obtain a desired object or service in a market economy, money must be given in exchange. Generally speaking, this appears to be a simple matter to those accustomed to such an economy, and the transaction may be completed almost automatically. What the person operating at the level of common sense does not take into consideration, however, is the set of laws and principles that govern a capitalist economy. Ask most people on the street who Adam Smith was or for any economic theory more complex than supply and demand, and one is likely to be met with blank stares or the question, "Why should I know that?"

Although common sense is not concerned with the comprehensive understanding that characterizes human knowing on the level of theory, it is still a matter of human intelligence. The skills and strategies that enable human persons to go about their daily lives are learned through the operations of experiencing, understanding, and judging as they encounter certain situations. They learn how to obtain goods and services, they learn how to interact with one another, and they learn skills which make it possible to earn a living. Through the living of daily life, individuals acquire routines which provide the desired results, though without a complete understanding of what they are doing.[37]

Moreover, as with the cognitional operations performed in the intellectual pattern of experience, common sense knowing is a self-correcting process. Through a process of determining which strategies or insights into daily life were successful or unsuccessful, human beings learn better how to operate in their social milieu. Perhaps they have learned a painful lesson by not paying enough attention to their surroundings, making a purchase from an untrustworthy individual, or heard of such stories from family and friends. The self-correcting process of knowing on the level of common sense enables them to become ever better at functioning in a particular social context.

As its name implies, common sense is not the achievement of a particular individual. Rather, it describes the wealth of practical knowledge possessed by the community in which persons are located. "There are as many brands of common sense as there are languages, social or cultural differences, almost differences of place and time."[38] Thus, individuals who are quite capable of functioning in one particular social context may be at a loss as to the manner in which they must operate in another. The European is accustomed to taking the train to visit relatives hundreds of kilometers away, but the American insists on driving a car and thus may find travel in Europe confusing. Although this example may seem of little import, the clashes of common sense can become much more serious in such matters as negotiations between nations with regard to natural resources or fair treatment of laborers.   Individuals operating with different brands of common sense will approach the concrete issues of daily life differently and often arrive at different, sometimes conflicting answers.

The distinction between common sense and theory, however, is not limited to the practical and intellectual patterns of experience. For instance, Lonergan writes the following with regard to common sense and patterns of experience.

> Common sense occurs, ordinarily, in the dramatic and practical patterns of experience.   The aesthetic pattern of experience also has its common sense. Scientific knowledge proceeds from common sense knowledge, but starts moving away from it because of its own aims; it has its specific end. Common sense, as a mode in which insight develops, is something common, I prefer to say, to some of the patterns.[39]

A distinction is present, therefore, between the professional art historian who takes a theoretical approach to the painting in the museum and the visitor to the museum who has no training in art history. Whereas the professional may see the brush strokes as indicative of the intent of the author to convey emotional turbulence, untrained persons may only be aware of the emotional effect of the painting. In the first instance, the concern is with general artistic theory, and in the second, individuals are engaged solely with the concrete instance of their encounter with the painting.

A similar distinction is also present with regard to the mystical pattern of experience. Whereas Thérèse of Lisieux and Julian of Norwich were concerned only with describing the workings of their personal spiritual lives, Teresa of Avila and John of the Cross were intent on presenting a general understanding of the human soul and its role in the human person's relationship with God. Moreover, those who encounter these writings may do so at the level of either theoretical knowledge or common sense knowing. The question of the scholar may be, "Where does this individual fit into the mystical tradition of the Western Christian church?" or, "What does this writer tell us of mysticism in general?" The concern of someone seeking personal spiritual edification is more a matter of the applicability of the mystic's writings to the specific content of the individual's relationship with the Divine.

The Relationship between Common Sense and Theory

Though different in concern and scope, theoretical and common sense knowing are not isolated realities, for a relationship exists between them. First, as the previous quotation indicates, theoretical knowing takes common sense as its starting point. The quest for general theories regarding the nature of the data of experience always starts from the concrete reality of individual persons. The Copernican revolution, for instance, was ultimately a result of the investigation as to why the sun appears to move across the sky. The answer, famously, is that the sun does not, in fact, travel around the earth, but the earth around the sun. With regard to mysticism, the split soul mentality is a result of a similar process, albeit one that went awry through an inadequate understanding of the relevant data. As described in the introduction of this book, the split soul is the result of a long process in which philosophers and theologians investigated the nature of the mystical experience and its relation to worldly affairs. These scholars perceived an incompatibility between the spiritual life and the practical concerns of human socio-political reality and developed theories which sought to explain this incongruity. The present discussion is similarly the result of a common sense concern moving to the realm of theory. Through my encounter with the mystics, I became convinced that the current situation in which the mentality of the split soul holds such sway is inadequate to the reality of Western Christian mysticism. Therefore, I have undertaken this project in an effort to provide a solution on the level of theory to the mentality of the split soul through the application of Lonergan's notion of self-appropriation to the issue of mystical-political theology.

Secondly, common sense has the potential to derail theoretical knowing through a mistaken claim to general theoretical applicability. Common sense does develop general principles, but these generalizations are concerned solely with the concrete, practical affairs of a specific context, not with universal principles from which scientific inquiry advances as it seeks to deduce further knowledge. "The generalizations issued by common sense are not meant to be premises for deductions. Rather they would communicate pointers it is well to bear in mind."[40] Assuming that the manner in which human persons operate in a particular milieu are adequate at all times and places has the potential to lead individuals into trouble both with regard to making their way in the world and in the pursuit of scientific inquiry. The first may lead to embarrassment or offense, and the later is sloppy science. When people are unclear as to whether they are operating on the level of common sense or theory, they run the risk of applying common sense answers that are inadequate to the situation.[41]

Thirdly, common sense may mistakenly claim that theoretical investigation of a matter is pointless and again try to insinuate itself into matters that are only sufficiently addressed by theory.

> It [common sense] is concerned with the concrete and particular. It entertains no aspirations about reaching abstract and universal laws. It easily is led to rationalize its limitations by engendering a conviction that other forms of human knowledge are useless or doubtfully valid.[42]

Without comprehensive exploration of the matter at hand, potentially fruitful ideas and questions are avoided, and a given society may find itself driven into a downwards spiral wherein insufficient insights are followed by further deficient insights until the process is broken by the conscious decision to examine the matter completely.[43]

Fourthly, the relationship between common sense and theory also proceeds from theory to common sense. Scholars do not simply develop their theories and keep them to themselves. Rather, they try to communicate them to society as a whole through the publication of books, articles, appearances on talk shows, etc. Although the cynic may propose that this is all a matter of marketing the ideas of the academics, it is also the attempt to disseminate the scholarly achievements of those individuals who dedicate their lives to intellectual pursuits. If these achievements are truly worthwhile, they become a part of the communal store of knowledge that comprises common sense. The heliocentric nature of the universe is no longer in dispute, and, unfortunately, the split soul mentality has become similarly rooted in societal attitudes toward mysticism. In a perfect world (from my perspective), my argument in this book regarding the inadequacy of the split soul and the relevance of self-appropriation to resisting this mentality would become part of the commonly held fund of knowledge. Henceforth, my readers would address socio-political concerns from the position of the unity of the human subject despite the manifold patterns of experience that are present in human consciousness.

Decision

Once human persons have pronounced judgment regarding the veracity of their understanding, the additional question of what to do with the judgments they have reached arises. This, Lonergan claims, is the level of decision, and, for authentically operating human subjects, this is a matter of consistency between what they have learned and what they do. If they surrender this consistency, then they relinquish their claim to authenticity.[44]

In this sense, a similarity exists between judging and deciding, for both acts are matters of either affirming or negating. In the case of judging, subjects affirm or negate their understanding of the thing under consideration, and in the act of deciding they are pronouncing judgment regarding the proper course of action. However, a difference between knowing what to do and actually doing it is also present.[45] The latter is an act of will rather than of intellect, and this act requires not only the decision regarding the proper course of action and the willingness to do so but also the requisite freedom to act accordingly.

Freedom in Deciding

For Lonergan, all human persons are both essentially and effectively free. The former is a recognition of the myriad of possible courses of action in any given situation, and the latter consists of the actual, or realistic, courses of action available to the person in the given situation. Within the will of the human subject essential freedom exists insofar as any number of courses of action are open to consideration by any human being. In reality, however, only a limited number of actions are available, and this more limited range of options comprises Lonergan's notion of effective freedom. A first effective limitation of human freedom is the concrete situation in which the person is located.[46] Children who live in Mexico cannot expect to build a snowman in their backyard, prisoners cannot come and go as they please, and the oppressed of Zimbabwe cannot fully participate in the socio-economic order. Such external conditions, however, are far from static, and in some cases, these limitations may be overcome. If prisoners wish to regain their freedom, exemplary behavior may result in early release. The Mexican children may travel to a more northerly climate. The oppressed Zimbabweans may liberate themselves through the heroic struggle for justice.

Secondly, the affective state of persons may limit the actuation of their freedom. Obsessions and anxieties may limit freedom insofar as they prevent individuals from taking certain actions.[47] Fear of the outside world may prevent persons from leaving the house, even though no physical obstruction to the act exists. Just as a disordered affectivity threatens to derail the authentic performance of the human subject's operations through bias, it may also restrict the freedom of persons in the effort to live authentically.

Thirdly, human freedom is determined in part by the intellectual functioning of human persons. Individuals can take action responsibly only after assessing the situation, considering alternative strategies, and judging which possibility is appropriate to the state of affairs under consideration.[48] Thus, a parallel exists not only with the act of judging, but also with the entirety of the human subject's operating. Persons cannot authentically affirm or negate a course of action without the prior decision to attend to the data and understand the possible outcomes of various strategies. Individual persons, however, are limited by certain factors in the performance of these operations. Cultural factors may prevent certain solutions from coming to mind, individuals may be better or less able to attend to the data or understand the situation, and bias may derail the entire process of deciding, just as it does with the cognitional process. Thus, the very operations that enable human subjects to transcend themselves are also a source of limitation regarding personal freedom.[49]

Fourthly, and lastly, the willingness of individuals to take action may limit their effective freedom. As the previous three limitations indicate, a certain, often high, level of commitment to the actuation of freedom is required on the part of individuals who wish to function authentically. Their particular external situation, affective state, and intellectual functioning are quite often formidable barriers, and people may not possess the will to overcome these difficulties. According to Lonergan, only when the willingness of human persons reaches the level of the unrestricted desire to know and love do they become free from internal and external restraints, and only then does their effective freedom reach its largest expanse.[50]

Kataphatic Mysticism and the Operations of the Human Subject

In the previous discussion of Lonergan's position regarding the mystical pattern of experience I bracketed the discussion of a kataphatic mysticism in order to clarify Lonergan's thought regarding the operations of the human subject. The human subject, according to Lonergan, experiences the data, seeks to understand the data, and passes judgment on that understanding. With regard to Lonergan's stance on mysticism, mystics encounter a cloud of unknowing, and only through later reflection does the experience come to have meaning. As noted, however, such a position does not take into account the kataphatic strand of mysticism wherein the mystical experience contains definite content, often through visions or voices, regarding the nature of God or the relationship between God and the individual.

At first, the manner in which the operations of the human subject gains access to the meanings of a kataphatic mystical experience seems a simple matter. Mystics encounter the Divine, and in this experience they encounter certain data, the meanings of which are discerned through later reflection and judgment upon that reflection. While this is true, such a position fails to take into consideration that the search for meaning with regard to the mystical pattern of experience cannot be conducted in the purely intellectual pattern of experience if the full depth of the mystical encounter with the Divine is to be appreciated. Mysticism, as the previous chapters attest, speaks not only to the head, but also to the heart, and it often does so through highly symbolic language with which the person operating in the intellectual pattern of experience cannot deal adequately. Therefore, what is needed is a critical control over the effort to gain access to the meanings contained in the affective and symbolic elements of the mystical experience. Such a resource, however, would not be a matter of the human subject operating in a manner different from the pattern of experiencing, understanding, and judging. Rather, it would enable persons to attend to the affective dimension of the mystical experience that is neglected or cast aside as a potential source of bias by the intellectual pattern of experience. Similarly, the critical control of meaning would aid the mystic in the attempt to understand the content of the experience, and, finally, to assist in the pronouncement of judgment upon that understanding.

I contend that such a resource may be found in the work of Robert Doran regarding the notion of psychic conversion and its relationship to the interpretation of symbols. Lonergan defines a symbol as, "an image of a real or imaginary object that evokes a feeling or is evoked by a feeling."[51] Thus, any object serving as a symbol is not functioning solely as that object. For instance, the cross is not merely two perpendicular pieces of wood. While that is an objective description, it fails to take into consideration the wealth of feelings associated with the cross. The symbol of the cross evokes feelings of love, gratitude, or comfort in a Christian person, but it may arouse repulsion or horror as an instrument of domination from a Native American, Jewish, or Muslim perspective. Symbols, according to Lonergan, "obey the laws not of logic but of image and feeling."[52] Thus, they are not restricted to the intellectual operations of the subject, but rather involve the affective aspect of the human person. Interpretation of the symbol must therefore recognize the entrance of feelings into the attempt to discern the meaning(s) contained in the symbolic language of texts arising from kataphatic mystical experience.

Symbols thus operate at two levels of meaning: the pre-reflective, in which the symbol affects its recipient in a way that is conscious, but not known, and the reflective, in which the meanings of the symbol become known through the authentic performance of the operations of the human subject. Lonergan writes the following in this regard.

> It is an elemental meaning, not yet objectified, as the meaning of the smile prior to the phenomenology of the smile, or the meaning in the purely experiential pattern in a work of art... It is a meaning that has its proper contexts in the process of internal communication in which it occurs, and it is to that context with its associated images and feelings, memories and tendencies that the interpreter has to appeal if he would explain the symbol.[53]

In other words, human persons have a certain access to the meaning of a symbol even before it is formulated in explanatory language. When a friend smiles at me, a meaning of benevolence or affection exists even before I consider the meaning logically. But to interpret the symbol, I must express the elemental meaning linguistically, articulating through language that which was previously felt, and in so doing I am able to explain to others what is communicated through the smile of my friend.

As Lonergan indicates, a great many thinkers have tried to establish a framework through which symbols may be interpreted and given linguistic expression.[54] None of these, however, approach the matter through the intentional operations of human consciousness. What work has been done, moreover, is the product of relatively recent endeavors and has been largely confined to the academy. Therefore many mystics and persons who approach the writings of the mystics do not have the means by which their experiences and accounts may be interpreted fully. Thus, they have been forced to report merely what they have encountered without the later process of understanding what has been experienced.

To illustrate the point, I propose the example of the 72nd chapter of Julian of Norwich's *Showings*. Here she describes the deadly nature of sin, yet reassures her readers that they will always be in the sight of God.

> And therefore it often seems to us as if we were in danger of death and in some part of hell, because of the sorrow and the pain which sin is to us, and so for that time we are dead to the true sight of our blessed life. But in all this I saw truly that we are not dead in the sight of God, nor does he ever depart from us; but he will never have his full joy in us until we have our full joy in him, truly seeing his fair, blessed face. For we are ordained to this by nature, and brought to it by grace.[55]

While this reassuring passage from her work expresses God's eternal presence with the symbol of Divine vision, it raises theological issues that are not resolved in the passage itself. What does it mean to be "in the sight of God?" What does it mean for God to "not have his full joy?" Does this passage tell us anything about eternal life? Not everyone gets to heaven according to Julian.[56] The revelation received by Julian in her vision is related, but she makes no attempt here to understand her vision theologically. The challenge, then, is the elaboration of an analytical tool that facilitates the understanding of the mystical encounter with the Divine, and I contend that Robert Doran's work on psychic conversion provides such an instrument.

In his published doctoral dissertation entitled, *Subject and Psyche*, Doran takes the following statement from Lonergan as a guide.

> Besides the immediate world of the infant and the adult's world mediated by meaning, there is the mediation of immediacy by meaning when one objectifies cognitional process in transcendental method and when one discovers, identifies, accepts one's submerged feelings in psychotherapy.[57]

For Doran, this discovery, identification, and acceptance of one's submerged feelings "entails both a methodical consciousness instructed through intentionality analysis and a post-critical symbolic consciousness, the self-articulated unfolding of which would be a transcendental aesthetic."[58] In other words, psychic conversion guides the attempt to discern the meaning of feelings just as recognition of the operations of the human subject guides recognition of meaning in other instances of human living. Just as human beings are able to transcend intellectually their particular situation and arrive at the truth of the matter, psychic conversion allows them to deal authentically with the feelings involved in the encounter with symbol. Are my feelings appropriate to the symbol, or are they the result of bias or cultural insensitivity? Why, for instance, are some persons proud of the Confederate flag despite its history as the symbol of an institution that condoned the practice of slavery? Perhaps, the response of those who take pride in the Confederate flag is affected by a group bias that wishes to protect the supposedly 'gentlemanly' nature of the Southern United States of America. Psychic conversion allows individuals to transcend their particular situation in their approach to symbols and arrive at Doran's 'transcendental aesthetic.'

Before I undertake an explication of the relevance of Doran's work on psychic conversion to mystical theology consonant with the work of Lonergan, three clarifications are in order. First, although Doran takes the above statement by Lonergan as his guiding principle, he does not restrict the relevance of the psychic to feelings that are submerged in the depths of the psyche. Feelings and the symbols associated with them, he notes, are present in virtually every moment of human consciousness.[59] Oftentimes symbols confront human persons head on, but people do not know how to deal with them, and their interpretation of the symbols may become threatened by bias. Psychic conversion, then, is a tool that provides a level of critical control to the interpretation of the affective dimension of human existence.

Secondly, both Doran and Lonergan acknowledge the role played by psychotherapy in the ability of persons to interpret symbols. Although Doran understands psychoanalysis of the subject to be the most effective manner in which the subject gains competency in the interpretation of symbols, he does leave room for other avenues to psychic conversion. He writes, "One way of recovering the dispositional aspect of primordial immediacy is through psychotherapy."[60] Although he limits his discussion of such recovery to the work of Carl Jung and Paul Ricoeur, the presence of the qualification, "one way" indicates an openness to other avenues.

Limiting psychic conversion to psychotherapy, moreover, would restrict people's ability to interpret the affective dimension of human living roughly to the 20th century or later and only to those with the means to see a psychotherapist. Such a position, however, fails to acknowledge the effect that symbols have had throughout human history. The symbols and metaphors of Teresa of Avila's *Interior Castle* have borne fruit for its readers for several centuries. Indeed, symbols have played a prominent role in non-mystical religious experience as well. According to noted scholar of world religions, Mircea Eliade, the inability to deal competently with symbol and religious story is a 20th century phenomenon, and inability which I believe to continue here in the 21st.[61]

Thirdly, in some cases the writings of the mystics themselves indicate advancement in understanding of their experiences. Thérèse of Lisieux, for instance, recorded no less than three manuscripts of her mystical life,[62] and Julian of Norwich produced both a long and a short text of her *Showings*. In these cases, the mystics returned to the task of understanding their experience of the immediate presence of God, which resulted in further discernment of meaning. Quite possibly, new levels remain unexplored in the writings of the mystics, and these may become accessible to readers who possess a greater symbolic fluency than previous scholars and other readers. Given Lonergan's assertion that a thing is never completely understood, advances in the understanding of mystical texts or experiences are always possible. If the interrelation between the mystical and political life is to be cultivated, then psychic conversion becomes a valuable tool in this important endeavor.

Within every symbol, however, resides a hermeneutical conflict that results from the fact that the symbol refers to something other than itself.[63] As previously mentioned, for the Christian a cross is not just two perpendicular pieces of wood. It carries with it a wide variety of feeling and interpretations. It may evoke feelings of joy or triumph on one end of the spectrum, or sadness and pain on the other. Symbols point beyond themselves to deeper meanings that may or may not be immediately apparent to those who encounter the symbol. Moreover, symbols not only evoke feelings in the present, but also contain a history. Any attempt to interpret a symbol, therefore, must take into consideration not only its meaning for today but also the intention of the symbol at the time of its creation.[64]

To aid the resolution of the hermeneutical conflict of symbol, Doran proposes that psychic conversion be described as the appropriation of the 'imaginal' as operator. Such appropriation refers to "what becomes known when one learns to relate disposition to elemental symbolization through the symbols spontaneously produced by the psyche in dreams and fantasies."[65] Appropriation of the imaginal recognizes the affective state and relates it to the symbols encountered in life. Interpretation of symbols is thus by no means an easy matter. It requires the development of a symbolic competency through psychic conversion which, as intellectual conversion does with knowing, enables individuals to know what they are doing when interpreting a symbol and thus become better able to do so.[66] With the symbolic competency enabled by psychic conversion in place, the writings of the mystics open to deeper levels of meaning than when approached in an exclusively intellectual or even religiously converted manner.[67] The secondary mediation of meaning facilitated by psychic conversion opens these layers to human persons as they go about the business of authentic human living.

Perhaps the best way to understand the role played by psychic conversion in the interpretation of symbols is to recall the earlier discussion regarding theory and common sense. Recall that common sense, though it proceeds through the levels of experience, understanding, and judgment and is thus intelligent, lacks the critical control provided by adherence to transcendental method in the operations of the human subject. Common sense is concerned with the particular rather than the general and is not concerned with the broader or long term implications of the inquiry. As such, common sense only discerns a particular meaning. Similarly, a common sense approach to the interpretation of symbol is concerned with the interpretation of the symbol only in the context of the moment, failing to take into consideration the hermeneutic tension inherent in all symbols. Thus, individuals often possess no critical control of the meanings that result from the affective encounter with symbol and are left with only neuralgic responses that run the risk of falling victim to bias and may lead to misguided behavior. The psychically converted person, however, acknowledges the intricacies of symbol interpretation and seeks to objectify and mediate the meanings of the feelings evoked by the encounter with the symbol. Psychic conversion thus provides a manner of critical control to the interpretation of symbols much as appropriation of the operations of the human subject does for intelligent inquiry.

Psychic conversion, however, is not merely a means to improve symbolic competency. It also serves a theological function insofar as it affects the operations of the theologian. Doran identifies the following five areas in which psychic conversion contributes to theology.

> [P]sychic conversion may influence (1) one's choice as to what qualifies as data for theology, (2) the base from which one engages in interpretation and history, (3) the horizon determining one's view of and influencing one's decision about, the tensions of religious and theological dialectic, (4) the bases from which one derives theological categories, positions, and system, and (5) the way in which one regards the mission of religion in the world.[68]

Thus, with regard to the specific task of a mystical theology, the critical control over the encounter with the symbols of mystical texts may: (1) lead to the recognition of new data as relevant to theological inquiry, (2) enable the theologian to better interpret the symbols produced by the mystical writers and historical movements within the mystical tradition of the church, (3) bring a new resource to the dialectic of opposing views found within mystical texts or their interpreters, (4) aid the recognition of mysticism as informative of the theological category of political theology, and (5) enable the theologian to better acknowledge mysticism as a force for progressive social change in the world.

To conclude this section, Lonergan's work on the operations of the human subject provides the missing piece to the mystical theology presented in Chapter One of this book. In the work of Underhill and Johnston, emphasis is placed on the particulars of the mystical experience and its effect on the lives of the individual mystics. For Lonergan, the manner in which the human subject pursues authentic existence is of paramount importance. Through attention to data (or lack thereof), formulation of explanatory hypotheses, and subsequent judgment, the meaning of a mystical experience becomes objectified and serves as the focus of further reflection and study. This process is aided, moreover, by the symbolic competency delivered by Robert Doran's work on the notion of psychic conversion, which provides a second mediation of meaning by which critical control of the affective dimension of the mystical experience is gained. The meanings of the mystical life are thus able to enter the foundational reality of human living, the basis on which human subjects function in every day life.

Unity in Differentiation: The Spiritually Integrated Subject

As I have tried to demonstrate in the preceding pages, Lonergan maintains that the functioning of the human subject begins with the act of attending to the data of consciousness, an act which he names, experiencing. This act, moreover, may involve the appropriation of the data in several different patterns of experience: intellectual, worshipful, practical, dramatic, biological, aesthetic, and mystical. Despite human subjects' encounters with such variation in the patterns of experience, however, they remain a unity and face the question of what to do with what has been encountered in the data of consciousness.

The first option in the attempt to recognize the unity of the human subject is to compartmentalize the functioning and experiences of human persons. In such a position, the human person is understood as operating differently in the different patterns of experience. Here assertions of specialized knowledge according to the given situation are operative. Thus, the person is required to learn as many different cognitional structures as there are patterns of experience, and communication between individuals immersed in different patterns of experience becomes difficult, if not impossible. Mystics know only mysticism, and matters of socio-political concern are left to the politicians or social activists. People leave the intellectual pattern at work or school, maintain distance between the affect and the intellect, and acknowledge the worshipful only on Sunday. This option is exemplified in the mentality of the split soul that dominates the state of mystical theology, and it runs counter to the manner in which the human person operates. Such a state of affairs may be adequate when people are operating at the level of common sense, where the concern is merely the particular situation, but to reject consciously some data from consideration when the concern is theoretical knowledge deliberately runs the risk of derailing the subsequent operations of understanding and judgment. If individuals are seeking a level of knowledge beyond that of common sense, all relevant data must be considered, and all pertinent questions must be pursued.

Moreover, if people hold the data experienced, understood, and judged to be true only in the particular patterns of experience in which they occurred, the risk of cutting short the investigation into the application of that data in other matters arises once again. Perhaps, which is my claim, that which is affirmed to be true in the mystical pattern of experience bears directly on matters of political theology. If Christians are called to live in love with one another, then the experience of mystical union with the God who is Love can tell them quite a bit about the social structures which organize human communities. If Christians do not attend to mystical experience, social and political structures may inhibit rather than encourage the flourishing of human living.

The second option is to recognize that both the functioning of the human subject and the content of the patterns of experience accompany individuals as they move from one pattern to another. Regardless of the content of the experience, the structure of the operations remains constant as people seek to understand the data and affirm their understanding. Therefore, the knowing that occurs as individuals seek to appropriate the reality encountered in the various patterns of experience is not restricted to specialists who have attained a proficiency in such matters. The structure of the operations remains constant; only the content changes.

In addition to the consistency of the structure of the operations, the content of the experience also remains with human subjects, and this content becomes a part of the consciousness of the person. As Lonergan writes:

> There is the relation of the present to the past. Thus, past judgments remain with us. They form a habitual orientation, present and operative, but only from behind the scenes. They govern the direction of attention, evaluate insights, guide formulations, and influence the acceptance or rejection of new judgments.[69]

If this were not the case, then human persons would constantly have to relearn what has already been known, and human living would be a matter of continually reacquiring the skills and knowledge pertinent to a given situation. The relation of past to present allows the wisdom and knowledge gained in reflection upon the mystical pattern of experience to remain with individuals as they proceed to matters of socio-political concern.

Because of the unity of the human subject, the goal of authentically operating persons is to recognize this integral nature and to appropriate the data of consciousness accordingly. Human beings achieve this goal by reaching what Lonergan calls the 'differentiation of consciousness.'[70] This notion involves the ability of persons to recognize the situation in which they are located, as it is formed by conversion (to be discussed in the next chapter) or the lack thereof, intent (be it common sense or theoretical knowing), pattern of experience, and the operations involved in the appropriation of the data contained in the given situation. As the patterns of experience indicate, certain moments require attention to or defense against feelings. Differentiation of consciousness enables human beings to know: 1) the situation, 2) the operations germane thereto, and 3) the relationships that exist between patterns of experience and the functioning of persons as they move from one pattern to another. Once human subjects have achieved the differentiation of consciousness, they are better able to investigate further questions.

When individuals have achieved differentiation of consciousness with regard to the patterns of experience and operations appropriate to the obtaining of meaning in those experiences, they come face to face with what Tad Dunne names the "spiritually integrated subject." The spiritually integrated subject, he claims, is able to move intelligently among five realms of meaning: common sense, theory, method, transcendence, and historical and literary scholarship. He writes the following:

> The limitations of common sense require the higher viewpoint of the realm of theory. The realm of theory, in turn, needs the higher viewpoint of the realm of method, that is, of philosophic or generalized empirical method. Within the realm of method we can understand the realm of religious transcendence and see how it possesses the power to heal the world of its ills. Finally, the question of redemption raises the need to examine the realm of historical and literary scholarship in order to listen to and tell the stories that touch the transcendent in ordinary living.[71]

In a spiritually integrated subject, then, the meanings gained in any of the five realms may be expressed in or affected by the other four. All of the realms bear on one another, and mystical wisdom is no longer relegated solely to the realm of transcendence.

Because the realm of common sense consists of the relation of objects, persons, and activities in relation to individual selves, individuals are concerned at this level only with going about daily life, that is, how to function in a given society or just generally get along. This is not to say, however, that issues such as 'the good' or 'truth' are absent in the realm of common sense.[72] To state that getting along in a society does not involve such matters would be mistaken. The point here is simply that many people go about their lives without formulating a logically developed position with regard to everyday life. I suspect that if the majority of the people living in the United States of America were asked, they would state that being honest is an important element of our society. If, however, they were asked what 'truth' is or what is meant by 'real,' the result would be a great number of blank stares as people fumbled about to come up with an answer. This is the case for any number of issues. Millions of Christians believe in the Trinitarian nature of God, but how many of them can engage in a theological discussion of the matter? On a more concrete level, I know that my car runs because its engine burns gasoline and uses the energy of this combustion to propel my car forward, but if you ask me about the chemical or atomic properties of gasoline, I am lost.

The search for logical clarity in such matters leads to the realm of theory. Here, individuals seek to understand objects, ideas, and persons not only in relation to themselves as subjects, but also in the relations of these with each other or of these realties in and of themselves.[73] As human subjects operate in the realm of theory, they are faced with the issues neglected by common sense; they search for definitions of truth, wrestle with notions of subjective or absolute truth, struggle with the notion of being, the meaning of a Trinitarian faith, and research the properties of fossil fuels.

The search for logical clarity, however, cannot go on without some attention to guiding principles which assure people that they are going about it in a proper fashion, and this is the concern of method. For Lonergan, human subjects in this realm cease to look outside in order to focus on their interior functioning. The issue is crucial if human subjects are to trust the logical clarity sought in the realm of theory, and the following quotation expresses this importance.

> So man is confronted with the three basic questions: What am I doing when I am knowing? Why is doing that knowing? What do I know when I do it? With these questions one turns from the outer realms of common sense and theory to the appropriation of one's own interiority, one's subjectivity, one's operations, their structure, their norms, their potentialities.[74]

Only by being attentive to these questions can persons successfully achieve the logical clarity sought in the realm of theory, for without attention to their operations, individuals leave themselves open to error, or even worse, to bias.

The human person, however, is not a solitary being. Generally speaking, human beings live and function within a societal setting shaped by relations with a great number of people, objects, or animals, and those of a religious inclination would speak of living in acknowledgment of the presence of the Divine. People operate within the realm of transcendence when their consciousness is focused not on the relationship of others to themselves (as in the realm of common sense) or to each other (as in the realm of theory), but on *loving* concern for others.[75] In this realm of meaning issues of morality and ethics arise. Even the investigation into the mechanics of the internal combustion engine takes on a different tenor when it is performed with the love of God and neighbor in mind.[76]

According to Dunne, in transcendent concern for God and neighbor the human subject must find a manner of communicating what has been learned in the preceding levels of meaning, and this, he claims, is the role of scholarship. In so doing, scholarship functions as a storyteller who announces to the community at large where it collectively stands, where it appears to be going, and whether these are good or bad things. He writes,

> Without stories, we would have no way to symbolize, let alone to understand, what happens to us. Stories bear both the known and the unknown, both the cogent and the ambiguous, both sin and grace. They allow us to deal with truth even when we cannot understand it. And they bind us together in a common desire to hear the truth spoken in love.[77]

When persons operate within this level of meaning, they are attempting to tell others what has been determined to be truly good and what has been found to be wanting so that the world may become a better place. For this reason the great mystics of the Christian tradition have attempted to communicate the benefits of the interior life to the world, and countless persons have grown spiritually as a result of their encounter with the writings of the mystical tradition.

With specific reference to the spiritually integrated mystic then, the wisdom gained in the mystical encounter would become a part of all levels of meaning. To be more concrete, I ask the reader to consider the example of Ignatius of Loyola whose spiritual life was marked in part by a desire to trust in God for the provision of his needs. The following is recorded in his third-person autobiography.

> So at the beginning of the year '23 he set out for Barcelona [as part of his pilgrimage to Jerusalem] to take ship. Although various people offered to accompany him, he wanted to go quite alone, for his whole idea was to have God alone as refuge... For he wanted to practice three virtues – charity, faith, and hope; and if he took a companion, he would expect help from him when he was hungry; if he fell down the man would help him get up. He himself, too, would trust the companion and feel attachment to him on this account. But he wanted to place that trust, attachment, and expectation in God alone.[78]

As Ignatius continued his pilgrimage, he received money in Rome to buy passage from Venice to Jerusalem. However, Ignatius felt this to be a violation of his desire to trust solely in God and gave much of it to the poor, keeping only what was necessary for one night of lodging. He eventually gained passage after impressing a wealthy gentleman with his knowledge of God, and this person then petitioned the civil authorities to guarantee passage for Ignatius to Jerusalem.[79]

When this concern for placing trust in God alone, which arose from his encounter with the transcendent (the fourth level), is examined further in light of Dunne's definition of spiritual integration, the following comes to light. The concern for absolute trust in God became an aspect of the manner in which Ignatius sought passage to Jerusalem, an activity performed on the level of common sense (the first level). Moreover, his giving of the money to the poor was the result of a theoretically developed notion (the second level) of what such trust involved. Although the account does not contain details regarding Ignatius's attention to his knowing (the third level), he does bring his concerns for living a life of complete faith to his confessor, who guides Ignatius in his decision making.[80] Finally, what Ignatius learned about trust in God has been recorded in his autobiography so that others may draw upon his example and his wisdom (the fifth level), and thus Ignatius serves to some extent as an example of spiritual integration.

Conclusion

In this chapter I have presented a second piece to Lonergan's notion of self-appropriation by describing the operations of the human subject and the importance of recognizing them as individuals seek to discern meaning in the various patterns of experience that comprise human living. The operations consist of the human subject's experiencing of the data of consciousness, the act of understanding that data, and the passing of judgment on that understanding. In this fashion persons come to know the data offered by the particular experience in which they are located. This appropriation of the data then forms the basis from which decisions may be made, a subject to be addressed in more detail in Chapter Four with regard to moral living.

The data of human experience, however, is not limited to the sensible world. Human beings can also become aware of their functioning as human subjects in the endeavor to find meaning in their surroundings. Thus, human persons are able to know their knowing and affectivity as they go about the business of discerning meaning. With regard to mysticism, self-appropriation allows individuals to become aware of the intersubjectivity unique to the mystical experience, and in those instances wherein the Divine directly communicates something of the Divine nature, Mystics are better able to appropriate what has been learned of God in the mystical pattern of experience.

Moreover, self-appropriation leads to what Tad Dunne calls the spiritually integrated subject who is able to apply the meanings of the spiritual life in all five realms of meaning. Beginning at the level of common sense, mystics may be concerned only with the application of mystical wisdom to the concrete particularity of their situation. Once mystics discover this relevance, they may seek to develop a theoretical understanding not only of the specific experience but of mysticism in general. To do so, however, requires the application of method so as to avoid the entrance of bias into the attempt, and the results of their endeavor is the production of scholarly literature on the subject. Self-appropriated persons may then approach this literature in a manner informed by method so as to form a theoretical understanding of the writings of the mystic, which then may be applied to the particular concerns of common sense. Both directions are a matter of the performance of theology, but before that topic is addressed, a third and final piece must be added to the presentation of Lonergan's notion of self-appropriation, that of the foundational reality out of which persons undertake the task of determining meaning in the world, and this is the focus of the next chapter.

NOTES

[1] Bernard Lonergan, *Method in Theology*, 2nd ed. (New York: Herder and Herder, 1973; reprint, Toronto: University of Toronto Press, 1990, 1994, 1996), 73-76.

[2] Lonergan names the four realms of meaning as common sense, theory, interiority, and transcendence. Ibid., 81-85, 257-262. To this list Tad Dunne adds the realm of literary and historical scholarship. I will undertake a discussion of this additional realm of meaning later in this chapter.

[3] Bernard Lonergan, "Philosophical Positions with Regard to Knowing," in *Collected Works of Bernard Lonergan*, vol. 6, *Philosophical and Theological Papers 1958-1964*, eds. Robert C. Croken, Frederick E. Crowe, and Robert M. Doran (Toronto: University of Toronto Press, 1988), 224.

[4] Although Lonergan asserts the presence of the cognitional operations in all of human activity, he does leave room for the performance of those activities already learned. If people had to relearn the appropriate skills every time they wanted to do something, human living would come to a standstill. Lonergan names those previously acquired skills, habits, but even in the performance of those skills people must attend to the data, reach some level of understanding, and then pass judgment. *Collected Works of Bernard Lonergan*, vol. 5, *Understanding and Being: The Halifax Lectures on "Insight,"* eds., Elizabeth A. Morelli and Mark D. Morelli (Toronto: University of Toronto Press, 1990), 5-6.

[5] Frederick E. Crowe, S.J., "Origin and Scope of *Insight*," in Frederick E. Crowe, S.J, *Appropriating the Lonergan Idea*, ed. Michael Vertin (Washington D.C.: The Catholic University of America Press, 1989), 15. Vernon Gregson agrees with Crowe on this point as he writes, "Becoming aware of one's experiencing, understanding and judging gives one the possibility of methodical controls of those operations. Not that our knowing process itself changes, but awareness of the aberrations and possible truncating of the process can facilitate our not falling into these traps." Vernon J. Gregson, *Lonergan, Spirituality and the Meeting of Religions*. Studies in Religion, vol. 2 (New York: College Theological Society, 1985), 11.

[6] *Collected Works of Bernard Lonergan*, vol. 3, *Insight: A Study of Human Understanding*, eds., Frederick E. Crowe and Robert M. Doran (Toronto: University of Toronto Press, 1992), 299.

[7] Lonergan, *Method*, 18, 231.

[8] Lonergan, *Insight*, 28.

[9] Lonergan, *Method*, 18, 231.

[10] Lonergan, *Insight*, 298-299.

[11] Lonergan, *Method*, 18, 231.

[12] Lonergan, *Insight*, 305; Lonergan, *Understanding and Being*, 118-120.

[13] Though the judgment regarding religious faith is the concern of religious conversion, Lonergan does present in *Insight* an argument for the existence of God based on the intelligibility of reality. His argument runs as follows. First, the real is intelligible; otherwise judgment could not be reached, and things could not be known. Secondly, reality is *completely* intelligible, otherwise the desire to know would be restricted. Thirdly, the complete intelligibility must exist, or it remains merely an object of thought. Fourthly, the act of unrestricted understanding that demonstrates complete intelligibility can only be described as God. Lonergan, *Insight*, 692-699.

[14] Lonergan, *Insight*, 305; *Understanding and Being*, 118-120.

[15] Frank Paul Braio, *Lonergan's Retrieval of the Notion of Human Being: Clarifications of and Reflections on the Argument of "Insight," Chapters I-XVIII* (Lanham, MD: University Press of America, 1988), 341.

[16] Lonergan, *Insight*, 402.

[17] Thomas Naickamparambil, *Through Self-Discovery to Self-Transcendence: A Study of Cognitional Self-Appropriation in B. Lonergan*, Tesi Gregoriana Serie Filosofia, no. 5 (Rome: Gregorian University Press, 1997), 185.

[18] Lonergan, *Insight*, 404.

[19] Ibid., 405-406.

[20] Ibid., 35-36.

[21] Ibid., 35.

[22] *Collected Works of Bernard Lonergan*, vol. 10, *Topics in Education*, eds. Robert M. Doran and Frederick E. Crowe (Toronto: University of Toronto Press, 1988), 126.

[23] Lonergan, *Insight*, 35-37; *Topics in Education*, 126; *Understanding and Being*, 45-47.

[24] *Webster's Ninth New Collegiate Dictionary* (Springfield, MA: Merriam-Webster, 1988), 1200.

[25] Lonergan, "Natural Knowledge of God," in *A Second Collection*, ed. William F.J. Ryan and Bernard J. Tyrrell (Philadelphia: Westminster Press, 1974), 123.

[26] Lonergan, *Insight*, Ibid., 325.

[27] Ibid., 310.

[28] Lonergan, *Insight*, 337-338, Lonergan, *Understanding and Being*, 67-68.

[29] Lonergan, *Method*, 101-103

[30] Lonergan, *Insight*, 311-312, 314-316

[31] Ibid., 308.

[32] Ibid., 310.

[33] Bernard Lonergan, "Natural Knowledge of God," 124-125.

[34] Lonergan, *Method*, 76-77.

[35] Lonergan, *Insight*, 197-198.

[36] Ibid., 200.

[37] Lonergan uses the example of a school child who, although capable of obtaining correct answers to mathematical problems, does so only through the performance of drills which do not require an understanding of the principles at work. Bernard Lonergan, "The Form of Inference," in *Collection: Papers by Bernard Lonergan* ed. F.E. Crowe, SJ (Montreal: Palm Publishers, 1967), 4.

[38] Lonergan, *Method*, 276.

[39] Lonergan, *Understanding and Being*, 306.

[40] Lonergan, *Insight*, 199.

[41] Lonergan, *Method*, 53.

[42] Lonergan, *Insight*, 251.

[43] Ibid., 251-260.

[44] Ibid., 636-637.

[45] Ibid., 636.

[46] Ibid., 645.

[47] Ibid., 645. Here lies another application of Robert Doran's notion of psychic conversion, for if individuals are able to gain some level of critical control over the affective dimension of their personality, they are better able to overcome the limitations that a disordered psyche places upon them. Doran describes this process as consisting of a "transformation of the psychic component of what Freud calls 'the censor' from a repressive to a constructive agency in a person's development." Robert Doran, *Theology and the Dialectics of History* (Toronto: University of Toronto Press), 59.

[48] Lonergan, *Insight*, 640-42.

[49] Ibid., 645-655; Lonergan, *Understanding and Being*, 230-233.

[50] Lonergan, *Insight*, 646-647.

[51] Lonergan, *Method*, 64.

[52] Ibid., 66.

[53] Ibid., 67.

[54] Ibid., 67-69.

[55] Julian of Norwich, *Showings (Long Text)*, 72, in *Julian of Norwich: Showings*, trans. Edmund Colledge and James Walsh, The Classics of Western Spirituality: A Library of the Great Spiritual Masters (New York: Paulist Press, 1978), 320.

[56] Ibid., 181-182.

[57] Lonergan, *Method*, 77, quoted in Robert Doran, *Subject and Psyche*, 2nd ed., Marquette Studies in Theology, vol. 3, Andrew Tallon, ed. (Milwaukee, WI: Marquette University Press, 1994), 11.

[58] Doran, *Subject and Psyche*, 32.

[59] Ibid., 115-117.

[60] Ibid., 125. In recent communication with Robert Doran, he offered me the strategies found in Eugene Gendlin's *Focusing* as an example of an aid to psychic conversion outside the context of psychotherapy. See, Eugene Gendlin, *Focusing* (New York: Bantam Books, 1991).

[61] Mircea Eliade, *Myths, Dreams, and Mysteries: The Encounter between Contemporary Faiths and Archaic Realities* (New York: Harper & Row, 1960), 7-12.

[62] Many of Thérèse's revisions were the result of requests by her friends and superiors. The point remains, however, that as she revisited her autobiography, her understanding of the significance and particularities of her spiritual life grew over time. John Clarke reports that Manuscript B was the result of a request on the part of Sister Marie for an account of Thérèse's doctrine of her "little way." Similarly, Manuscript C resulted from Mother Marie de Gonzague's desire for an account of Thérèse's religious life that was not present in Thérèse's first manuscript. John Clarke, O.C.D., "Introduction," in Thérèse of Lisieux, *The Story of a Soul: The Autobiography of St. Thérèse of Lisieux*, 3rd ed. trans. John Clarke, O.C.D. (Washington, D.C.: ICS Publications, 1996), xvi-xvii.

[63] Doran, *Subject and Psyche*, 131.

[64] Ibid., 137-141.

[65] Ibid., 169. The production of symbols is not limited to instances of dreams and fantasy, however. Doran argues that in human consciousness an "ever-present flow of mood" exists that accompanies every aspect of human living. As human persons go about their lives, feelings come to the surface as a result of what they encounter and their attempts to deal therewith. This constant stream of mood, which Doran terms 'dispositional immediacy,' is given expression through the construction of symbols by the imagination of the subject, and

the meaning of these symbols may be mediated through the process of psychic conversion. Ibid., 117-127.   Therefore, the symbols whose meanings are discerned through psychic conversion are present in everyday life as well as in dreams and fantasies.

[66] Joan Timmerman defines someone who has reached a level of symbolic competency as, "one who can read the many layers of meaning that inhere in things." Joan Timmerman, "The Sacramentality of Human Relationships," *The Way Supplement* 94 (1999): 11.   While I agree with this definition, my goal in this book is to provide a further level of clarity as to how the human subject is able to discern the "many layers," especially as this discernment pertains to mystical-political theology.

[67] I am not suggesting here that psychic conversion is the only resource necessary for adequate interpretation of symbol. If human persons do not approach symbols intelligently or attend to the religious dimensions of symbols, they run the risk of missing certain levels of meaning. For example, an intellectual approach to the Christian cross may reveal meanings such as perpendicular pieces of wood or the history of one the tradition.   Religiously speaking, however, the cross is an expression of God's love for the world. The awareness of Divine Love adds to the meaning of the cross. Similarly, psychic conversion adds the additional level of understanding what that love means. Knowing that God loves creation and being aware of loving God in an unrestricted fashion is one thing; discerning meaning from it is quite another.

[68] Robert M. Doran, S.J., "Psychic Conversion," in *Theological Foundations*, vol. 1, *Intentionality and Psyche*, (Milwaukee: Marquette University Press, 1995), 64-65.

[69] Lonergan, *Insight*, 302.

[70] Lonergan, *Method*, 286-287.

[71] Dunne, 182-183.

[72] Lonergan, *Method*, 82.

[73] Lonergan, *Method*, 82-83.

[74] Ibid., 83.

[75] Dunne, 107-109.

[76] The topic of moral decision making will be addressed in the following chapter.

[77] Dunne, 152.

[78] Ignatius of Loyola, *The Autobiography*, 3:35, in *Ignatius of Loyola: Spiritual Exercises and Other Works*, ed. George E. Ganss, S.J., The Classics of Western Spirituality: A Library of the Great Spiritual Masters (New York: Paulist Press, 1991), 82.

[79] Ibid., 84-85.

[80] Ibid., 83.

CHAPTER FOUR

Self-Appropriation III: Conversion and the Dialectic of the Subject

Introduction

The present chapter is dedicated to a deeper understanding of the basis from which the authentic human subject proceeds. Whereas the previous chapter focused upon the operations of the human subject in the search to discern the meaning(s) present in the various patterns of experience, the current chapter will focus upon a more fundamental aspect of the human subject, the foundational reality out of which that functioning occurs. Before human beings attend to the data of consciousness, a certain set of presuppositions or guiding principles underlies and shapes their functioning as subjects. Even the act of experiencing, which begins the cognitional process, is subject to this foundational reality. If individuals are to understand their functioning, that is, to undergo self-appropriation, they must come to an understanding of that underlying reality which affects the manner in which they perform the operations of consciousness. To fail to do so is to run the risk of skewing the process of self-appropriation, which would then fail to serve as a point from which other matters may be pursued.

The first part of this chapter, then, is dedicated to Lonergan's work regarding foundational reality, which he describes as consisting of intellectual, moral, and religious conversion. Conversion, according to Lonergan, is the act of deciding for what and whom individuals stand, and against what and whom they position themselves. "It is a fully conscious decision about one's horizon, one's outlook, one's world-view."[1] As such, conversion, or lack thereof, affects every aspect of functioning as a human subject. Intellectually converted persons will not be satisfied by: 1) a failure to attend to the entirety of the data, 2) incomplete understanding, or 3) a refusal to pass judgment when the data demands a verdict. Religiously converted individuals will always take the dynamic state of being in love with God into consideration as they go about the business of their lives.

Morally converted individuals, to be described later in this chapter, cannot continue to live a life based on satisfaction rather than value. Thus, moral conversion dramatically alters human experiencing, understanding, judging, and the subsequent act of deciding what to do with what has been affirmed or denied. Religious persons will acknowledge the reality of God as relevant to the process of attending to the data whereas atheists will not, intellectually converted persons will insist on passing judgment when relativists refuse, and morally converted individuals insist that judgments of value are possible and necessary in any deliberations regarding courses of action.

The second part of the chapter will be dedicated to the fundamental tension that exists in the human person between transcendence, in which human persons achieve authenticity,[2] and the limitation that comes with the fact that human beings are created beings. This tension, according to Lonergan comprises the dialectic of the subject, which must be resolved if the person is to function authentically in the foundational reality comprised of conversion or lack thereof.

This chapter adds a third element to Lonergan's notion of self-appropriation. If human persons are to know what they are doing while performing the operations of consciousness, they must not only be aware of the pattern of experience in which they are located and the operations they are performing, but also the underlying stance from which those operations proceed. Converted individuals possess different first principles than unconverted persons, and the status of the resolution of the dialectic of the subject similarly affects human beings as subjects. To live authentically, human persons must acknowledge these factors.

Conversion

Perhaps no other term is as closely associated with the work of Bernard Lonergan than the notion of conversion, for through intellectual, religious, and moral conversion human beings, as subjects, transcend themselves, which, in turn, is at the heart of authenticity. Through intellectual conversion, human beings discover the unrestricted desire to know, and in pursuing this desire in a detached, disinterested fashion they come to know things not only as they appear from their particular perspective but as things truly are. Through moral conversion, they make the transition from living a life based on personal and selfish preferences to living according to judgments of value that identify what is truly good. Religious conversion is the result of falling in love with God in an unrestricted fashion, and this state of being in love becomes the first principle in every moment of religiously converted persons' lives. In all three cases, individuals leave behind the egocentric position of encountering the world from a stance in which their personal perspective or benefit is paramount to a standpoint in which human persons live by concerns or realities greater than themselves.[3]

Intellectual Conversion

Intellectual conversion, according to Lonergan, consists of the recognition and embrace of the operations of human cognition discussed in the previous chapter, namely, experiencing, understanding, and judging. Human persons achieve their full intellectual potential according to the extent to which they adhere to this pattern.[4] Intellectual conversion, however, is not merely a matter of becoming a better knower. Intellectual conversion also involves a radical shift in people's manner of existing, and this change carries with it an enormous responsibility. "Errors, rationalizations, ideologies fall and shatter to leave one open to things as they are and to man as he should be."[5] If human subjects fail to live up to this new manner of living, then they are living inauthentically, and this affects not only those who neglect intellectual conversion, but also those with whom they come into contact. At its heart, bias is a matter of the more or less conscious decision to be incorrect or the refusal to answer all pertinent questions, and bias grows inasmuch as individuals who hold a biased position interact with other human persons. The incomplete performance of intelligence affects others insofar as those persons who fail to execute authentically the operations of consciousness present their incorrect results as correct and convince others of their sufficiency. Those who have undergone intellectual conversion, on the other hand, are not satisfied with incomplete questioning or hasty judgments. They are dedicated to the pursuit of truth, to the knowledge of things as they truly exist, that is, to knowing being, and just as bias grows, so too does truth.

Intellectual conversion, then, is not merely a matter of coming to know something that was not known earlier, namely the manner in which human subjects operate. Rather, it consists of a commitment to these operations in the process to discover meaning(s) contained in a given experience. As such, the change wrought in the manner of performing the cognitional operations goes far beyond so-called life changing experiences, for the details of a given experience may fade; but once human persons undergo intellectual conversion, that fundamental change in the manner in which they inhabit the world is operative in all other experiences. Intellectual conversion becomes an aspect of every moment of human consciousness.

Religious Conversion

Just as intellectual conversion entails a radical shift in the manner in which persons go about their lives, so, too, does religious conversion. The state of being in love with God in an unrestricted fashion becomes, according to Lonergan, the "first principle, from which flow one's desires and fears, one's joys and sorrows, one's discernment of values, one decisions and deeds."[6] For religiously converted individuals, then, the love of God becomes an element of every moment of consciousness, coloring each and every experience, regardless of the pattern in which they may occur. Even such a practical matter as the purchase of a car entails the acknowledgement of the state of being in love with God. Is, for example, a vehicle which consumes an inordinate amount of gas consistent with the unrestricted love of God? If the answer is no, then individuals buy the car only at the risk of living an inauthentic existence.

Moral Conversion

Because religious conversion involves living life according to the love of God, it implies the ability of the human person to determine such notions as 'the good' and the ability to pronounce judgment regarding the value of a given experience or its contents. Generally speaking, if religiously converted persons live their lives according to their relationship with the Divine, then following the will of God is good, a judgment of value. Determining Lonergan's notion of the good, however, requires some discussion for, as Frederick Crowe notes, Lonergan significantly altered his thinking on the subject in the time between *Insight* and *Method*. Crowe claims that in the former, which first appeared in 1957, Lonergan's presentation of the good focuses upon the adherence of the subject to the transcendental method, which enables the person to make rational decisions that are reflective of value.[7] Lonergan writes, "[I]t is in rational, moral self-consciousness that the good as value comes to light, for the value is the good as the possible object of rational choice."[8] Thus, choosing the good seems to be a matter of evaluating choices of action in light of the good, which stands as the intelligible and rational.[9]

In the later *Method*, which first appeared in 1973, Crowe identifies a shift in emphasis in which Lonergan makes room for the impact of feelings on the performance of ethical thinking and acting.[10] Whereas in *Insight* feelings are primarily viewed as contributing to bias, which threatens the authenticity of the operations of the human subject,[11] *Method* allows for the entrance of feelings into the notion of value in a positive manner.[12] The question, therefore, is the role played by feelings in the apprehension of value, which, in turn, provides the framework for moral conversion as the transition to a life in which decisions are made on the basis of value rather than satisfaction.

Feelings

Feelings, according to Lonergan, fall into two general categories, intentional and non-intentional. The latter refers to those states and trends that have causes and goals, and they arise spontaneously rather than as the result of the operation of intelligence. To use Lonergan's example, people may feel hungry, and the performance of the operations follows to determine the cause and the remedy.[13]

Intentional feelings, on the other hand, are the result of an orientation to a world of meaning. As such, they are directed toward objects, in the broadest sense of the term to include people and ideas, rather than causes or trends, and they drive the functioning of the human subject. Because of feelings, human presence in the world goes beyond the cold, clinical operations of daily activities.

> We have feelings about other persons, we feel for them, we feel with them. We have feelings about our respective situations, about the past, about the future, about evils to be lamented or remedied, about the good that can, might, must be accomplished.[14]

Such intentional feelings may then be examined to determine whether they are representative of value or merely fall into the categories of the agreeable or disagreeable. For what is agreeable may in fact be destructive, and what is disagreeable may actually be reflective of value.[15]

The experience of feelings in human persons leads to the apprehension of value.[16] As individuals experience feelings for a given object, person, or social structure, the question must be faced as to whether or not their feelings are misguided. Perhaps, what at first seems inspiring and noble is in reality a perversion of human dignity. To help in such evaluation, Lonergan distinguishes ascending categories within the broader notion of value: vital, social, cultural, personal, and religious. Vital values are those factors which contribute to a physically healthy life, but these are subordinate to social values such as the good of order or the distribution of health services, which contribute to the well-being of other members of the community. Cultural values reside beyond the living and functioning which pertain to vital and social values. However, going about the business of living as automatons, performing only those functions which sustain human life and society is insufficient for Lonergan. Human persons develop meaning and value in their lives, and the function of culture is to express and develop these notions. Fourthly, personal value "is the person in his self-transcendence, as loving and being loved, as originator of values in himself and in his milieu, as an inspiration and invitation to others to do likewise."[17] Lastly, religious values provide ultimate meaning to human life and are revealed in the relationship with the Divine.[18] Although Lonergan identifies an ascending level of priority in his identification of five types of value here, they do not exist independently of one another.[19] Individuals cannot be instruments for the advance of social values if they are not healthy enough to do so. Likewise, no culture exists if a society does not exist in which cultural values arise, and so on. The relationship between the various values also develops down the scale. The higher values imbue the lower levels with added meaning. [20] When viewed in light of religious value, the manner in which human beings treat their bodies (vital values) takes on meaning beyond the sustenance of human life. Created in the image of God, human beings possess a special dignity that merits respect and care so that human life may be lived to the fullest.

Mystical experience stands to make a valuable contribution to the discernment of religious value, and thus to the other levels of value as well, because of the nature of the experience. If Christians are called to live in love with one another (a religious value), who better to serve as a resource than those who have experienced the immediate presence of God? Through mystical experience, the mystic learns more of Divine love, and Christians are to love as Christ loved his friends (John 13:34). The writings of the mystics are filled with wisdom regarding the nature of God's love for the world, and thus they may serve as an aid in the apprehension of values on all of the levels identified by Lonergan.

The intentional response to values, according to Lonergan, leads human persons to self-transcendence and forms the basis for moral conversion, which is the transition from making decisions on the basis of satisfaction to doing so based on value.[21] This is not a simple matter, however, for as discussed previously, even though the perception of values is closely linked to the feelings about certain people or things, feelings also play a role in the functioning of bias, which inhibits the authentic performance of human life.

Lonergan's solution to this issue is his development of a transcendental notion of value. As the operations of human intelligence intend being, the discernment of which actions are truly good in a given situation intends value. In other words, just as knowing a thing as it exists independently of the subject is possible, so also is knowing the good as it is distinct from the individual feasible.[22] The goal of morally converted persons, then, is to go about the business of judging the extent to which a course of action is based upon and reflective of value. Although such judgment differs in content from judgments of fact and "are objective or merely subjective inasmuch as they proceed from a self-transcending subject,"[23] the structure is the same. Individuals encounter an experience in which feelings give rise to the discernment of value, seek to understand the value revealed by these feelings, and then pass judgment on that understanding.

As judgments of value and fact are similar in structure, they are also similar insofar as they are both self-correcting.[24] Human learning is a matter of the advance of knowledge in which new questions are asked in light of new data and new human situations. As this process goes forward, human understanding, though never complete, moves ever closer to comprehensive knowledge of a thing. In the same manner, human beings can advance in their judgments of value, although this endeavor, like questions for intelligence, can be derailed by bias.

Barring such interference, human persons advance in their moral understanding of a given situation, and this forward movement may lead to a revision or outright rejection of previously held positions. Although others may accuse individuals in such instances of being inconsistent, such persons are actually coming to a fuller understanding of the matter. Just as judgments of fact may be based on previous erroneous judgments and require correction, so too judgments of value may require persons to revisit prior judgments and adjust their moral decision making and action. Lonergan writes the following in Chapter Ten of *Method*.

> One has to keep developing one's knowledge of human reality and potentiality as they are in the existing situation. One has to keep distinct its elements of progress and its elements of decline. One has to keep scrutinizing one's intentional responses to values and their implicit scales of preference. One has to listen to criticism and to protest. One has to remain ready to learn from others. For moral knowledge is the proper possession only of morally good men and, until one has merited that title, one has still to advance and learn.[25]

Although the possibility of human persons reaching the point at which they have nothing more to learn seems rather unlikely, Lonergan's point here is that moral conversion is a life-long process, that it takes work, and that like intellectual conversion with regard to knowing and religious conversion with regard to the presence of the Divine affecting every aspect of life, moral conversion requires persons to advert consciously to the choices and actions that comprise moral living.

Without the self-correcting nature of moral decision making, according to Crowe, human beings would run the risk of falling into the same difficulty encountered with regard to judgments of value as with judgments of fact.[26] This difficulty consists of determining the point at which they have reached a virtually unconditioned, that is, when all relevant questions have been answered. As discussed with regard to human knowing, determining the point at which an unconditioned has been reached is no easy matter, especially considering Lonergan's position that a thing can never fully be understood. Individuals must resolve this issue, however, or be left with the two unsatisfactory options of either pronouncing judgment rashly, before accounting for all the data, or being indecisive, not pronouncing judgment for fear of new questions or data.

Implications of Moral Conversion

As previously noted, the unity of Lonergan's work on the notion of value judgments lies in the self-correcting nature of moral decision making. This element of consistency enables the combination of both the intellectual and affective elements of the human person with regard to moral conversion. Lonergan's later work on feelings and their relation to the apprehension of value allows morally converted persons to advert to the entirety of their moral living, and the intellectual rigor of his earlier work serves the valuable function of providing a level of control to the process of making judgments of value. In addition to informing perception of value, emotions and personal experiences are often the source of bias, and the controls provided by the transcendental precepts "Be attentive. Be intelligent. Be reasonable." help people to adhere to the fourth precept, "Be responsible."

For this book, the implications of Lonergan's presentation of moral conversion are twofold. First, it prevents relativist positions from blocking any pronouncement of judgment regarding the creation of just human societies and the contributions that mystics may make to that endeavor. Despite the contention of relativism that human beings cannot judge a society as a good or poor representative of value, persons who acknowledge transcendent value will recognize that in today's world not every human community operates in a manner that promotes the flourishing of all human persons. A transcendental notion of value enables persons to resist those social practices that may be justified as culturally acceptable but are in actuality destructive of authentic human existence. Societal elements such as the condoning of racial inequality or the glorification of violence cannot be justified as a societal particularity in light of the transcendental notion of value, for such a notion goes beyond societal individuality and enables judgments regarding the truly good.[27]

Secondly, because religious values occupy the highest place in Lonergan's ascending categories of value, mysticism stands to make a contribution not only to the discernment of religious value, but also with regard to the dynamic relationship that exists between morally converted individuals and God. Morally converted persons who are making decisions and taking actions based on religious value are doing so as a response to the unrestricted act of falling in love. Feelings arise out of this relationship that lead to the apprehension of religious value. But feelings in any relationship are not static realities, and this is also the case with regard to the act of falling in love with God in an unrestricted fashion. Feelings may wither and die off, and in some cases they may grow to deeper levels.[28]

> But there are in full consciousness feelings so deep and strong, especially when deliberately reinforced, that they channel attention, shape one's horizon, direct one's life. Here the supreme illustration is loving. A man or woman that falls in love is engaged in loving not only when attending to the beloved but at all times. Besides particular acts of loving, there is the prior state of being in love, and that prior state is, as it were, the fount of all one's actions.[29]

I believe that in the Western Christian tradition, no better record of such a loving relationship between God and humanity may be found outside of the mystics. The mystics of the tradition acknowledge their relationships with God as the basis of all their actions,[30] and this recognition frequently propelled them to great moral action. Moreover, morally converted individuals who are acting on the basis of religious value would do well to turn to the mystics for guidance regarding the deepening of their relationship with the Divine. The growth of a loving relationship is not automatic, and the mystics have lived lives dedicated to the fostering of the love between humanity and God. The fruits of their labors stand before humanity today as an aid to the struggle to live a life informed by religious value.

As is the case with the previously discussed intellectual and religious conversions, moral conversion also affects every aspect of human living. For the morally converted, life is no longer a matter of making decisions according to satisfaction but doing so according to value. They may encounter many things that are satisfying but are not representative of value or the truly good, and the decision to live in accordance to value is not an intermittent guiding principle, but, rather, an aspect of the foundational reality out of which individuals live and operate as authentically functioning subjects.

The Relationship between the Conversions

To the previous chapters' treatment of self-appropriation with regard to patterns of experience and the operations of the human subject, the present chapter has added Lonergan's notion of conversion as it occurs intellectually, religiously, and morally.   Although Lonergan goes to great lengths to distinguish between these notions, they do not exist independently of one another. First, a relation exists between the three conversions insofar as religious and moral conversions affect the data deemed to be relevant by the human subject operating in the intellectual pattern of experience and subsequent understanding and judging.[31]   Because moral and religious conversion entail the discernment of value, morally and religiously converted individuals may consider certain data to be important to a given line of investigation whereas someone who approaches a given line of investigation from a strictly intellectual basis will reject the relevance of that data.[32] Secondly, as human persons experience, understand, and judge the data of consciousness, what they learn stays with them and affects subsequent operations with regard to all three types of conversions. For instance, once individuals have fallen in love with God in an unrestricted fashion and assented to this relationship in a specifically Christian context, they can no longer encounter the created world as simply a collection of flora and fauna. Rather, creation has become a means by which the Divine may become manifest, and even the considerations of the biochemical processes of an organism such as a bird must take this into account.

Causally speaking, according to Lonergan, religious conversion is generally first, for the gift of God's love awakens human persons to the reality of self-transcending truth, beauty, and value. This awakening, in turn, may lead to moral conversion as they begin to make decisions based on newly discovered religious values as these come to expression in the faith community. The acceptance and understanding of these articulations may lead them to recognize that the universe is indeed intelligible. Human beings are not limited to passing judgment on what is good or right.   Human intellectual activity is such that human persons are able to know things not merely as they appear, but as they truly exist independently of one another.[33]

Although the order of the three conversions generally proceeds along the pattern of religious, moral, and intellectual conversion, the manner in which they shape the foundational reality of human persons progresses in the opposite direction. Intellectual conversion, according to Lonergan, consists of overcoming the 'ocular myth' in which knowing is understood as taking a close look. Through the appropriation of their cognitional operations, individuals are able to come to know things as they truly exist rather than as they appear. Moral conversion adds an additional dimension to intellectual conversion insofar as it enables individuals to apprehend and pass judgment upon value and the truly good.

> So moral conversion goes beyond the value, truth, to values generally. It promotes the subject from cognitional to moral self-transcendence. It sets him on a new, existential level of consciousness and establishes him as an originating value.[34]

The promotion of self-transcendence of which Lonergan is writing here does not obliterate the previous achievement of intellectual conversion, however. Rather, moral conversion opens human intellectual functioning to deeper realities. Human subjects continue to experience, understand, and judge the data of consciousness, but now the discernment of value enters the picture. Moral conversion also adds a level of responsibility to the performance of the cognitional operations. Adherence to intellectual conversion may be difficult or unsettling, but when the investigation involves matters of value and the truly good, morally converted individuals are compelled by moral conversion to do so authentically. Though it may be unpleasant, morally converted persons cannot go about the business of knowing sloppily or lazily.

Similarly, religious conversion builds upon the achievements of moral conversion, for religious conversion awakens individuals to the highest level of value. Taken together, the various conversions, or lack thereof, comprise the foundational reality from which persons pursue authentic existence in their life. Conversion becomes the basis of all of their functioning.

Because foundational reality comprises the framework out of which the operations of the human subject proceed, the patterns of experience discussed in Chapter Two are open to new interpretation. If, for instance, someone has fallen in love with God in an unrestricted fashion, then this state of being in love is present in every subsequent pattern of experience. Therefore, scientists who are investigating the nature of the cosmos may fall into a worshipful pattern of experience as they discover more fully the wonder of creation in all of its complexity. In such a case, perhaps a better manner of describing the experience is to identify a hybridization of the patterns of experience.[35] In the case of such scientists, they are operating within an intellectual-worshipful pattern of experience. Because of this hybridization, self-appropriation becomes all the more important. If persons fail to acknowledge the impact that their moral and religious sensibilities have on the manner in which they attend to the data available in the various patterns of experience, they run the risk of inadequately performing the operations of consciousness. Human persons live in a world mediated by meaning, and these meanings are present on many different levels according to the pattern of experience in which they are located. Only through self-appropriation can individuals become aware of this manifold of meanings, and only through this awareness can they live authentically. Such authenticity recognizes the unity in differentiation that characterizes human beings, and overcoming the split soul mentality becomes possible.[36]

Dialectic of the Subject

At first glance, Lonergan's notion of conversion may appear a simple notion even if conversion in all its forms is a difficult task. The fruit of authenticity is self-transcendence, and persons achieve self-transcendence through: intellectual conversion, in which they come to know things as they truly exist, through moral conversion, which involves the transition to a life lived according to value, and through religious conversion, wherein individuals fall in love with God in an unrestricted fashion. Once they undergo these conversions, they may seem to be off and running to an authentic life. Unfortunately, this is not the case, for just as individuals may make progress, so too may they regress.

> Besides conversions there are breakdowns. What has been built up so slowly and so laboriously by the individual, the society, the culture, can collapse. Cognitional self-transcendence is neither an easy notion to grasp nor a readily accessible datum of consciousness to be verified. Values have a certain esoteric imperiousness, but can they keep outweighing carnal pleasure, wealth, power? Religion undoubtedly had its day, but is not that day over? Is it not illusory comfort for weaker souls, an opium distributed by the rich to quiet the poor, a mythical perfection of man's own excellence into the sky?[37]

Authentic existence, then, requires continuous vigilance and effort on the part of human persons if authenticity is to become the rule of their lives rather than the exception. Human beings exist in a state of dialectical tension between the ability for self-transcendence on the one hand, and the limitations placed on persons because of external circumstance, affective elements of the personality, lack of intellectual development, and a willing resistance to authenticity.[38]

According to Robert Doran, however, a difficulty exists in *Insight* with regard to the manner in which Lonergan uses the term, 'dialectic.' This word, Doran claims, may be used either to indicate a 'dialectic of contraries,' wherein two opposing terms or notions stand in creative tension with one another or a 'dialectic of contradictories,' in which the opposition of the terms or notions is such that a choice must be made in favor of one position or the other.[39] Authentically operating persons, therefore, must not only attend to their knowing, but also to the dialectical choices that they encounter in adverting to their operations as human subjects. In some cases, the demands of authenticity allow these choices to coexist, but in others, this is not possible.

The primary example of a dialectic of contraries within the human subject, Doran claims, is the tension that exists between conscious and unconscious neural demands.[40] The functioning of human subjects is not merely a matter of coldly and clinically experiencing the data, understanding that data through the formulation of explanatory hypotheses, judging the veracity of such theories, and then taking action on the basis of these judgments. Rather, feelings often enter the matter, and if individuals are to live authentically, they must attend to these feelings, for they are the building blocks for the apprehension of value. The difficulty lies in the fact that the content of the experience regarding the affective dimension of the human person is of a different order than the content of the intellectual pattern of experience. Whereas the intellect functions with concepts and logic through which sense is made of the data, human affectivity operates with symbols and emotion, and these often defy attempts at conceptual understanding. Moreover, human affectivity may derail the cognitive operations through bias, and it may do so surreptitiously that people seeking to discern meaning in the experience wander far afield. A key role of psychic conversion, therefore, is to gain a level of critical control over the meanings contained in the psychic activity of the human person. Not only does this lead to the accessing of these deeper levels of meaning, but it also seeks to avoid the disintegration of the human subject into two opposed poles of the intellect and affect. The authentically operating human person recognizes the tension between the intellectual and affective elements of the subject and is able to allow each to positively affect one another.

A secondary example of a dialectic of contraries is the aforementioned tension that exists between the limitations imposed by the concrete situation in effective freedom and the reality desired by individuals in essential freedom. They are free to imagine and desire any number of alternatives to the present situation, but only a limited number of those possibilities are actually available to them. Lonergan treats the attempt to make the transition from "what is" to "what ought to be" under the notion of 'The Law of

Genuineness,' which requires a recognition of the tension that exists between the two concrete situations. If, on the one hand, people lean too heavily toward the limitations imposed by the current situation, they run the risk of acquiescing to the status quo regardless of the fact that the present arrangement may stand in desperate need of correction. Or, as is more likely the case, they may be prevented from taking action because certain courses of action or theoretical solutions may never occur to them because they are mired in the schemes of recurrence that reinforce limitations on their ability to act or think. On the other hand, persons may become so enamored with the desired set of circumstances that the particularities of the given situation are lost, and the aspiration to a new situation vanishes in utopian dreams and fantasies.[41] These limitations create a moral impotence that goes beyond the restraints of the socio-historical situation to a limitation of individuals which prevents solutions from rising in their consciousness.

> To assert moral impotence is to assert that man's effective freedom is restricted, not in the superficial fashion that results from external circumstance or psychic abnormality, but in the profound fashion that follow from incomplete intellectual and volitional development.[42]

In other words, the limitation that forms one pole of the dialectic goes far beyond the restraints placed upon human freedom by socio-political structures, upbringing, or even genetics. The lack of development on the part of persons morally or intellectually serves to hinder the achievement of the desired situation insofar as it prevents them from conceiving of possible avenues for change.

How, then, are human beings to overcome the limitations of moral impotence if that very incapacity prevents alternatives from arising in their consciousness? In light of the self-correcting nature of the operations of the human subject with regard to judgments of both fact and value, a similar solution would seem to be applicable here. When moral impotence rears its head, however, such self-correction is impossible because no further questions or insights into the unsatisfactory state of affairs come to mind. Individuals are left staring blankly at a situation from which no escape seems possible. Even worse, solutions may arise that only serve to exacerbate an already unsatisfactory state of affairs.

> Essentially the problem lies in an incapacity for sustained development. The tension divides and disorientates cognitional activity by the conflict of positions and counterpositions. This conflict issues into contrary views of the good, which in turn make good will appear misdirected, and misdirected will appear good. There follows the confounding of the social situation with the social surd to provide

misleading inspiration for further insights, deceptive evidence for further judgments, and illusory causes to fascinate unwary wills.[43]

In light of the incapacity for development as a result of moral impotence, a higher integration of the human person is necessary, one which is capable of overcoming the inertia caused by moral impotence and enabling positive change.

For Lonergan, this higher integration is the fruit of a healing vector that enters human history and is able to transform the human condition situation in such a manner as to restart the creative element of human living in the creation of meanings, institutions, and culture.[44] This vector has its origin in God, and whereas the cognitional operations of human persons operate from below upwards in order to create the expression of the meanings contained within the data of consciousness, healing proceeds from the top down, radically changing all that it encounters. The healing vector descends upon the human situation, and the love of God present in that healing transforms the operations of human beings, and thus new strategies for overcoming moral impotence and moving the human condition forward are thereby revealed. In so doing, the healing vector is able to provide the remedy for those situations where the lack of human development or the dialectic of the subject has caused human persons to run into a stumbling block.

> For human development is of two quite different kinds. There is development from below upwards, from experience to growing understanding, from growing understanding to balanced judgment, from balanced judgment to fruitful courses of action, and from fruitful courses of action to the new situations that call forth further understanding, profounder judgment, richer courses of action.
>
> But there is also development from above downwards. There is the transformation of falling in love: the human love of one's tribe, one's city, one's country, mankind; the divine love that orientates man in his cosmos and expresses itself in his worship.[45]

As such, certain principles or options for the achievement of the desired situation are chosen or rejected in light of the transformation effected by love. Moreover, this transformation may involve new solutions that were previously unavailable due to moral impotence. As persons examine these principles more deeply, their understanding of them grows, and the creative process that has been derailed by a lack of higher integration may be restarted.

Perhaps the best illustration of this transformation of human living by the healing vector is the change wrought by religious experience, for religious conversion draws into itself and expands upon both intellectual and moral conversion. In the act of falling in love with God as a response to God's flooding of the human heart with love through the Holy Spirit, people take a stance in the world. This is a concrete expression of the whole of their life – a decision for and against certain values. For the Christian, it is a stance for the God who is love (1 John 4:8). This conscious stance in the world comes to expression in certain affirmations regarding the reality and nature of that Love. Doctrinally speaking, the God who is love became incarnate in the person of Jesus Christ so that sin and death might no longer hold the upper hand in human affairs. Other affirmations may not be doctrinally formulated by the church but are true nonetheless. For instance, some may affirm that because they are in love with God in an unrestricted fashion, they should treasure and protect that which God has created in all its forms. Such affirmations would be impossible without the prior act of falling in love with God. People may certainly come to an atheistic environmental ethic, but that ethic would be informed not by love of God, but by such factors as awe at the complexity of the natural environment or a recognition that a healthy planet is necessary for a healthy humanity. But for religiously converted persons, an environmental ethic is affirmed because of the entrance of Divine love through the healing vector, and their judging has been radically altered.

Once individuals have affirmed such truths, they continue to develop downwards in the level of understanding.[46] What does it mean that God became incarnate in the person of Jesus Christ? What does it mean to love God's creation? Through such reflection, persons come to deeper levels of understanding in both the meaning of the affirmations and the implications of these truths for their stances in the world. As with acts of judging, understanding takes on a different tenor in the downwards vector of healing. According to Lonergan, the religious experience holds an affective dimension that is normally resisted in the performance of the cognitional operations. For the religiously converted, this affective dimension is operative as they seek to understand previously affirmed truths. In order to understand the doctrine of the Incarnation or God's love for all of creation, Christians must not only use the reason of the head but also the reasons of the heart.[47] As with the understanding of the data in light of the gift of God's love present in the upwards vector, understanding of judgments in the downwards vector is transformed into something other than pure reason.

The transformation wrought by the healing vector bears fruit, then, as individuals take up the creative task of the upwards vector. Experiencing, understanding, judging, and deciding are now open to new possibilities that free persons from the stagnation present prior to the entrance of the healing vector.[48] They now attend to data in a new way, informed by the values revealed by the love of God entering human affairs through the healing vector. Their understanding is more expansive as they have awakened to new possibilities, and they now possesses a broader awareness of the good, the true, and value from which they may affirm or negate explanatory hypotheses.

The dialectic of the human subject is thus a matter of the interplay between the two vectors of consciousness. If individuals stubbornly stick to their own operations for the solution to every problem, they will remain blind to the integration offered by the healing vector. Conversely, if persons sit idly by waiting for Divine intervention to provide all of the answers, they may be sitting for a very long time indeed. Only by allowing the healing offered by the Divine to enter their operations as human subjects are persons able to let the tension between limitation and transcendence of the dialectic of the subject bear fruit and offer an integrated approach to authentic human existence.

Mysticism and the Healing Vector

The dialectic of the human subject provides insight into the nature of the mystical experience by meeting possible objections to the applicability of Lonergan's notion of self-appropriation to mystical theology because of his emphasis on the cognitional operations of the human subject. When the functioning of the human subject is the focus in the appropriation of the data, or lack thereof, in the mystical experience, a danger emerges; the notion of the infused nature of mystical wisdom may be lost. From a perspective informed by Lonergan's work on the human subject, mystics encounter and recognize the mystical pattern of experience, attend to the data present therein, seek to understand that data, pass judgment on the understanding, and then make decisions based upon that affirmation or negation. Such a position would seem to grasp the mystical experience as one in which the human subject does all of the work of discerning meaning in the experience.

This position, however, fails to take into account the change effected by the loving relationship with God upon the operations of the human subject. Within the loving relationship between the mystics and God, the healing vector is present, and this, I believe, is how the infused nature of the mystical experience may be best understood. Mystics do not passively receive the content in the mystical experience. Rather, mystics attend to the data of the experience but do so in a manner transformed by the love of God in the healing vector, and this opens the consciousness of the mystics to new insights which would be unavailable without the presence of the healing vector. Grace is present in the mystical experience in a profound manner, and Grace expands and refines the operations of authentic human persons, thus allowing for the flourishing of the human community as a whole.[49]

Moreover, what may be perceived by others as inactivity on the part of the mystic, thus contributing to the notion that mysticism is a passive matter, may in fact be part of this healing vector. As mystics encounter this movement from above downwards, they may pause, perhaps resting in the truth of the experience[50] or seeking to understand these truths before going about the business of applying these truths and understandings thereof in the practical matters of life. Before they are able to act upon the content of the mystical experience, they must understand that content, and if the accounts of the mystical experience are taken seriously, this may take quite some time.[51] Once mystics gain understanding of their experiences, they are better equipped to approach the challenges of the day or relate the particularities of their spiritual lives for the benefit of others.

Lastly, the healing vector is able to serve as a resource for those persons whose spiritual life, though it may be profound and rich in truths, goes somewhat awry in its concrete expression. Consider, for example, the extreme ascetical practices of Henry Suso or Catherine of Siena. Might it be the case that in such cases these individuals concentrate so heavily on the healing vector or the transcendent dimension of the dialectic of the subject that they lose the creative vector or the aspect of limitation? In such instances, the mystics lose contact with the element of the dialectic that grounds them in the world and worldly matters, which for Henry and Catherine may have been care of the body. Conversely, some people may rush off to social action too hastily, without allowing for the healing vector or transcendent dimension to inform their actions. As with all human persons, mystics must come to a resolution of the dialectic of the subject, which consists of allowing the two poles and two vectors to live in creative tension with one another.

A Clarification by Contrast

A potential difficulty arises with regard to the healing vector when it is compared with Lonergan's assertion that insights also arise unbidden in the mind of the human subject as a response to human inquiry into experience. He writes:

> What we have to grasp is that insight (1) comes as a release to the tension of inquiry, (2) *comes suddenly and unexpectedly,* (3) is a function not of outer

circumstances but of inner conditions, (4) pivots between the concrete and the abstract, and (5) passes into the habitual texture of one's mind.[52]

Therefore, when deliberating about a certain situation, possible solutions arise in the mind of human persons, but the question remains: is this the action of the healing vector of Divine love, or is this an insight into the situation arising unexpectedly from the tension of human inquiry?

The fundamental difference between the two lies in their origin. Insights are the result of human activity, whereas the healing vector originates in God and comes to expression in human living. As such, the certainty experienced by the human person differs in the two instances. After having an insight into a matter, the next step is to understand it through the asking of all relevant questions and then to pass judgment as to the insight's potential for addressing the given situation.

The healing vector, however, proceeds not up through the operations of the human subject but down. Beginning therefore in the level of judgment, a certainty arises immediately as religiously converted persons affirm the Divine origin of the solution. The next step in such a case is to understand and formulate in language what the solution means and then to seek to implement it.

The difference between the two is not only fundamental in nature but also of great consequence. Not all divine revelation occurs in the healing vector. People may hear the voice of God, understand what God has told them, affirm that understanding, and take appropriate action. If they treat their insights as the activity of Divine love, they make the dangerous claim that their as yet untested insights hold the absolute objectivity associated with the level of judgment. If they do not hold their understanding up to the scrutiny of judgment they run the risk of allowing bias to threaten authentic human existence.

To clarify the distinction between the activity of Divine love in the healing vector and insight into the will of God, I offer the examples of Francis of Assisi and Ignatius of Loyola. Both of these great spiritual figures experienced difficulty with the decision to answer God's call to service. For Francis, this struggle took place over many years and came to resolution in the church in San Damiano. At this time he encountered God's famous call to, "fix my church,"[53] and Francis answered, dedicating his life to service to God.

In light of the downward progression of Lonergan's notion of the healing vector, Francis immediately affirmed the truth of the experience. He relates that he perceived the voice of God as speaking directly to him from the crucifix on the wall of the church. His efforts at understanding the experience were not, as in the case of moving up through the levels, dedicated to understanding the content of the experience and then moving to the level of judgment. Rather, his understanding *followed* the affirmation that his experience came from God, and then he focused on the implications of the directive for the rest of his life. For Francis, that meant severing his ties to his family's wealth and a life of poverty in imitation of Christ as he sought to obey God's command to "fix my church."

Ignatius, on the other hand, struggled with the direction of his life following a debilitating injury suffered in war. As he recuperated from this injury, he began to read the *Golden Legend* by Jacobus de Voragine and *The Life of Christ* by Ludolph of Saxony. During this time Ignatius found that when he thought or read about Christ he was filled with joy, but when his mind was on other matters, his life was dissatisfying.[54] Through his attempts at understanding his experiences in this stage of his life, Ignatius came to the decision to dedicate his life to following God, and after his recovery, he set out on a pilgrimage to Jerusalem.[55] For Ignatius, then, the acceptance of the call to religious life was the result of a long process of understanding the experiences he had while reading religious texts, an understanding he affirmed as true. Unlike Francis whose experience involved the immediate judgment regarding the call of God, Ignatius had to sort through his experiences and come to an understanding regarding their content.

Despite the fact that Francis immediately recognized the truth of his experience at San Damiano, development downwards importantly continued after judgment. For Francis, the task of understanding what was revealed to him took some amount of time. First, he took the command to "fix my church" literally as he set out to fund the restoration of the church in which he heard the call of God.[56] Upon further reflection, Francis recognized his call to be one of church reform in a wider sense. To act immediately upon a judgment in the movement downwards through the levels of human consciousness may be to obey unintelligently, and thus, inauthentically.

Conclusion

In this chapter, I have presented Lonergan's notion of the foundational reality out of which the functioning of the human subject proceeds and the dialectical tension of the subject that allows development both from below upwards in the creative vector and from above downwards in the healing vector. This foundational reality consists of conversion, be it intellectual, moral, or religious, or the lack thereof, and comprises the principles according to which people perform the operations of the human subject.

Intellectual conversion is a matter of overcoming the myth that knowing consists of taking a good look as well as recognizing the fact that human cognition is a process of experiencing the data, seeking to understand the data, and affirming or negating that understanding in the act of judging. This process is completed as individuals proceed to the level of decision wherein they decide what to do with what has been learned. Moral conversion is the transition from making such decisions on the basis of personal satisfaction to doing so based on judgments of value, which are similar in structure to judgments of knowing but differ in content. Religious conversion, finally, is the act of falling in love with God in an unrestricted fashion. For the religiously converted, every dimension of life is affected by the relationship with the Divine.

These conversions, moreover, are interrelated insofar as moral conversion sublates intellectual conversion and religious conversion sublates both moral and intellectual conversion. This sublation, however, is not a matter of negating previous achievements. Rather, Lonergan uses this term to indicate that moral and religious conversion take up into themselves and expand upon intellectual conversion. For morally converted persons, knowing is not merely an exercise of rationality but a responsible decision where they pursue the truth out of a sense of value regarding the task. For religiously converted individuals, the data of consciousness takes on a different, deeper tenor because the reality of the Divine and their relationship therewith becomes an omnipresent factor in their lives.

Human subjects operate within their foundational reality in the dialectical tension between transcendence and limitation. At times, the self-correcting nature of human cognition is sufficient to address the problems of knowing things or determining what is truly good. In such instances they may be said to be operating within the creative vector of human existence for they are creating and inhabiting a world mediated by the meanings achieved through authentic human existence. At other times, however, the limitation of human beings is such that only a higher integration is able to jumpstart or correct the process of creating and mediating meaning. Such integration, according to Lonergan, is available through the healing vector of Divine love, which enters the process and affects human judging and understanding so as to place the functioning of human subjects back on track. Moreover, if individuals concentrate too heavily on either side of the dialectic, they runs the risk of, on the one hand, believing human agency to be sufficient in all matters or, on the other, sitting idly by waiting for Divine intervention. Ideally, then, if human beings recognize the foundational reality in which they are operating and are willing to operate within the tension between limitation and transcendence, they are better able to exist authentically in the world, and become positive forces therein.

The value of self-appropriation is that it provides a framework from which persons can deal with additional questions. In other words, if people are conscious of: 1) the pattern of experience in which they are located, 2) whether they are operating on the level of common sense or theory, 3) their foundational reality as it is shaped by the presence or absence of conversion, and 4) the extent to which they are true to this foundational reality in the dialectic between limitation and transcendence, then they are poised to address authentically subsequent questions. If they fail to appreciate any or all of these factors which shape the functioning of the human subject, then they are not operating authentically, and the results of the investigation of later questions will reflect this inadequacy.

The complexity of Lonergan's thought regarding the nature of self-appropriation, with its various patterns of experience, conversions, and the extent to which the human subject operates authentically, may lead the reader to the position that this concept does nothing to address the split soul mentality that seeks to separate the mystical life from the socio-political affairs of the world. If, after all, the experiencing of the human subject may be divided into such a wide variety of patterns of experience and if certain individuals deem different data of consciousness to be relevant according to their conversions, is Lonergan not separating human consciousness into distinct means of operating that are appropriate to each given pattern?

The answer to the above question is negative, and I make this response on the basis of two elements of Lonergan's thought. First, even though the content of the human experience may fall into different patterns, persons perform the same operations regardless of that content as they seek to know what has been encountered. Thus, even though more affective patterns of experience such as the worshipful or aesthetic are more heavily laden with feeling, individuals experience the data, seek to understand it, and pass judgment on that understanding. Though the content judged to be relevant differs, the structure remains the same.

Secondly, human beings carry the knowledge gained in one experience to all subsequent experiences. What has been learned in the mystical pattern accompanies people as they search for answers to social ills in the intellectual pattern. Spiritual integration, moreover, indicates that various levels of meaning may be present in any given experience and enables individuals to apply these meanings appropriately. Taken collectively, human living comprises a horizon, which Lonergan describes as the range of knowledge and interests. Whereas foundational reality provides individuals with a stance from which the functioning of human subjects proceeds, the notion of a horizon indicates the knowledge, values, and meanings that their functioning has delivered to their consciousness. Thus, once mystics have reached the conviction that the spiritual life does indeed bear directly on the practical affairs of human existence, that position becomes an element of their horizon, and they will pursue further investigation into political theology with that principle in mind. A horizon, moreover, develops and expands (or regresses and collapses) as individuals add to their store of knowledge and interests. At certain points, people must reject previously held positions or refine them in order to accommodate newly found knowledge.[57] For example, my hope is that through reading this book, my readers will reject the mentality of the split soul and add to their horizon the conviction that mystical life has much to contribute to socio-political matters.

The knowledge gained in various patterns of experience thus accompanies individuals they encounter new experiences and seek to learn the data contained therein. Self-appropriation is not merely a matter of becoming aware of the particularities of their existence at a given point in time and functioning accordingly. Rather, it is a matter of being aware of these particularities so that their horizon may be formed by truth instead of error, the good instead of the merely apparently good, and the healing brought about by love rather than the fractured relationships caused by fear and hatred.

NOTES

[1] Bernard Lonergan, *Method in Theology*, 2nd ed. (New York: Herder and Herder, 1973; reprint, Toronto: University of Toronto Press, 1990, 1994, 1996), 268.

[2] Ibid., 104.

[3] Ibid., 104-105.

[4] Bernard Lonergan, "The Response of the Jesuit as Priest and Apostle in the Modern World," in *A Second Collection*, ed. William F.J. Ryan and Bernard J. Tyrrell (Philadelphia: Westminster Press, 1974), 165; Bernard Lonergan, "The Future of Christianity," in *A Second Collection*, ed. William F.J. Ryan and Bernard J. Tyrrell (Philadelphia: Westminster Press, 1974), 152.

[5] Lonergan, *Method*, 52.

[6] Ibid., 105.

[7] Frederick E. Crowe, SJ, "An Exploration of Lonergan's New Notion of Value," in *Appropriating the Lonergan Idea*, ed. Michael Vertin (Washington D.C.: The Catholic University Press of America, 1989), 52-54. This identification of a shift in Lonergan's thought is echoed by Walter E. Conn in Walter E. Conn, "Bernard Lonergan on Value," *The Thomist* 40 (1976): 243.

[8] *Collected Works of Bernard Lonergan*, vol. 3, *Insight: A Study of Human Understanding*, eds., Frederick E. Crowe and Robert M. Doran (Toronto: University of Toronto Press, 1992), 624.

[9] Bernard Lonergan, "*Insight* Revisited," in *A Second Collection*, ed. William F. Ryan, SJ and Bernard J. Tyrrell, SJ (Philadelphia: Westminster Press, 1974), 277.

[10] Crowe, "An Exploration of Lonergan's New Notion of Value," 53.

[11] Lonergan, *Insight*, 629.

[12] Lonergan treats feelings in pages 30-34 of *Method* and the notion of judgments of value on pages 34-41. For a more in-depth examination of the progression of Lonergan's thought on value and the good, see M. Shawn Copeland, *A Genetic Study of the Idea of the Human Good in the Thought of Bernard Lonergan* (Ph.D. diss., Boston College, 1991), 150-253.

[13] Lonergan, *Method*, 30. Lonergan is relying here upon the work of Dietrich von Hildebrand. Dietrich von Hildebrand, *Christian Ethics* (New York: David McKay, 1953).

[14] Lonergan, *Method*, 31.

[15] Ibid. See also Tad Dunne's discussion of the role of feelings in the moral life in Tad Dunne, *Lonergan and Spirituality: Toward a Spiritual Integration* (Chicago: Loyola University Press, 1985), 70-77.

[16] Lonergan, *Method*, 37.

[17] Ibid., 32.

[18] Ibid.

[19] Ibid., 31.

[20] Conn, "The Desire for Authenticity," 41.

[21] Lonergan, *Method*, 240.

[22] Ibid., 34-36; Conn, "Bernard Lonergan on Value," 250.

[23] Lonergan, *Method*, 37.

[24] According to Frederick Crowe, this self-correcting nature of moral decision making provides an underlying unity to Lonergan's transition from ethics as a matter of the highly intellectual endeavor of determining the intelligible and rational to a notion of moral conversion that recognizes and appreciates the role played by feelings in the discernment of value. Crowe, "An Exploration of Lonergan's New Notion of Value," 59.

[25] Lonergan, *Method*, 240.

[26] Crowe, "An Exploration of Lonergan's New Notion of Value," 61.

[27] Although Lonergan's notion of value emerges as a transcendent notion and the structure of the human good is invariant, Lonergan at no point suggests that one true embodiment of the human good exists toward which all human beings should aspire. As Copeland notes, virtually all of Lonergan's post-*Insight* essays are concerned with the transition from classicism to historical mindedness. Copeland, 206. In such a transition, the idea of such a supreme instance of human culture is rejected. The human good may be embodied in any number of manners, and the function of the transcendental notion of value is to enable human persons to evaluate the socio-political structures that govern human living in light of that transcendental notion. This shift, moreover, allows for the progress of human history and the changes it effects on human societies. See Bernard Lonergan, "The Transition from a Classicist World-View to Historical Mindedness," in *A Second Collection*, ed., William F.J. Ryan, S.J. and Bernard J. Tyrrell, S.J. (Philadelphia: The Westminster Press, 1974), 1-9.

[28] Ibid., 113.

[29] Lonergan, *Method*, 33.

[30] This is most evident in those mystics who have achieved the unitive life as described by Underhill.

[31] Importantly, the data of the experience does not change. Rather, moral and religious conversion concern values. Thus, their impact on the act of attending to the data of a given experience is limited to affecting which data is determined to be relevant to a given line of inquiry.

[32] Consider, for example, those who wish to tackle the issue of the United States of America's reliance on foreign oil in response to the global threat of terrorism. From a strictly intellectual point of view, extensive drilling in the Gulf of Mexico or in the Arctic could be addressed from the point of view of cost, productivity, and profit. Religiously and morally converted persons, however, may consider the results of studies regarding the environmental impact of drilling to be important because of their moral or religious discernment of the value of the natural world.

[33] Ibid., 242-243.

[34] Ibid., 242.

[35] Lonergan mentions the blending of the patterns of experience in Chapter Fourteen of *Insight*. Lonergan, *Insight*, 410.

[36] Robert Doran, *Theology and the Dialectics of History* (Toronto: University of Toronto Press), 161-163; Dunne, *Lonergan and Spirituality*, 183. With regard to the hybridization of the patterns of experience, Lonergan hints at such a notion in *Understanding and Being* with regard to the aesthetic and dramatic patterns of experience. He writes the following in response to a question posed to him in a question and answer session. "I use the aesthetic pattern to indicate the possibility of a transition from the biological to other patterns of experience. Also to provide an underpinning of the dramatic. The dramatic is, as it were, a specialization, or extension of the aesthetic." *Collected Works of Bernard Lonergan*, vol. 5, *Understanding and Being: The Halifax Lectures on "Insight,"* eds., Elizabeth A. Morelli and Mark D. Morelli (Toronto: University of Toronto Press, 1990), 307. Just as the dramatic is an extension of the aesthetic, the worshipful can serve as an extension of all other patterns of experience as a result of religious conversion.

[37] Lonergan, *Method*, 243.

[38] Lonergan, *Insight*, 645-646.

[39] Doran, *Theology and the Dialectics of History*, 68.

[40] Ibid., 46

[41] Lonergan, *Insight*, 500-503.

[42] Ibid., 650.

[43] Lonergan, *Insight*, 653. By the term 'social surd,' Lonergan is indicating an underlying lack of intelligibility that is present in the social fabric when a society is in decline. This lack of intelligibility is evident insofar as certain social strategies and institutions continue to exist

despite their failure to address adequately the condition(s) toward which they are directed. The general bias of commonsense prevents societies from realizing these inadequacies through the application of commonsense answers to theoretical questions. Therefore, the social surd is part of the underlying conditions which simultaneously cry out for redress and prevent those calls from being answered. Ibid., 250-257.

[44] Bernard Lonergan, "Healing and Creating in History," in *A Third Collection*, ed. Frederick E. Crowe (New York: Paulist Press, 1985), 100-102.

[45] Ibid., 106.

[46] Those readers familiar with Lonergan's theological method will recognize the goal of understanding previously affirmed doctrines as the theological functional specialty of systematics. Lonergan, *Method*, ch. 13.

[47] When Lonergan refers to the reasons of the heart he is relying upon the work of Pascal. Lonergan, *Method*, 115.

[48] Doran, *Theology and the Dialectics of History*, 32-33.

[49] Ibid., 32; Lonergan, *Method*, 290.

[50] I owe the phrase "resting in the truth" to a conversation with the Lonergan scholar Fr. John Haughey of Loyola University in Chicago.

[51] I again draw the reader's attention to the example of Julian of Norwich whose additional understanding of her spiritual life led her to rewrite her account thereof.

[52] Lonergan, *Insight*, 28. Emphasis mine.

[53] Arnoldo Fortini, *Francis of Assisi*, 2 vols., trans. Helen Moak (New York: Crossroad, 1981), 216. Although I write here of an immediate recognition of the source of the voice emanating from the crucifix, I acknowledge that Francis's conversion, as discussed in Chapter One, was an extended process.

[54] Ignatius of Loyola, *The Autobiography*, 1:1-12, in *Ignatius of Loyola: Spiritual Exercises and Selected Works*, ed. George E. Ganss, S.J., trans. Parmananda R. Divarkar, S.J., George E. Ganss, S.J., Edward J. Malatesta, S.J., Martin E. Palmer, S.J., The Classics of Western Spirituality: A Library of the Great Spiritual Masters (Mahwah: Paulist Press, 1991), 71-73.

[55] "General Introduction," in *Ignatius of Loyola: Spiritual Exercises and Selected Works*, ed. George E. Ganss, S.J., trans. Parmananda R. Divarkar, S.J., George E. Ganss, S.J., Edward J. Malatesta, S.J., Martin E. Palmer, S.J., The Classics of Western Spirituality: A Library of the Great Spiritual Masters (Mahwah: Paulist Press, 1991), 15,19.

[56] Fortini, 216-217.

[57] Lonergan, *Method*, 235-237.

CHAPTER FIVE

Self-Appropriation and the Theologian

Introduction

The fruit of self-appropriation is that it provides a basis from which further questions may be pursued. In this chapter I will examine how these fruits are borne in the field of theology. Lonergan writes, "A theology mediates between a cultural matrix and the significance and role of a religion in that matrix."[1] This definition admits a great many specializations through which academics dedicate themselves to a pursuit of a particular interest or specialty, such as the concern of this book, mystical-political theology. Lonergan's primary contribution to theology, however, is not the development of a specific theology but the manner in which theologians go about the task of theology. Theology, Lonergan claims, consists of two phases. The first is a mediated phase wherein theologians investigate the tradition in search of the truths of the past and the truth regarding the past. Moreover, perhaps theologians have lost certain aspects of previous theologies through the course of history or have misunderstood some elements of the tradition. In either case, the first phase of theology, according to Lonergan, is an attempt to avoid or correct such oversights in order to provide the groundwork for a second, mediating phase of theology in which theologians try to reach new understandings or applications of the results of the first phase so as to keep theology relevant to the changing reality of the human situation.[2]

As such, Lonergan does not develop a specifically mystical-political theology but rather provides the framework from which subsequent theologians may undertake such an endeavor authentically. According to Lonergan, method is of utmost importance because of the Hegelian problem in which human subjects pursue ideals. Initially, ideals are merely implicit because they have not yet been formulated; but when articulated, they become explicit. However, a problem remains insofar as these ideals are abstract in their formulation. They are not found in the concrete situation of human living, even as they are pursued by individuals situated in a particular socio-historical context. A state of alienation arises between the ideal and the concrete reality of the human situation, and human persons must seek to mediate between the explicit formulation of the ideal and the situation, which results in a more adequate reconciliation between the ideal and concrete reality.[3]

But, a difficulty remains insofar as the formulation that emerges from the process of reconciliation is still, to some extent, inadequate to the situation because that situation continuously changes. Because the human condition is constantly in motion, ideals similarly undergo transformation as persons seek to grasp ideals under a new set of circumstances. Thus, the process repeats itself, and the end result is that as soon as individuals reconcile the alienated explicit formulation of the ideal with their situation, that formulation is to some extent outdated and in need of further reconciliation.[4] Positively speaking, the Hegelian problem allows for the advance of human knowing insofar as human persons continually seek to update the various ideals operative in their lives so as to address the ever changing human situation. Negatively, it prevents the definitive resolution of any matter, and human accomplishments are relegated to obsolescence almost as soon as they are reconciled to the human situation.

This Hegelian dynamic may, in fact, be a contributing factor to the split soul mentality. Chapter One presented the work of both mystical and political theologians who recognized the connection between the two disciplines, but their positions have not gained the upper hand. I propose that their lack of attention to the human subject has not only contributed to the mentality of the split soul by focusing too heavily on mystical or political experience, but has also left them searching for an ideal of mystical-political theology that becomes alienated from the human condition almost as soon as it comes into existence. If, as the Hegelian problem asserts, an explicitly formulated ideal becomes outdated to some extent as the human situation changes, the ideals developed by Johnston, Underhill, Sölle, and Gutiérrez may have become obsolete. Underhill, for instance, wrote at the beginning of the 20th century, and the world is vastly different here in the beginning of the 21st. Many liberation theologians such as Gutiérrez, moreover, rely upon some level of Marxist analysis, but, as Nancy Fraser documents, since the fall of European communism, Marxist analysis is largely discredited as a failure. The left, she claims, needs to develop new alternatives to laissez-faire capitalism, but no such viable option has yet come to the surface.[5] Lonergan's contribution to this problem is his appeal to the operations of the human subject, which may reveal the inadequacies of unbridled capitalism and its shortcomings with regard to what is truly good or representative of values without simply placing a new ideal next to the old one.[6]

Lonergan's emphasis on method thus avoids the problem of pursuing the ideal of a mystical-political theology. By focusing on the operations of the theologian, Lonergan enables mystical-political theologians to proceed not by pursuing a definition of mysticism's relevance to socio-political matters by which socio-political structures may be measured, for such a task runs the risk of becoming quickly outdated, but through the examination of these arrangements by appealing to the operations of the human subject. Through the authentic examination of the concrete human situation, people may judge certain realities to be only apparently rather than truly good. Mysticism's wisdom is a valuable resource in this task, for if Christians are called to live in love with one another, who is a better resource than those who have experienced union with the God who is love?

In an effort to document the relevance of self-appropriation to mystical-political theology, Chapter Three documented Lonergan's contribution with regard to the operations of the human subject located in the mystical pattern of experience as developed in Chapter Two. Chapter Four added the additional pieces of Lonergan's notion of foundational reality and the manner in which this underlying element affects human functioning as human subjects. The present chapter will investigate the ability of Lonergan's work to contribute to an explicitly political theology and to the role to be played by mystical theology therein.

I must be clear at this point at the risk of sounding redundant. This chapter will not result in a new mystical-political theology to be placed alongside previous efforts in the field. To do so would be to repeat the process of pursuing an ideal that is incapable of adequately addressing the constantly changing concrete reality of the human situation. Rather, this chapter will consist of a clarification of the manner in which Lonergan's work on the human subject clears the way for investigation into the socio-political structures that exist within that concrete reality. Just as self-appropriation allows mystics to come to know authentically the meaning(s) of mystical experience, so too does self-appropriation guide persons working in the area of political theology. Self-appropriation thus enables political theologians to authentically investigate the extent to which the socio-political reality of the day reflects and/or promotes the Kingdom of God.

Self-Appropriation and the Mystical Theologian

Theologians may undertake the task of theology, then, from one of two stances: one concerned with self-appropriation, the other unconcerned with the effort to be an integrated subject. In the case of the latter, quite likely investigations may go astray as certain data is ignored, misinterpreted, or overlooked completely. For theologians undertaking the task of self-appropriation, awareness of intellectual, moral, and religious conversion and of the patterns of experience in which they are located enables them to go about the task of theology more authentically. Theologians are better able to function intellectually if they know their knowing, they are able to improve their moral decision making and actions if they advert to the transition from living life on the basis of satisfaction to doing so according to value, and they are better able to discern the impact of their religiosity on cognitional and moral functioning if they recognize their falling in love with God in an unrestricted fashion. Theologians carry out the theological enterprise better if they know what they are doing when they do it as well as the framework (comprised of their foundational reality and the particular pattern of experience) in which they pursue the task. Or, as Vernon Gregson aptly puts it, Lonergan's work on the functioning of the human subject provides a 'therapy for the theologian' insofar as it helps theologians become more aware of aberrations in their work as the result of bias.[7]

Moreover, self-appropriated theologians are also in the position to draw upon the fruits of other areas of study. Transcendental method is not only transcendental because it allows individuals to know things as they truly exist, but also because it is operative in all instances of human knowing. Lonergan writes:

> It is in the measure that special methods acknowledge their common core in transcendental method, that norms common to all the sciences will be acknowledged, that a secure basis will be attained for attacking interdisciplinary problems, and that the sciences will be mobilized within a higher unity of vocabulary, thought, and orientation, in which they will be able to make their quite significant contribution to the solution of fundamental problems.[8]

As such, transcendental method allows mystical-political theologians to investigate the contributions of scholars working in other disciplines. A mystical-political theology would be well served by incorporating research done with regard to the distribution of goods in a global economy or the structural elements of the United States that keep the marginalized from gaining a louder voice on social issues that directly affect them. Indeed, contributions from other avenues of study have already become evident in the refinement undergone by political theology in the past 40 years. It has become apparent, for instance, that Latin American theologies of liberation, while important to those in the United States, do not speak adequately to the concerns of African Americans. Thus, theologians such as James Cone have developed liberation theologies expressly directed at this particular situation.[9] Likewise, German political theologians such as Sölle differ from Latin American theologians in the primacy of theory over praxis.[10] Thirdly, sociologists of religion such as Cheryl Gilkes and Stephanie Y. Mitchem have built upon the contributions of feminist and African American theologians in an effort to speak to the experience of African American women in what has come to be known as womanist theology.[11] All of these subdivisions of political theology have been aided by research in areas outside of theology. Through such avenues as sociology, economics, and political science the framework of political theology can be filled out and given concrete expression. If such collaboration required the learning of a new way of knowing in every approach to a new discipline, the correlation of the findings to a theological enterprise would become so daunting as to discourage any number of well-intentioned theologians.

The authentic performance of mystical theology, then, proceeds from the standpoint of self-appropriation, both with regard to theologians' own conversion and their recognition of the pattern of experience in which they find themselves. An important distinction is in order here regarding the difference between theology and philosophy of God. According to Lonergan, only those individuals who, as a response to the prior gift of God's love flooding their hearts, seek to know the source of this love better through the investigation of the history and/or teachings of the tradition to which they belong may perform the task of theology. Philosophers of God, on the other hand, are more interested in the "thought and affirmations or negations concerning God that are not logically derived from revealed religion." [12] Thus, although a philosopher of God may indeed be a Christian, strictly speaking, an explicitly Christian philosophy of God does not exist because Christianity involves revelatory aspects. Although this distinction may at first appear to be an exercise in the parsing of words, its importance lies in the fact that, whereas Christian mystical theologians go about their task from the specific context of Christian mysticism, philosophers of God who undertake the study of mysticism would be more interested in an understanding of mysticism which does not rely upon the specific revelation of a given religious tradition. Therefore, whereas the authentic functioning of theologians requires advertence to their state of being in love with God in an unrestricted fashion, this may not be the case for philosophers of religion. Philosophers of religion may be able to study the phenomenon of mysticism, but they likely will not be able to interpret mystical texts and doctrines as fully as theologians because mystical experience and accounts involve the affectivity and discernment of religious value that accompany religious conversion, which is understood by Lonergan as falling in love with God. Again, knowing the focus of the investigation, the purpose of that inquiry, the pattern of experience in which the investigation is carried out, and the role played by conversion in the task are all important aspects of self-appropriation.   Self-appropriation enables scholars to gain a better understanding of these issues and allows human beings to proceed in a greater degree of authenticity.

Mystical Theology as Reflection upon Personal Mystical Experience

The first manner in which mystical theology may be articulated is by critically reflecting upon personal mystical experience. This, generally speaking, is the path taken by the great mystics of the tradition. Although many of these individuals were highly educated, they based their mystical writings primarily upon their personal encounters with the Divine.[13] These remarkable persons are representative of the notion that the truths of the mystical experience are imparted by God. Then, mystics relate the truths and wisdom received in the mystical experience to their friends, spiritual directors, or later readers.

But this idea, as stated previously, concentrates so heavily upon the experience that little, if any, attention is paid to the human subject who encounters the immediate presence of God. Self-appropriated mystics are able to recognize the pattern in which they are located and are thus better able to attend to the data of the experience. The presence or lack of conversion also plays a role in their attending to the experience. As Ignatius reminds his readers, that which appears to be from God may in fact be a destructive force in one's life or the world.[14]   Only by reflecting on experiences in light of the state of being in love with God in an unrestricted fashion is such discernment possible.[15] Moreover, those who have not undergone religious conversion may be less able (or willing) to accept the source of the experience as the Divine. St. Francis of Assisi, for instance, speaks of his extended conversion experience; only after reflection upon his spiritual life was Francis able to recognize the role of God in his life.[16]

Religious conversion is a response to the gift of God's love flooding the human heart, and this is only sometimes an instantaneous experience. As human persons search for authenticity in their lives, they come to the question of the ground of all being, and religiously converted individuals find that the only answer to this question is God.[17] Religious conversion can be a long and rather tortuous affair, for it reorients people in their world and alters the meanings that constitute that world.   Moreover, religious conversion may entail the loss or rejection of what has been so carefully built up over the course of a lifetime. If individuals have not undergone religious conversion or are only encountering the first stirrings of God's love in their hearts, they may encounter greater difficulty recognizing and attending to the data of the mystical experience.

Once mystics have attended to the data of the experience, they strive to understand that experience, and self-appropriation contributes to the performance of this task as well.   For the mystics, the content of the immediate presence of God contains a highly affective dimension that is not as profoundly present in the intellectual or practical patterns, but if they are to understand authentically the encounter with Divine Love, this element must be considered. For example, Julian of Norwich writes the following of God's role as mother in the Trinity.

> As truly as God is our Father, so truly is God our Mother, and he revealed that in everything, and especially in these sweet words where he says: I am he; that is to say: I am he, the power and goodness of fatherhood; I am he, the wisdom and the lovingness of motherhood...[18]

Can the maternal role of God be understood without all of the feelings that are associated with motherhood?   If Julian had approached the mystical experience of God without recognizing the pattern of consciousness as mystical in nature, then her understanding of the content of that experience would have been hindered because of a lack of attention to the affective dimension of the human person, and this impediment would have curtailed her authenticity.[19]

Just as self-appropriation aids mystical theologians in attending to the data and understanding thereof, it also helps in passing judgment regarding the understanding of the data. Thérèse of Lisieux, for example, writes of her great consternation as to why some come to Christ early in life and thus spend a great deal of time in loving closeness to God while others convert later in life.   In response, she writes that Jesus showed her the 'book of nature' wherein some flowers bloom early in spring, and others later in the year. Such a vision lends itself to two different understandings. First, it may imply that some are more favored by God and hold a special place in the heart of Christ.   Secondly, and this is the interpretation which Thérèse adopts, gardens and fields retain their beauty through a variety of plants which flower at different times. Through this variety, the splendor of nature remains throughout the year. Similarly, through conversions at various times in life the glory of God remains more visible.[20]   In her account of this experience, Thérèse does not write that Jesus told her which interpretation to choose, but that she came to understand and affirm this interpretation of her mystical vision. What led her to this judgment? I contend that her prior mystical life, which contains great emphasis on the love of God for all, helped her to affirm the latter interpretation, for the image of the flower provides the primary metaphor for her spiritual life. Without her previous mystical experiences and her appropriation thereof, Thérèse would have been less likely to affirm the second interpretation, one which is more representative of the loving God of the Christian tradition.

Next is the level of decision on the part of the mystics. What are they to do with the truths of the mystical experience that they have affirmed in the level of judgment? In some cases, they decide to record their spiritual lives in texts to which people still turn for guidance today.[21]   Others turn to the foundation of monasteries,[22] while still others begin to teach or serve as spiritual mentors,[23] and still others become involved in the practical affairs of the world.[24] In all of these cases, mystics are faced with the question of what to do with the meaning(s) of their mystical experience. To the extent they live authentically, self-appropriation provides mystics with the framework from which they can make responsible decisions on the basis of that meaning. If mystics are unclear as to the pattern in which they are operating or are unaware of their conversions, or lack thereof, then their decision making will be hampered. Self-appropriation, then, is a valuable resource for those who perform the task of theology from the standpoint of their personal experience.

As documented in Chapter One, Evelyn Underhill describes the unitive life as characterized by a constant state of union with the Divine. I believe that a way of expressing this unity within the framework of Lonergan's notion of self-appropriation is that in the unitive life mystics are continually aware of the mystical level of meaning in every moment of their lives. In human living, the patterns of experience intertwine with one another, and any given moment may contain any number of meanings according to the patterns present at the given instance. Religiously converted astronomers may encounter a deep sense of awe at God's creation as they study the heavens, and the worshipful pattern enters their consciousness. They may even experience mystical union with the Divine as they ponder the vastness of space and the immensity of being. Most persons, however, lose sight of the presence of the Divine from time to time as practical concerns require their time and energy. Only when individuals move from the intermittent awareness of the illuminative stage to the unitive life do they live in constant awareness of and advertence to the mystical pattern of experience and the meanings contained therein.

Mystical Theology as the Study of Mystical Texts

Secondly, scholars of mystical experience may undertake the theological endeavor by examining the texts of those mystics who have gone before them. Scholars like Bernard McGinn approach mystical theology from the intellectual rather than mystical pattern of experience. As implied by the previous paragraphs regarding self-appropriation's usefulness as a tool for mystical theologians who reflect upon the content of their personal spiritual lives, self-appropriation serves this second category of mystical theologians by clarifying the pattern of experience in which they are located and by guiding the performance of the operations of the human subject in this pattern. By seeking the passionless pursuit of the truth characteristic of the intellectual pattern of experience, theologians of this ilk are better able to attend to the entirety of the data present in the texts under consideration and to avoid the bias that threatens to derail the investigatory process.

Likewise, theologians may perform operations of understanding and judging more authentically. Mystical texts are filled with affective and symbolic dimensions, and if theologians do not approach these texts authentically, these elements may impede both the understanding of the mystical writing and subsequent judgment regarding that understanding.[25] The mystical theologian, for example, may approach the writings of Teresa of Avila with an ecumenical openness, but must deal with her decided disapproval of the Reformation. She writes, "At that time news reached me of the harm being done in France and of the havoc the Lutherans had caused and how much this miserable sect was growing."[26] Here, theologians are faced with the choice of omitting this anti-Reformation sentiment from the investigation, accepting this statement as true, or carrying out research that considers the data relevant to the historical context in which Teresa lived. In so doing, theologians are forced to consider whether this statement was the product of Teresa's mystical life or her own personal feelings in light of her historical context. Therefore, self-appropriation serves as a tool for theologians to determine where the mystics themselves may have gone wrong in their understanding of the mystical experience. As William James contends, mystical texts often carry a certain authority because the mystics claim that the content is communicated directly from God or other divine figures such as angels or saints.[27] Such a position, however, fails to take into account that mystics also are rooted in their historical contexts and are inevitably limited by it. Self-appropriation aids theologians in the sorting out of these issues and prevents the biases of either the theologian or the mystical texts from disrupting the pursuit of truth.

Mystical Theology as Reflection on Personal Experience and Tradition

Thirdly, mystical theologians may undertake mystical theology both by reflecting upon their own mystical experiences and by researching the mystical tradition through the writings of other mystics. Evelyn Underhill and William Johnston are representative of this category. For scholars such as these, self-appropriation serves to steady their investigations insofar as they recognize and differentiate the data that arises from personal experience and that which comes from the texts they encounter in their research. The highly affective nature of mystical experience as well as admiration for mystics may derail the scholarly investigation through the bias that originates from desiring a certain outcome rather than allowing the data to speak for itself. For these scholars, self-appropriation is valuable insofar as it prevents them from mistaking a pattern of experience or allowing the content of their own experience to lead their research astray. The joy present in the mystical encounter with the Divine may serve as a distraction to the scholar's intellectual pursuits, and, conversely, a too heavy concentration upon the intellectual pattern of experience may prevent the scholar from listening to the inner voice of love.

In all three strategies, self-appropriation resists the effects of the split soul mentality by providing a comprehensive understanding of human knowing. As Michael Rende notes, Lonergan's great concern in *Insight* was to give his reader a cognitional theory that enables scholars to attend to all the data available for their various inquiries. Using the example of the human sciences, Lonergan claims that such investigations cannot follow exactly the natural sciences because the latter rely heavily on observation of such things as electrons and mechanical natural processes. The human person, however, goes beyond such quantifiable realities to include such things as soul, will, and spiritual concerns.[28] Similarly, traditional theology relies upon the intellectual investigation of previously affirmed doctrines of the church or of historical occurrences. Such explorations do not necessarily require the affective dimension of the human person, and thus the split soul may win out as this aspect of human existence is disregarded in the theological enterprise. When this is the case in mystical theology, however, valuable insights and wisdom are lost or placed into a category of existence separate from the concerns of political theology. Self-appropriation, therefore, allows the mystical theologian to regain these resources in the attempt to gain theological understanding and to resist the efforts of the split soul mentality.

Self-Appropriation and Political Theology

My contention is that the mystical theologian who proceeds from the integration provided by self-appropriation will come to the conclusion that the mystical and the political do not reside in opposed corners of human existence. The patterns of experience (worshipful, aesthetic, biological, etc.) often intertwine, and human subjects carry meanings discovered in one pattern to others. The foundational reality of the person, which is formed by conversion or lack thereof, guides this interconnection as a set of first principles that individuals ignore only at the peril of inauthenticity. The question then, is the manner in which the mystical pattern of experience bears upon the task of political theology.

In Chapter One I tried to show that Christian political theology, broadly speaking, is concerned with the development of theological reflection which leads to concrete action in human society that fosters justice and human flourishing, in consonance with Jesus' preaching of the Kingdom. Initially, Lonergan's work on the human subject may seem to be too narrowly focused on cognitional and intellectual proposals to be an aid to the task of political theology. But liberation theology recognizes that sinful social structures are somehow greater than the sum of the sins of the individual people living within such arrangements. Can Lonergan's focus on the human subject address broader social ills, or is his work limited to the development of persons rather than societies as a whole? Although Lonergan never explicitly refers to himself as a political theologian, his work does indeed lend itself to the task of political theology, for theology is a matter of mediation between a cultural matrix and the role played by religion therein.[29]

According to Frederick G. Lawrence, Lonergan's contribution to political theology is located in three areas of concern – economics, education and culture.[30] Lonergan's work on economics, Lawrence claims, emerges from a concern that economics will come to be the primary science by which political institutions are established and judged. A family wage is an instance of a moral economic policy, but its benefit to a national economy is vague.[31] If the economy were to be the determinative factor regarding the good of a given policy or institution, these realities would be deemed a success if they were economically beneficial rather than morally justifiable.

With regard to education, Lonergan was convinced that an education concerned primarily with the exigencies of economics could never replace the value of practical wisdom. Such wisdom would enable people to respond to issues of economic concern with integrity and an awareness of the moral implications of economic policies and structures.[32]   This concern for an element of practical wisdom in the education of young men and women is evidenced by the extensive treatment of the human good in his Cincinnati Lectures on the philosophy of education in 1959, which will be presented in more detail later in this chapter.[33]

Lawrence's third point concerns Lonergan's contribution in regard to political theology in the area of culture. Culture was a topic which intrigued Lonergan greatly in the latter part of his career, and he argued that a transition is needed from a 'classicist world-view' to a 'historical mindedness.' The former consists of the notion that one ideal culture exists toward which all human societies should strive, while the latter entails an empirical understanding of culture whereby a wide variety of cultural particularity may be recognized and affirmed.[34]

This move recognizes that human culture is an evolving reality in which certain forms and strategies are abandoned and new ones constructed to address the exigencies of the constantly changing human situation. A notion of a universal culture into which new problems are to be fit is a mistaken view. Such thinking often leads to great difficulties for members of a culture deemed to be inadequate when compared to the so-called ideal, which too often corresponds to the military superiority of a given culture. What is needed is an understanding of culture which recognizes the various strategies developed by particular cultures as representative of the truly good even as those strategies differ from culture to culture. Lonergan's notion of the good, as transcendent, allows for its pursuit through any number of cultural forms. Human culture is a concrete reality, and the cultural specificity of a given group of human persons may not be able to meet the needs of another community. Lonergan therefore develops an empirical notion of culture wherein culture "is the set of meanings and values that informs a way of life. It may remain unchanged for ages. It may be in the process of slow development or rapid dissolution."[35] An empirical notion of culture enables cultures to evolve to meet the exigencies of new situations as they arise without surrendering their claims of pursuing the truly good.

For Lonergan, the key to such cultural progress is adherence to the transcendental precepts. Being attentive involves not only paying attention to the immediate surroundings in which persons are located, but also to the social context in which they live.   Being intelligent involves not only explanatory hypotheses, but also the production of creative alternatives to the current situation.   Being reasonable not only involves judgment as to the veracity of a given proposal, but also analysis as to which proposals probably would or would not work.   Being responsible, finally, involves not only decisions made on the basis of individuals' personal lives, but also taking into consideration the effects of their decisions on others.[36]   Authentically operating human subjects perform these operations with intellectual, moral, and religious conversion in mind.   What do their religious convictions tell them regarding that to which they have attended, understood, and judged? What potential courses of actions are reflective of value rather than satisfaction?   Have they authentically examined the given situation?   The role of theology is to mediate the meaning of religion in these activities which, for the Christian, includes working for a human society open to the coming of the Kingdom of God.

Besides progress, however, cultures can experience decline. Unsatisfactory answers may be found for the problems encountered by a given culture.   The precepts may be violated, or bias may derail intelligence, sympathy, and action as human persons strive for progress.   Poor decisions lead to misguided actions, and the given society soon finds itself in a downward spiral from which escape is very difficult.   Here, theological reflection is of the utmost importance, for authentic human subjects are self-transcending, and "a religion that promotes self-transcendence to the point, not merely of justice, but of self-sacrificing love, will have a redemptive role in human society inasmuch as such love can undo the mischief of decline and restore the cumulative process of progress."[37]   The redemptive role of religion, however, is not self-evident.   It must be mediated in the cultural matrix, which is the role of theology.   When theologians reflect upon the redemptive effects of religion on society, inspiring the human community to ever greater justice and peace, they engage in political theology.

Lonergan's work toward an empirical notion of culture does not specify those structures and strategies reflective of openness to the Kingdom of God. Yet he offers political theologians two resources.   First, with regard to moral conversion, judgments of value are possible.   According to Jesus' teaching, the Kingdom of God is characterized by justice and righteousness.   From a Christian perspective, religiously and morally converted persons are capable of making judgments as to which aspects of a given society are exemplifications of the Kingdom, and which are not.   Secondly, Lonergan provides the theologian with a concrete structure of the human good that serves as an analytical tool for the examination of social structures and institutions in light of their contribution to cultural progress or decline.[38]

Structure of the Human Good

As with much of his work, Lonergan's presentation of the human good demonstrates considerable development over the course of his career. This discussion will therefore treat Lonergan's work on the structure of the human good in terms of his early and later career. His early contribution corresponds to the notion of the good as it appears in *Topics of Education* and *Insight*, and his later period is marked by his treatment of the issue in *Method*.

The Early Period

In his early period, Lonergan identifies three levels of the human good: the particular good, the good of order, and the good of value.[39] The particular good, according to Lonergan, consists of an isolated instance in which individuals identify specific desires, which may be things or events.[40] These wishes may be mundane, as in longing for a new house, or altruistic, yearning for the liberation of oppressed people. At either end of the spectrum, particular goods are restricted to concrete desires in specific situations.

The second level of the good consists of the manner in which the attainment and/or delivery of particular goods are organized by a particular society, and Lonergan identifies four aspects of the good of order. The first facet is that the good of order is a recurrent scheme. "If X is a good thing and occurs, it will recur when there is a good of order."[41] If production of more fuel efficient automobiles is determined to be an instance of the good, then production of such vehicles will continue. If this is concluded not to be the case, then fabrication will cease.

Lonergan develops the notion of schemes of recurrence and their significance for the good of order in *Insight*.[42] Here, Lonergan points out that certain events are interrelated to the extent that the occurrence of one leads to another, which may lead to another, and so on.

> If A occurs, B will occur; if B occurs, C will occur; if C occurs, … A will recur. Such a circular arrangement may involve any number of terms, the possibility of alternative routes, and in general any degree of complexity.[43]

In the above example of fuel-efficient cars, a long list of factors reinforce or resist the production of such automobiles, including the availability of the necessary raw materials, required skilled labor, and the profit margins of the manufacturer. In a scheme of recurrence, the fulfillment of one element of the scheme leads to another, and when the process seems to reach its end with the purchase by consumers, the course repeats itself in the production of more cars.

In addition to the interrelated events of schemes of recurrence, defensive mechanisms also exist by which the scheme is insulated, to some extent, from change. Lonergan writes:

> Schemes might be complemented by defensive circles, so that if some event *F* tended to upset the scheme, there would be some such sequence of conditions as 'If *F* occurs, then *G* occurs; if *G* occurs, then *H* occurs; if *H* occurs, then *F* is eliminated.'[44]

Continuing the example of the fuel efficient vehicle, the increased cost of assembling such an automobile may tend to discourage its production. However, people may come to the conclusion that the environmental benefits of such a car outweigh the increased cost, and the production of such cars continues. The defensive mechanism has protected the process, and the good of order, as manifested in the recurring scheme of producing fuel efficient automobiles continues.

Lonergan identifies the second aspect of the good of order as the coordination of human activity. Goods and services do not appear out of thin air, but are the result of a functioning human society that has developed coordinated strategies and processes through which particular goods are obtained.[45] Examples on the small scale would include the purchase of groceries or social etiquette that makes possible and governs social interaction. On the larger scale, certain procedures have been established to facilitate trade between nations and diplomatic courses of action that seek to maintain peace and communication between the countries of the world.

Such coordination, however, is not automatic. According to Lonergan, all human cooperation relies upon the fulfillment of certain conditions, namely, habits, institutions, material equipment, and personal status.[46] By habits, Lonergan means those activities for which persons have the necessary knowledge, desire, and skills to perform a given task. "If every time something had to be done people had to take a year off to learn, or to be persuaded, or to acquire the skills, nothing would ever be done."[47] The habits of living in a given society contribute to the maintenance of coordinated human effort, which, in turn, supports the good of order.

174   *Chapter Five*

The institutions that support human cooperation may be governmental or social mechanisms for the making of decisions. These structures consist of general agreement as to the manner in which a given society functions. People agree to drive according to certain regulations and rely on others to do so as well. Similarly, they fill their familial roles according to a common understanding. If those involved fail to agree on the guidelines that govern driving or living in a particular family, they run the risk of physical injury or the disintegration of the family. Without institutions, community living would be chaotic, and personal behaviors would be governed only by the will of the individual.[48]

The third condition of human cooperation in the good of order consists of the materials necessary for the functioning of habits and institutions.[49] Speaking of the habits that guide the purchase of material goods would be meaningless if those goods or the necessary resources were unavailable. Speaking of the institution of city government would similarly be nonsensical if buildings or supplies for the recording of laws were not available.

Lonergan's fourth and final condition for the coordination of human effort is personal status.[50] As the good of order is established, people find their niche within society. As Copeland notes, however, Lonergan's sociological understanding of personal status is not the usual notion of measuring two or more people against one another. Rather, for Lonergan, status "may be derived from an individual's social or economic class, from familial background, from profession and employment, and from engagement in some public or official role."[51] The role of status, then, is to define one's relationships according to the position in society held by others. My relationship with my mother, for instance, is quite different from my interaction with a police officer or my students.

The next aspect of the structure of the human good in Lonergan's early period is value, and three subdivisions are present in this notion. First, Lonergan identifies value as associated with aesthetics.

> Aesthetic value is the realization of the intelligible in the sensible: when the good of order of a society is transparent, when it shines through the products of that society, the actions of its members, its structure of interdependence, the status and personality of the persons participating the order.[52]

If the persons, structures, and organizations of a society are functioning appropriately, the good of order can be determined. Camaraderie and concern for the other is noticeable, and quality of life shines forth in the health and happiness of the people as well as in the quality of goods produced in the society.

The second element of value is ethical value, which is "the conscious emergence of the subject as autonomous, responsible, free."[53] At this level people take stands for what is true and right. They recognize their responsibility for the realization of the good and act accordingly.

Lonergan's final aspect of value is religious value, which comes to light when individuals place their relationships with other persons before God.[54] As Copeland writes, "From the human subject's deliberate and decisive appropriation of religious value, the structure of religious value, the structure of the human good becomes integrated into the supernatural destiny of human beings."[55] Whereas non-religious persons may possibly become aware of and act in accordance with ethical value, they possesses a limited view of the good, but for those who operate within a horizon that includes relationship with the Divine, the good takes on a transcendental character.

I have presented in the preceding paragraphs a brief sketch of Lonergan's early work on the notion of the human good. It consists of an invariant but dynamic structure comprised of particular goods, the good of order, and value, and as Copeland notes, it provides an analytical tool by which persons can examine the degree to which certain societies or parts thereof are reflective of the human good.

> Lonergan emphasizes that practical intelligent activity is the basis of the human good as developing object and developing subject. He roots the practicality of activity in the activity of intelligence, asking and answering the questions: What should I/we do? (question for intelligence); Should I/we do it? (question for reflection); Is it worthwhile? (question for evaluation and deliberation).[56]

Moral action, then, would be a matter of a rational choice as it regards the structure of human good.[57] Does a certain action contribute to this structure, or does it take away from the realization of the human good? The decision, moreover, should be made by means of the transcendental method, which treats affectivity primarily as a source of bias.

In discussing Lonergan's notion of the human good as an analytical tool, however, care should be taken always to bear in mind his notion of historical mindedness. A normative culture does not exist, either in reality or ideally, in which the human good is best actualized. According to Lonergan, the human good is always realized in a particular finite situation and is thus necessarily limited. Things are good, according to Lonergan, insofar as they participate in the infinite good that is God, and "anything that is good by participation is finite, and because it is finite it is not perfect in every respect."[58] Therefore, no instance of the realization of the particular good is impervious to criticism on the part of others, nor are individuals required to adopt a particular embodiment of the human good. The structure of the human good is invariant, but it may be embodied by any number of societies and cultures. Therefore, although the achievement of a particular good or social order may appear to be desirable from one perspective, this is not necessarily the case for those living in a different set of circumstances.

The Later Period

The later period of Lonergan's career is marked by a shift away from the highly intellectual character of the human good, as he presented the issue in *Topics in Education* and *Insight*, toward a notion of the good which involves human affectivity. Even Lonergan's understanding of the role played by God on the level of value takes on a highly intellectual cast in his early period, for, as previously noted, the reality of God can be demonstrated, according to Lonergan, by the performance of transcendental method, which does not require the presence of grace.[59] Later, however, Lonergan describes God in a much more affective manner, as gift, and religious conversion is depicted as falling in love with God in an unrestricted fashion.[60]

In his later period, particularly in *Method*, Lonergan discusses the human good as "a transcultural and transhistorical structure within which solutions to the problems of human living are worked out."[61] The question that arises here is how the addition of an affective element to the notion of the human good influences Lonergan's understanding of that structure. The issue of feelings and their relationship to the apprehension of values has already been treated in Chapter Four. Feelings may be intentional or non-intentional, and psychic conversion aids human persons in a second mediation of meaning wherein their feelings are appropriated. Once the meaning of their feelings becomes known and they operate accordingly, they may undertake the discernment of the values toward which the feelings point, and moral action may be taken.

The structure of the human good as it appears in *Method* is characterized by a greater complexity than was evident in *Topics in Education*. Lonergan has here identified no less than eighteen elements involving both individual and social matters that together form the structure of the human good. To help make sense of this nest of terms and relations, Lonergan provides his reader with the following diagram.[62]

Individual		**Social**	**Ends**
Potentiality	*Actuation*		
capacity, need good	operation	cooperation	particular
plasticity, order	development,	institution,	good of
perfectibility	skill	role, task	
liberty value	orientation,	personal	terminal
	conversion	relations	

With regard to the first line, individuals have needs, understood in the broadest sense so as to include wants, as well as the capacity to fulfill them. Acting to satisfy their needs is an instance of obtaining a particular good. Such fulfillment, moreover, may involve any number of other persons cooperating in the pursuit of the particular good.[63]

The second line of the chart begins with the notion that human capacities are plastic and perfectible. Individuals grow more competent in fulfilling their needs as they develop and improve their strategies toward that fulfillment. The development of skills, when viewed in a social context, leads to the erection of social institutions in which the cooperation of individuals is concretized in the good of order, consisting of the social patterns of cooperation in which particular goods are obtained.[64]

Thirdly, the perfectibility of the capacity to fulfill needs is manifest in the liberty of persons. They are free to choose whether or not to improve. This basic stance is the realm of conversion, for in liberty people choose to live authentically or inauthentically. On the social level, human liberty is lived amidst a nest of interpersonal relations, which gives rise to a great plethora of feelings. Feelings regarding the persons with whom individuals interact give rise to the apprehension of value in those relationships. For instance, some people may come to view others as possessing ontic rather than merely instrumental value. Authentically operating subjects exercise liberty in a community whose constitutive members and social institutions more or less reflect terminal value as instances of the truly good.[65]

Lonergan's schema of the human good may also be read vertically. The human person's capacity is perfectible, which then leads to the exercise of liberty in the meeting of human needs. Secondly, people may refine and develop the skills utilized in the fulfillment of their needs, which leads to an orientation in the world. Thirdly, human persons live in groups that operate collectively through a cooperative pattern which becomes more or less codified in a given society, and these social institutions inform interpersonal relations within that society. Finally, the meeting of a particular good directly involves the good of order that facilitates that fulfillment, which leads, in turn, to discernment as to whether that order is truly reflective of a transcendental notion of the good.[66]

Lonergan thus provides his readers with a structure by which concrete instances of individual and societal functioning may be analyzed in light of the extent to which they are reflective of the truly good. He has expanded his early work, which was characterized by a highly intellectualist cast, to allow for the apprehension of value as it originates through feeling, and through an organic process of revision and refinement, the implications of his notions of being and human community became more clearly defined.[67]

The analytical tool provided by Lonergan's structure of the human good is able to serve the task of political theology well. Without such a concrete notion of the roles played by individuals and institutions in society, Christian openness to the Kingdom becomes a vague notion of a utopian society which humanity is blindly chasing. An important reminder is in order here at the risk of redundancy. Lonergan never makes the assertion that only one concrete instance of the human good exists. As different cultures evolve in different times and places, new strategies are developed to meet the exigencies of the particular situation. The point of Lonergan's empirical notion of culture is that the truly good may be manifested in the human community in a great variety of manners. The invariant structure of the human good serves not as a device to coerce cultural change through the imposition of a certain social order upon others, but rather, it is a tool to aid in the discernment of the extent to which societal factors encourage progress, decline, or redemption. The structure of the human good thus provides guidance for the theologian working for openness to the Kingdom among all nations and peoples.

Self-Appropriation and the Human Good

Lonergan's explicit contribution to political theology may be understood more easily by drawing connections between his notion of self-appropriation and the structure of the human good. First, the authentic operations of the human subject enable discernment of the truly good. Intellectual conversion allows people to examine socio-political realities in a state of 'passionless calm' in order to avoid the entrance of bias into the endeavor. Certain policies or institutions may have their origin in an emotional response to such matters as terrorism or some people's supposed need for the thrill of a fast car. The rigor of intellectual conversion would resist the manipulation of public policy, both foreign and domestic, on the basis of such affectively biased positions. Moral conversion sublates the contribution of intellectual conversion by adding not only the discernment of value, in which the notion of the good emerges as a distinct notion, but also by providing the commitment to act responsibly in response to knowing reasonably. Morally converted political theologians perform their task in a manner consistent with judgments of value, in which feelings, unlike purely intellectual judgments, play and important role. Religious conversion, finally, demands that the responsible undertaking of political theology be performed in accordance with the love of God flooding the hearts of theologians. Thus, the structure of the human good not only guides political theologians in the analysis of the concrete human reality but also emerges from their authentic operation as human subjects.

Next, self-appropriation allows political theologians to be aware of the patterns of experience in which they are investigating a given issue. If theologians are considering a particular social institution in light of mystical experience, for instance, self-appropriated theologians are able to perform the task by drawing upon the entirety of the data in a manner consonant with the affective nature of the experience. Theologians who lack self-appropriation may miss certain data or cast it aside as irrelevant to political theology.

Finally, theologians may utilize the fruits of self-appropriation as they address the three areas of contribution identified by Frederick Lawrence. Self-appropriated political theologians who desire to play a role in economics cannot do so without adhering to transcendental method and the structure of the human good. Is a certain economic policy reflective of or contributing to the concrete good in its multivalent complexity? With regard to education, self-appropriated political theologians will examine pedagogical structures in light of their ability to encourage the presence of wisdom and value in the classroom. An educational system concerned only with the acquisition of knowledge or the preparation of students for financial success fails to meet the characteristics of the human good. Without the structure of the human good and the self-appropriation that enables political theologians to undertake their task authentically, they will face greater difficulty in analyzing the concrete human reality.

In my judgment, Lonergan's structure of the human good stands to make its greatest contribution to political theology in the area of cultural analysis, the third area of potential contribution identified by Lawrence. Culture, according to Lonergan, provides meaning and value for its constitutive members.[68]   Objects and ideas play different roles in different cultures. Some in United States may be baffled by cultures in which all members of the extended family live under the same roof. Conversely, members of other cultures may be confused by the so-called 'gun culture' of the United States. Some cultures place a higher value on education, whereas others encourage their children to work at an early age so as to help provide for the family. Given the wide-reaching impact of culture's function as provider of meaning and value, political theologians who study the structures and institutions of a given culture face a daunting task indeed.   In some cases, social arrangements such as polygamy serve a societal function. In others, such arrangements may be destructive of the social fabric. The structure of the human good provides the political theologian with a valuable tool in the analysis of culture, but as with economics and education, only through self-appropriation can theologians use this resource authentically.

Conclusion

In this chapter I have presented the contribution to be made by Lonergan's notion of self-appropriation to the performance of theology, especially as it pertains to mystical and political theologies. To this end I first presented the relevance of self-appropriation to mystical theology, which consists of three areas of pertinence. First, adherence to the transcendental method enables mystics to utilize other areas of knowledge in the attempt to comprehend the content and nature of the mystical experience. Secondly, self-appropriated mystics are better able to know the content, or lack thereof, and meaning of the mystical experience itself.   Through attention to the nature of the mystical pattern of experience and their operations as subjects, mystics are better able to keep bias or inattention to the data from derailing the attempt at knowing what was encountered. Thirdly, self-appropriation enables mystical theologians to approach authentically the mystical texts of the tradition.

The chapter then moved to a discussion of Lonergan's contribution to political theology, which, according to Frederick Lawrence, consists of the areas of economics, education, and culture, and these are to be analyzed by political theologians in the context of the structure of the human good. As in the case of mystical theology, self-appropriation provides both the framework from which such analysis may proceed and the guidelines by which political theologians may do so authentically.

The final task for this chapter is the connection between mystical theology and political theology and the role played by self-appropriation therein. First, an authentic mystical theology performed from the standpoint of self-appropriation leads to the recognition of the fact that the mystical experience and political action are part and parcel of the same subject. Not only does the tradition demonstrate the presence of the mystics in the socio-political affairs of their time, but the self-transcendence encountered in mystical experience is a matter of authentic existence, for human persons achieve authenticity through transcendence. Therefore, the significance of insights arising from mystical experience which contribute to the understanding of God's relationship with humanity extends beyond that particular relationship with God. Teresa of Avila's *Interior Castle* is relevant not only to her life, but to the lives of her readers. The implications of mystical experience transcend the particular situations of individual mystics, and therefore mystical wisdom is capable of becoming a positive, transformative force in the world.

Secondly, self-appropriation allows mystics to gain access to the meanings contained in the mystical experience itself, or the meaning of a lack of meaning. In the search for mystical wisdom persons are not limited to examining the lives of those who have gone before them. They can also look within, and by being aware of the pattern in which they are located and guided by conversion, they are able to gain insight as to the relevance of the meaning(s) of a particular mystical experience to political matters. What at first seems to have little or no consequence for human community may, in fact, contribute to the construction of just human societies. The mentality of the split soul has maintained for centuries that the spiritual life has no bearing on the political realm. The loving relationship between God and human persons is a personal matter to be kept separate from social concerns. If, however, Christians are commanded to love one another (John 13:34-35) and to work for the coming of the Kingdom of God, then they would do well to reflect upon the nature of love. And to whom better can Christians turn in their reflection than to those who have encountered mystical union with the Divine? If Christians do not attend to the pattern of experience in which they are located, they may miss mysticism's contribution to this effort. The integration provided by self-appropriation enables human persons to discern the various levels of meaning in any given experience and to apply those meanings to the promotion of just human societies.

Thirdly, self-appropriation allows theologians to examine the relevance of the great mystical texts to the task of political theology. As indicated above, mystical experience transcends the particular moment and bears fruit beyond the life of the person experiencing the intersubjectivity of the moment. This often occurs as later persons read the mystical texts of the tradition and seek to apply the mystical wisdom of spiritual masters in their own lives. This is true for political theologians as well as for those individuals seeking spiritual edification. The task of political theologians is to reflect upon social institutions and structures in an effort to determine the extent to which such arrangements promote or hinder the coming of the Kingdom and to provide input as to how matters may be improved. If political theologians approach mystical texts with the split soul mentality in place, they remove from consideration a valuable resource for the performance of their task.

As an example of the connection between mystical and political theology, I suggest consideration of the plight of the poor in the United States. In so doing I am not claiming to provide a solution for the tragic conditions under which some persons are forced to live in the U.S. Rather, I am trying to show a thumbnail illustration of the contribution to be made by self-appropriation to mystical-political theology.

First, Christian political theologians must be aware of the pattern of experience in which they are reflecting upon the state of persons living in poverty. Primarily, this occurs in the intellectual pattern of experience, for they are examining the data – the causes and effects of poverty, seeking to understand those causes and effects, and passing judgment on that understanding. Political theology, however, is not merely an intellectual exercise. Theologians have fallen in love with God in an unrestricted fashion, and this dynamic state of being in love affects every aspect of life, including reflection upon political matters. For Christian political theologians, the love of God is not a private matter because the Christian faith has implications for human communities. Therefore, political theologians take God's love for all of humanity into account when investigating the plight of the poor in the United States.

Political theologians, then, do well to understand to the best of their ability the nature of Divine love and what it means to make this principle a guiding force in the construction of just societies. As I have claimed throughout this book, mystical experience stands to make a decided contribution to the effort to know God's love better, and political theologians may thus turn to the mystics of the tradition or to personal mystical experience for insight regarding the extent to which human communities reflect and promote the Kingdom of God. Self-appropriation guides political theologians here as they recognize deeper levels of reality and seek to discern the meanings contained therein through the performance of the operations of the human subject. Therefore, political theologians studying the causes and effects of poverty in the U.S. may benefit from allowing the affective element of the human subject, which is heavily present in mystical experience, to be a factor in their reflection. They become mystical-political theologians, and self-appropriation helps them to avoid bias in all of its forms and perform this task better.

However, the mentality of the split soul resists such efforts to integrate the mystical life into political theology; it is deeply entrenched and will not give up without a fight. Despite the work of such theologians as Evelyn Underhill, William Johnston, Gustavo Gutiérrez, and Dorothee Sölle, this dualism remains. How, then, do mystical-political theologians go about effecting a transition in political theology that enables them to apply the wisdom of the mystics to their work? The immediate answer is – through self-appropriation. By attending to their foundations and functioning as human subjects, theologians become able to integrate the data of the mystical life or of theology into all areas of theological operations.

I contend, therefore, that conversion is needed, not only on the level of individual human subjects regarding the relevance of mysticism to political theology, but also on the part of theologians as a community of seekers. Groundwork for such a shift can be found in the work of William Matthews, who treats the inherent drive of humanity to know on a communal level. According to Matthews, academic disciplines such as history are not solely descriptions of a given category of data to which human subjects may attend, reflect upon, and pronounce judgment. These disciplines name communities of learners who seek knowledge in the given area. These groups, however, often fail to communicate with one another, as their work is understood to be germane only to the given avenue of investigation. Moreover, people operating on the level of common sense have distanced themselves from academic pursuits. The result, according to Matthews, is a human community that is fragmented and whose constituents are unable to relate to one another. The end result is that understanding of reality is hindered because certain data are neglected by the various groups of knowers.[69] For example, can an environmental theology be developed without adequate attention to the fruits of biological and ecological study? Conversely, does theology have something to offer those scientists who are urging humanity to value and preserve the natural world?

Given the discordant voices of the various communities, Matthews's goal is to search for a guiding principle that can serve these groups in their appropriation of reality as a collection of individuals. According to Matthews, Lonergan's primary point in Chapter Twelve of *Insight* is that the unrestricted human desire to know aims to know being and that reality truly can be known and appropriated. This desire to know, moreover, is operative in the communities of thinkers such as historians, scientists, and people of common sense, for questioning drives the appropriation of reality. The advance of knowledge is very seldom the accomplishment of a single person. Scholars examine and reflect upon data not just in a given experiment, but also in relation to the results achieved by other scientists. Each realm of investigation has a common goal. Physicists research the mechanical workings of the universe. Chemists examine the interactions between chemical compounds. Mathematicians study the nature of numbers and statistical probability. Collaboration in pursuit of a common goal leads to communal advance of knowledge; and thus, just as self-appropriation is an issue of great importance for individual persons, the issue of communal self-appropriation is of significance for communities of learners.[70]

For Matthews, communal self-appropriation involves the identification of the types of questions asked by each group of knowers. Although the pattern of cognitional operations on the part of individuals within each community remains the same, namely, experiencing, understanding, judging, and deciding, each group focuses on different topics. Historians ask different questions than biologists, and mathematicians ask different questions than philosophers. The questions relevant to each group may be posed in many different contexts, but their basic form remains consistent. Historians may investigate different time periods, but their questioning is always in search of what was going forward in a given historical context. Just as personal self-appropriation consists of the objectification of the operations performed in human knowing, communal self-appropriation, then, would consist of the objectification of the recurring questions raised by each group.[71] Moreover, just as self-appropriation on the individual level enables human persons to live more authentically, doing so at the communal level would better enable community members to better pursue their particular avenues of investigation.

The relevance of Matthews's work for mystical-political theology is that communal self-appropriation on the part of mystical and political theologians would objectify the questions asked by each group, thus aiding the cooperation between the two. Such objectification, moreover, would expand the relevant data to which theologians could attend. If, broadly speaking, mystical theology is concerned with the immediate presence of God and the wisdom received therein, and if political theology is a matter of reflecting upon socio-political institutions in light of God's promised kingdom, mystical-political theologians are provided with clearly defined data from which they can proceed. They can attend to the data from mystical theology in a manner that investigates its relevance to the fostering of the Kingdom, and they can read the mystical texts of the tradition in light of Gutiérrez's assertion that all theology is inherently political.

Such cooperation between areas of investigation may be facilitated by Mark D. Morelli's notion of 'horizonal diplomacy.' According to Morelli, "The range of human endeavors has its own standpoint, mode of conscious and intentional operation, and world."[72] As such, theologians who address the issue of political theology do so from a given horizon, comprised of such factors as conversion, or lack thereof, personal experience and interests, and cultural particularity.[73] As theologians collaborate in one of Matthews's communities of questioners, a constellation of horizons forms, and these horizons may be complementary, genetic, or dialectically opposed. For Morelli, when different horizons encounter one another, a recognition of 'horizonal dissonance' in which the theologians involved apprehend this diversity of standpoints may occur, and further collaboration requires it to be addressed.[74]

At this point, Morelli claims, what is needed is the establishment of horizonal relations, which "may be conceived as functions of efforts made by subjects with different horizons to accommodate the perplexity generated by recognitions of dissonance."[75] To fail to establish such lines of communication is to risk the unity of the constellation of horizons in which a common human endeavor takes place. The unity of the common pursuit of political theology would thus be threatened if horizonal relations are not established. Latin American liberation theologians may be in one corner of the room, feminist theologians in another, European political theologians in still another, and so on. The end result of such isolation would be that the many subdivisions of the common category of political theology would become isolated entities with little or nothing to say to one another.

In the face of such a breakdown, Morelli proposes that horizonal diplomacy takes two basic forms.

> On the one hand, there is the ideal of differentiated unity, that is, the ideal of a harmonious blending of elements which retain their individual autonomy and integrity. On the other hand, there is the reductionist ideal of cultural unity, that is, the ideal of a monolithic unity which emerges subsequent to the annihilation or relegation to inferior positions of all but one of the elements.[76]

The problem is that neither of these basic forms resolves the tensions created by the encounter of different horizons. The ideal of differentiated unity tends toward a conglomeration of equally valued standpoints in which political theologians would go about their work. "You do your thing, and I will do mine, and we will co-exist quite nicely." This arrangement, however, does nothing to rectify the potential splintering of mystical and political theology into any number of categories. Mystical-political theology would then become just another way of approaching social ills or studying spirituality that other scholars who are unconvinced of the connection would bracket from their investigations. The ideal of reductionism is likewise unsatisfactory, for the goal of this position would be the capitulation to one horizon, which is deemed to be superior, thus eradicating the beneficial aspects of other horizons.[77] The specter of bias raises its head here as scholars may ignore certain questions or data that threaten the superiority of their position.

The solution to this difficulty, according to Morelli, lies in a horizonal diplomacy comprised of two stages. In the first phase, the diplomat would identify the particularities of each horizon in the constellation. Before constructive dialogue can be undertaken, the positions of those involved must be clarified. Secondly, the participants would undertake the task of examining their adherence or lack of attention to transcendental method.[78] Such clarification would serve a function similar to that of Lonergan's functional specialty of dialectics in which theological positions are illuminated and methodological flaws uncovered.

Horizonal diplomacy is not, however, dialectics, for it deals not with propositions and formulations but with horizons, the framework from which theologians proceed. The difference is subtle but important, for the doctrines that are affirmed as true from the possibilities posed in dialectics become a part of the horizon in which theologians approach later theological investigation. For mystical-political theologians, the doctrine that mysticism bears directly on the project of political theology has already been decided, at least in my mind. Therefore, later theological endeavors are performed with this doctrine already in hand. Theologians do not have to reinvent the wheel, so to speak, because the issue has already been decided. They may seek further understanding of the doctrine in the functional specialty of systematics, but the case no longer needs to be made. The doctrine has become part of the horizon in which they operate.

The horizonal diplomacy I have in mind here would consist of theologians from two camps sitting down to discuss the differences between them. The first group is convinced that mystical and political theologies are two unrelated matters, and the second is certain that the two bear directly on one another. These theologians would first lay out their cases for their positions, and then take the subsequent step of examining how they came to such conclusions. If this process is flawed by bias in any of its forms, then authenticity demands that these mistakes and oversights be corrected and the final position adjusted accordingly. In this book I have argued that the first group may have been influenced by a lack of self-appropriation or an inadequate notion of the human subject. Therefore, if I have made my case, then my contribution to horizonal diplomacy is to illustrate how the mentality of the split soul has derailed mystical and political theology over the years, and hopefully my work will inspire others to reevaluate their stance regarding mystical-political theology.

According to noted Lonergan scholar, David Tracy, however, no theology is complete without a corresponding element of praxis, and this is true especially of political theology, which seeks the transformation of the human community. Although theological use of the term praxis is widely varied, Tracy identifies a commonality insofar as it entails a personal involvement on the part of the theologian. A theology of praxis is not merely a matter of reflecting on theological issues in the ivory tower of academia. Rather, it is a matter not only of speaking the truth but of doing the truth. [79] A theology of praxis, therefore, both affects and is affected by the drama of human living – a drama in which political theology, from a Lonerganian perspective, seeks the ever more authentic existence for the human community and to which mysticism stands to make a valuable contribution.

NOTES

[1] Bernard Lonergan, *Method in Theology*, 2nd ed. (New York: Herder and Herder, 1973; reprint, Toronto: University of Toronto Press, 1990, 1994, 1996), xi.

[2] This brief sketch of Lonergan's two phases of theology is the basis for *Method*, which further subdivides the two phases into eight functional specialties which correspond to the operations of the human subject.

[3] *Collected Works of Lonergan*, vol. 5, *Understanding and Being: The Halifax Lectures on "Insight,"* eds., Elizabeth A. Morelli and Mark D. Morelli (Toronto: University of Toronto Press, 1990), 12.

[4] Ibid. This is the problem that leads Lonergan to concentrate on the functioning of the human subject rather than knowing as an ideal. To get around the Hegelian objection, Lonergan urges the taking of a step back from the attempt to explicitly formulate what knowing is to the operations of the human subjects as they go about the business of knowing, and this, Lonergan claims, is the process of self-appropriation. Ibid., 14-17.

[5] See Nancy Fraser, *Justice Interuptus: Critical Reflections on the "Postsocialist" Condition* (New York: Routledge, 1997).

[6] Bernard Lonergan, "The Transisition from a Classicist World-View to Historical Mindedness," in *A Second Collection*, ed., William F.J. Ryan, S.J. and Bernard J. Tyrrell, S.J. (Philadelphia: The Westminster Press, 1974), 3.

[7] Vernon Gregson, *Lonergan, Spirituality, and the Meeting of Religions*, College Theology Society Studies in Religion, vol. 2 (Lanham, MD: University Press of America, 1985), 10-11.

[8] Lonergan, *Method*, 23.

[9] See, for example, James Cone, *A Black Theology of Liberation: 20th Anniversary Edition* (Maryknoll, NY: Orbis Books, 1997).

[10] See, Dorothee Sölle, "Eine Erinnerung um der Zukunft willen," in Edward Schillebeeckx, ed., *Mystik und Politik: Theologie im Ringen um Geschichte und Gesellschaft; Johann Baptist Metz zu Ehren zum 60. Geburtstag* (Mainz: Matthias-Grünewald-Verlag, 1988), 17-18.

[11] See, for example, Cheryl Gilkes, *If It Wasn't for the Women--: Black Women's Experience and Womanist Culture in Church and Community* (Maryknoll, NY: Orbis Books, 2001); Stephanie Y. Mitchem, *Introducing Womanist Theology* (Maryknoll, NY: Orbis Books, 2002).

[12] Bernard Lonergan, *Philosophy of God, and Theology: The Relationship between Philosophy of God and the Functional Specialty, Systematics*, St. Michael's Lectures, Gonzaga University, Spokane, WA (London: Darton, Longman & Todd, 1972), ix.

[13] Examples include such individuals as Teresa of Avila, John of the Cross, and Ignatius of Loyola.

[14] Ignatius of Loyola, *The Autobiography*, 3:31, in *Ignatius of Loyola: Spiritual Exercises and Selected Works*, ed., George E. Ganss, S.J., The Classics of Western Spirituality: A Library of the Great Masters (New York: Paulist Press, 1991), 81.

[15] For example, Ignatius writes in his autobiography that he was grasped by an intense desire to pray during the night hours. However, such an active prayer left him too exhausted to help others during the day. According to Ignatius, even activities that are directed towards God must be examined in order to be certain that one is not being led away from God even while desiring to come closer. Ibid., 79.

[16] According to Arnoldo Fortini, only later in life when Francis was recovering from illness did he look back upon his time spent in the countryside and recognize the first stirrings of God's call. Arnold Fortini, *Francis of Assisi*, trans. Helen Moak (New York: Crossroad, 1981), 173. Moreover, the night before Francis traveled to Spoleto, he received a vision of an enchanted castle in which a beautiful woman appeared to him as his bride. Ibid., 183-185. Upon his return from this trip, he received another vision in which this same woman appeared, only this time she was dressed as a beggar maid. Ibid., 192-194. Only after conflict with his father regarding Francis's desire to give his share of the family fortune to the poor did Francis recognize this woman as Lady Poverty and accept her as his bride. Ibid., 228-229.

[17] Denise Carmody, "The Desire for Transcendence: Religious Conversion," in Vernon Gregson, ed., *The Desires of the Human Heart: An Introduction to the Theology of Bernard Lonergan* (New York: Paulist Press, 1988), 58-59.

[18] Julian of Norwich, *Showings (Long Text)*, 59, in *Julian of Norwich: Showings*, The Classics of Western Spirituality: A Library of the Great Masters, trans. Edmund Colledge, O.S.A. (New York: Paulist Press, 1978), 296.

[19] I am contending in this book that Lonergan's notion of self-appropriation is capable of serving as an aid to the task of mystical-political theology because self-appropriation allows persons to know what they are doing when they are functioning as human subjects. As such, all theologians, both the great mystics of the past and today's scholars, would benefit from the integration provided by self-appropriation. This is not to say, however, that all efforts at theology prior to Lonergan are insufficient because of an inadequate position regarding the human subject. Lonergan's point in *Insight* is that all human persons proceed through the operations of experiencing, understanding, judging, and deciding regardless of whether or not they acknowledge this pattern. Although self-appropriation is the awareness of these operations, authentic performance of the operations of the human subject is possible without advertence to their presence. As previously noted, "Method then is not essential to obtaining results, but it accelerates the process, eliminates misconceptions." Frederick E. Crowe, S.J., "Origin and Scope of *Insight*," in Frederick E. Crowe, S.J, *Appropriating the Lonergan Idea*, ed. Michail Vertin (Washington D.C.: The Catholic University of America Press, 1989), 15. Thus, I am not calling into question Julian's interpretation of her mystical life due to a lack of self-appropriation. Rather, I am merely contending that her efforts at understanding and communicating her mystical life would have been helped by self-appropriation, and in some cases she would have been better able to provide her readers with a more developed account of her experiences and insights. But this does not preclude her from performing the operations of the human subject authentically.

[20] Thérèse of Lisieux, *The Autobiography of Thérèse of Lisieux*, 3rd ed., trans. John Clarke, O.C.D. (Washington D.C.: ICS Publications, 1996), 14.

[21] Teresa of Avila's best known work, *The Interior Castle*, is intended to serve as a guide for those on the mystical path. Teresa of Avila, *The Interior Castle*, in *The Collected Works of St. Teresa of Avila*, vol. 2, trans. Kieran Kavanaugh, O.C.D. and Otilio Rodriguez, O.C.D. (Washington D.C.: ICS Publications, 1980), 261-452.

[22] Consider the example of Bernard of Clairvaux who initiated monastic reform in an effort to increase the degree to which monks lived according to *The Rule of St. Benedict*. For a discussion of Bernard's monastic theology, see G.R. Evans, *Bernard of Clairvaux* (New York: Oxford University Press, 2000), 22-41.

[23] John of the Cross fits into this category due to his role as spiritual mentor for students and nuns while at the University of Baeza. "General Introduction," in *The Collected Works of St. John of the Cross*, trans. Kieran Kavanaugh, O.C.D. and Otilio Rodriguez, O.C.D. (Washington D.C.: ICS Publications, 1991), 21.

[24] Ignatius of Loyola, for instance, became an advocate for governmental care for the poor. Ignatius of Loyola, *The Autobiography*, 9:89, in *Ignatius of Loyola: Spiritual Exercises and Other Works*, ed. George E. Ganss, S.J., The Classics of Western Spirituality: A Library of the Great Spiritual Masters (New York: Paulist Press, 1991), 106.

[25] Doran's notion of psychic conversion is of great help to the theologian engaged in the interpretation of mystical texts for it provides a level of critical control over the symbolic meanings contained in the text.

[26] Teresa of Avila, *The Way of Perfection*, 1:2, in *The Collected Works of St. Teresa of Avila*, vol. 2, ed., Kieran Kavanaugh, O.C.D. and Otilio Rodriguez, O.C.D. (Washington D.C.: ICS Publications, 1990), 41.

[27] William James, *Varieties of Religious Experience* (New York: Penguin Books, 1982), 381.

[28] Michael L. Rende, *Lonergan on Conversion: The Development of a Notion* (Lanham, MD: University Press of America, 1989), 54.

[29] Lonergan, *Method*, xi. I am concerned here with the explicit role of Lonergan's work in political theology. Recalling Chapter One, Gutiérrez claims that all theology is political insofar as it resists or accommodates the present socio-political situation. This chapter is concerned with Lonergan's contribution to a theology that consciously addresses the institutions and strategies present in human communities. One's theological endeavors unwittingly having a political impact is one thing. Undertaking such work with the political reality at the fore of one's mind is quite another.

[30] Frederick G. Lawrence, "Lonergan as Political Theologian," in Timothy P. Fallon, S.J. and Philip Boo Riley, eds., *Religion in Context: Recent Studies in Lonergan*, College Theology Society Resources in Religion, vol. 4 (Lanham, MD: University Press of America, 1988), 6-7.

[31] Ibid., 7.

[32] Ibid., 10-11.

[33] *Collected Works of Bernard Lonergan*, vol. 10, *Topics in Education*, eds. Robert M. Doran and Frederick E. Crowe (Toronto: University of Toronto Press, 1988).

[34] Lonergan, "The Transition from a Classicist World-View to Historical Mindedness," 1-7.

[35] Lonergan, *Method*, xi.

[36] Ibid., 53.

[37] Ibid., 55. This, as described in Chapter Four, is the role of the healing vector in human history.

[38] Lonergan's assertion of the human good as concrete avoids the Hegelian position regarding the insufficiency of ideals. In *Method*, Lonergan writes the following. "What is good always is concrete. But definitions are abstract. Hence, if one attempts to define the good, one runs the risk of misleading one's readers. The present chapter, then, aims at assembling the various components that enter into the human good." Lonergan, *Method*, 27. As such, the subsequent discussion of Lonergan's notion of the human good will indicate that this concept is not an attempt at defining the good but an analytical tool by which individuals may examine the concrete human situation to determine the extent to which it is reflective of goodness.

[39] Bernard Lonergan, *Topics in Education*, 33.

[40] Ibid., 33-34.

[41] Ibid., 34.

[42] Ibid., 34, ftnt. 22.

[43] *Collected Works of Bernard Lonergan*, vol. 3, *Insight: A Study of Human Understanding*, eds., Frederick E. Crowe and Robert M. Doran (Toronto: University of Toronto Press, 1992), 141.

[44] Ibid.

[45] Lonergan, *Topics in Education*, 35.

[46] Ibid., 35-36.

[47] Ibid., 35.

[48] Ibid., 35-36.

[49] Ibid., 36.

[50] Ibid.

[51] M. Shawn Copeland, *Lonergan on the Human Good* (Ph.D. dissertation: Boston College: 1991), 163. Compare Lonergan's notion of personal status with the dramatic pattern of experience.

[52] Lonergan, *Topics in Education*, 37.

[53] Ibid.

[54] Ibid.

[55] Copeland, 164.

[56] Ibid., 197.

[57] Walter E. Conn, "Bernard Lonergan on Value," *The Thomist* 40 (1976): 247.

[58] Lonergan, *Topics in Education*, 32.

[59] See Lonergan's proof for God on the basis of the intelligibility of reality in chapter 19 of *Insight*. Lonergan, *Insight*, 692-699.

[60] Copeland, 207. Lonergan himself notes this transition as he writes, "In *Method* the question of God is considered more important than the precise manner in which an answer is formulated, and our basic awareness of God comes to us not through our arguments or choices but primarily through God's gift of his love." Bernard Lonergan, "*Insight* Revisited," in *A Second Collection*, ed., William F.J. Ryan, S.J., and Bernard J. Tyrrell, S.J. (Philadelphia: Westminster Press, 1974), 277.

[61] Copeland, 261.

[62] Lonergan, *Method*, 48.

[63] Ibid., 48.

[64] Ibid., 48-49.

[65] Ibid., 50-51.

[66] Ibid., 48-52.

[67] Copeland, 188-189.

[68] Lonergan, *Method*, 32.

[69] William Matthews, "Method and the Social Appropriation of Reality," in Matthew L. Lamb, ed., *Creativity and Method: Essays in Honor of Bernard Lonergan, S.J.* (Milwaukee: Marquette University Press, 1981), 425-426.

[70] Ibid., 426-432.

[71] Ibid., 436-440.

[72] Mark D. Morelli, "Horizonal Diplomacy," in Matthew L. Lamb, ed., *Creativity and Method: Essays in Honor of Bernard Lonergan, S.J.* (Milwaukee: Marquette University Press, 1981), 460.

[73] Lonergan, *Method*, 235-237.

[74] Morelli, 460-461.

[75] Ibid., 462.

[76] Ibid., 463.

[77] Ibid., 464.

[78] Ibid., 468-469.

[79] David Tracy, "Theologies of Praxis," in Matthew L. Lamb, ed., *Creativity and Method: Essays in Honor of Bernard Lonergan, S.J.* (Milwaukee: Marquette University Press, 1981), 35-36.

CONCLUSION

The problem addressed by this book is the mentality of the split soul. I have argued that Bernard Lonergan's treatment of the human subject serves as a valuable tool for the project of resisting that mentality. To make this problem concrete, I have argued the relevance of mystical theology to the task of political theology. The introductory chapter documented the reality and history of the split soul mentality as it came to prominence through both theological and philosophical movements over the centuries. This mentality succeeded in cordoning off the mystical life from matters of socio-political matters by establishing a false dichotomy between spiritual and worldly matters. Chapter One refuted the mentality of the split soul by demonstrating not only that mysticism is able to inform one's stance regarding the practical affairs of human community, but also that mysticism is necessarily involved in such concerns. According to Evelyn Underhill and William Johnston, the mystical life cannot be separated from other areas of human living because mysticism reveals the true nature of Reality (Underhill) and emphasizes the role of God as the unifying force in all of creation and human living therein (Johnston).

Chapter One also took the further step of defining political theology as theological reflection upon the extent to which the concrete forms of human community reflect or participate in the Scriptural portrayal of the Kingdom of God. A community marked by such reflection would consist of structures and institutions that ensure the flourishing of all peoples, justice for all, and the meeting of life's needs for every human person. For Gustavo Gutiérrez, all theology is political insofar as it either supports or resists the established systems that govern human living, and therefore mystical theology is inherently political. For Dorothee Sölle, the salvation wrought by Jesus Christ involves an historical aspect in the establishment of the Kingdom, which leads to her claim of salvation *in* history rather than *from* history. The wisdom gained from the mystical experience becomes a resource for Christians who desire to participate in this historical salvific process by opening their eyes to the true state of things and the possibilities for a human community truly reflective of the Kingdom of God. The connection between mystical and political theology presented by these four theologians presents a position that stands in dialectical opposition to the split soul mentality, and I contend that careful scrutiny requires the decision to side with Underhill, Johnston, Gutiérrez, and Sölle.

Once this choice has been made, the question arises as to why, if a relationship between mystical and political theology necessarily exists, the split soul mentality is so successful in maintaining its dominance. As I stated earlier, the history of theology offers examples of many thinkers who have asserted the connection between mystical and political theology but this position has failed to unseat the mentality of the split soul. I contend that a primary reason for this unfortunate situation is a lack of attention to the functioning of the human subject in coming to know the content and the meanings present in mystical experience. The result has been that mystical experience is pushed into a distinct category of human existence that is only concerned with matters of the interior life.

In this book I have proposed that the work of Bernard Lonergan on the functioning of the human subject can serve as a valuable resource in the attempt to address the split soul mentality. Chapter Two took the first step in this endeavor, presenting Lonergan's notion of the patterns of experience that characterize human existence. The first step for individuals who seek to know their operations as subjects is to recognize the situation in which they are operating. Chapter Three then discussed the operations of the human subject as they are performed in the various patterns of experience. Individuals first attend to the data contained within each experience, seek to understand that data, and then pass judgment on that understanding. These operations, moreover, will utilize different aspects of the human person as the particularities of the given pattern of experience demand. The intellectual pattern of experience deliberately avoids the affective dimension of the person, whereas the mystical pattern involves feelings due to its highly symbolic nature.

Chapter Four presented Lonergan's stance on the human subject as it addressed the issue of conversion and the dialectic of the subject. The various conversions undergone by the individual, according to Lonergan, comprise the foundational reality out of which human beings perform the operations of consciousness in the concrete reality of the many patterns of experience. Intellectually converted people will adhere to the demands of the responsible performance of human cognition, the morally converted will take actions based on value rather than satisfaction, and the religiously converted will approach all of life's twists and turns in a state of being in love with God in an unrestricted fashion. Self-appropriation is thus a matter not only of identifying patterns of experience and performing the operations of the human subject but also of being aware of one's conversions or lack thereof. If individuals do not take the foundational reality that informs their existence in the world into account, they run the risk of missing some of the data, precluding an explanatory hypothesis, pronouncing judgment before all of the available data has been considered, or stubbornly refusing to affirm or reject their understanding. Decisions made from such an incomplete standpoint are much more likely to be destructive rather than constructive, and hurtful rather than healing.

The dialectic of the subject is a recognition of the tension that exists between the human ability for transcendence and the inherent limitation of being human. Because of the former, people seek to know things as they really are, not only as they appear to be from a given perspective. Because of the latter, some things are simply beyond their ken without some type of outside help. The source of that help is God's healing activity in the world, which opens human eyes to solutions that would otherwise be unavailable. Without help, the destructive power of sin and the communities formed on the basis thereof would continue to have the upper hand in human history. With the healing offered by the Divine, however, new answers come to mind, and the decline of the human condition may be arrested.

If I have presented Lonergan's thought on the topic of self-appropriation adequately, the relevance of this notion to the overcoming of the split soul should be apparent to my readers. Self-appropriation enables the human subject to integrate all of life's experiences through the clarification of the patterns of experience, the performance of the cognitional operations therein, and the determination of the aspects of the human person applicable to this task. Moreover, for the self-appropriated individual, the knowledge gained through the authentic performance of the operations of consciousness comes together to form a horizon within the human subject lives and works. The individual's horizon then provides the framework of stances and beliefs that inform one's further functioning.

For the sake of clarity regarding the distinction between Lonergan's notions of foundational reality and horizon, I must risk redundancy at this point. Foundational reality is a matter of recognizing and objectifying one's state of conversion, or lack thereof, and conversions concern the functioning of the human subject as intelligent, moral, or religious persons. Thus, Lonergan's functional specialty of foundations consists of the effort to determine one's basic stance in the world.[1] Horizons, on the other hand are comprised of the principles and knowledge gained from the attempts to come to know the reality in which individuals are located.[2] These principles, moreover, are the fruit of the authenticity provided by acknowledging the presence or lack of conversions (foundations), and horizons may undergo many changes and refinements as individuals goes through their lives, but conversion is the bedrock underlying their horizons, and a change in conversion requires the re-visitation of the main beliefs and doctrines that comprise their horizons.

With specific regard to the relevance of self-appropriation to the overcoming of the split soul mentality, individual mystics encounter the immediate presence of God in the experience of unitive prayer. After accurately identifying the encounter as fitting into the mystical pattern of experience, they reflect upon the content, or lack thereof, of the experience and seek to understand this data. Once all relevant questions have been answered, mystics then pass judgment upon this understanding. If their understanding is affirmed, then the wisdom of the mystical experience becomes an aspect of the horizon in which they operate. Therefore, the content of the mystical experience becomes a part of the resources upon which mystics may draw when addressing the socio-political concerns of their day. The mystical life is no longer cordoned off into a category separate from the exterior life, and the split soul mentality is demonstrated to be an inadequate expression of the nature of the human subject.

Without self-appropriation, mystics remain at the mercy of mentality of the split soul because they possess no clear way of explaining the relevance of the mystical experience to every day life. They run the risk of inadequately coming to know the wisdom of the mystical experience and/or applying this wisdom inappropriately in the external affairs of human living. Moreover, such mistakes, when perceived by others, would only serve to strengthen the split soul mentality by serving as an example of how mysticism has no place in the exterior life. Perhaps such unfortunate mistakes contribute to the strength of the split soul mentality's grip on theology today. If this is the case, it is not the fault of the nature of mysticism but of the inadequate attention to the operations of the human subject in the mystical experience and the manner in which the meanings of the mystical experience are applied to life in the world.

Chapter Five undertook the final task of this book by examining the relevance of self-appropriation to the explicit task of mystical-political theology. Beyond the affirmation of the relevance of mysticism to socio-political concerns, self-appropriation also aids the theologian who seeks to apply the fruits of the mystical experience to the flourishing of the Kingdom of God here on earth. The preliminary step to the development of an explicit mystical-political theology on the basis of Lonergan's notion of self-appropriation is the previously stated position that recognizes the integrity of the human person elucidated through self-appropriation as a more adequate understanding of the human subject than the mentality of the split soul. Once theologians make this affirmation, they are in a position to investigate the particularities and nuances of the connection between mystical and political theology.

At this point, theologians are entering Lonergan's functional specialty of systematics, for systematics is the attempt to understand the statements and principles previously affirmed in the specialty of doctrines.[3] These doctrines may arise from the personal experience of the theologian, from the accounts of other mystics, or from a combination of the two. In all three cases, self-appropriation guides theologians in their attempt at understanding. In the case of theologians who try to understand their personal experiences, self-appropriation guides them with regard to the aspects of the human person that are relevant to understanding the data contained in the mystical experience. Unlike the intellectual pattern of experience, the attempt to understand the content of the mystical experience requires attention to the affective dimension of the human person. For theologians who approach the writings of others, self-appropriation aids them by preventing their feelings from derailing the task of understanding the meaning of the text under consideration. Theologians may wish for a certain interpretation to be true, but the text may not warrant the desired reading. On the other hand, the highly symbolic nature of many mystical texts may require attention to the feelings aroused by the symbols used by the mystics to convey their spiritual life. Self-appropriation thus keeps theologians on the right track and resists the harmful influence of bias from entering the theological task.

The fruit of self-appropriation is that it provides a framework from which other questions may be addressed. This statement opens the door for the human subject to address any number of challenges or academic disciplines, for it identifies both the importance of grasping what people are doing when they are knowing and urges them to apply that awareness in scholarly and every day life. The significance of self-appropriation for theology lies in the implications of incorrect judgment regarding the ways of God and the teachings of the church. Poorly done theology has justified oppression, violence, and bigotry, and the Kingdom of God seems a remote reality indeed. Even such a glorious mystery as the Trinitarian nature of God has contributed to a devaluing of women due to gender specific language in Trinitarian theology. The earth, created by God, has been exploited as a result of a notion of 'dominion' that has been distorted by self interest and a desire for 'the good life.' In light of the profound effect of theology on human history, theologians are to be conscientious when exploring the mysteries of God, and self-appropriation serves as a valuable resource in this regard.

When theologians undertake the task of mystical-political theology, self-appropriation takes on added significance. Not only do selfishness and the highly affective nature of mystical experience threaten to lead their theology astray, the mentality of the split soul tends to relegate their accomplishments to a corner of human experience separate from everyday life. Self-appropriation, however, guides theologians through the potential minefield of affectivity and bias so that they may emerge on the other side with an appreciation of mysticism as connected directly to the practical concerns of human living. Not only does the history of Western Christian mysticism testify to this, but in mystical experience itself God speaks to individual mystics. The wisdom imparted therein accompanies mystics as they operate in the other patterns of experience. For the religiously converted, what is known of God becomes a factor in all decision making, and self-appropriation helps to determine just what role it plays. With all due respect to my colleague at St. Catherine's, if everyone was a mystic, everything would be done a whole lot better.

NOTES

[1] Bernard Lonergan, *Method in Theology*, 2nd ed. (New York: Herder and Herder, 1973; reprint, Toronto: University of Toronto Press, 1990, 1994, 1996), 130-132

[2] Ibid., 235-237.

[3] Ibid., 132.

BIBLIOGRAPHY

Alexander, Jon. "What Do Recent Writers Mean by Spirituality." *Spirituality Today* 32 (1980): 247-256.

Armstrong, Christopher. *Evelyn Underhill: An Introduction to Her Life and Writings*. Grand Rapids: Eerdmans, 1976.

Armstrong, Regis J. O.F.M. Cap., J.A. Wayne Hellmann, O.F.M. Conv., and William J. Short, O.F.M., eds. *Francis of Assisi: Early Documents*, 3 vols. New York, London, and Manila: New City Press, 1999.

Boisvert, Leandre. "Les images bibliques de dieu dans l'oeuvre de Gustavo Gutiérrez." *Église et theologie* 19:3 (1988): 307-321.

Bouyer, Louis. *Introduction à la vie spirituale: précis de théologie ascétique et mystique*. Paris: Desclée, 1960.

Braio, Frank Paul. *Lonergan's Retrieval of the Notion of Human Beiung: Clarifications of and Reflections on the Argument of "Insight," Chapters I-XVIII*. Lanham, MD: University Press of America, 1988.

Brame, Grace Adolphsen. "The Extraordinary within the Ordinary: The Life and Message of Evelyn Underhill (1875-1941)." In *Feminist Voices in Spirituality*. Edited by Pierre Hegy. Studies in Women and Religion, no. 38. 101-124. Lewiston, NY: Edwin Mellen, 1996.

Brown, Robert McAffee. *Gustavo Gutiérrez*. Makers of Contemporary Theology. Atlanta: John Knox Press, 1980.

_____. *Gustavo Gutiérrez: An Introduction to Liberation Theology*. MaryKnoll, NY: Orbis Books, 1990.

_____. "Spirituality and Liberation: The Case for Gustavo Gutiérrez." *Worship* 58 (1984): 395-404.

Browning, Don S. "Practical Theology and Political Theology." *Theology Today* 42 (1985): 15-33.

Bynum, Caroline Walker. "The Female Body and Religious Practice." In *Fragmentation and Redemption: Essays on Gender and the Human Body in Medieval Religion*. New York: Zone Books, 1991.

Byrne, Lavinia, ed., *Traditions of Spiritual Guidance*. Collegeville, MN: The Liturgical Press, 1990.

Cadorette, Curt. *From the Heart of the People: The Theology of Gustavo Gutiérrez*. Oak Park, IL: Meyer Stone Books, 1988.

Callahan, Annice. *Evelyn Underhill: Spirituality for Daily Living*. Lanham, MD: University Press of America, 1997.

_____. *Spiritual Guides for Today: Evelyn Underhill, Dorothy Day, Karl Rahner, Simone Weil, Thomas Merton, Henri Nouwen*. New York: Crossroad, 1992.

Capps, Walter Holden and Wendy M. Wright, eds. *An Invitation to Western Mysticism*. Harper Forum Books. San Francisco: Harper & Row, 1978.

Carmody, Denise Lardner. "The Desire for Transcendence: Religious Conversion." In *The Desires of the Human Heart: An Introduction to the Theology of Bernard Lonergan*. Edited by Vernon Gregson, 57-73. Mahwah, NJ: Paulist Press, 1988.

Cone, James. *A Black Theology of Liberation: 20th Anniversary Edition*. Maryknoll, NY: Orbis Books, 1997.

Conn, Walter E. "Bernard Lonergan on Value." *The Thomist* 40 (1976): 243-257.

_____. "The Desire for Authenticity: Conscience and Moral Conversion." In *The Desires of the Human Heart: An Introduction to the Thought of Bernard Lonergan*. Edited by Vernon Gregson, 36-56. New York: Paulist Press, 1988.

_____. "Passionate Commitment: The Dynamics of Affective Conversion." *Cross Currents* 34 (1984): 329-336.

Copeland, M. Shawn. *A Genetic Study of the Idea of the Human Good in the thought of Bernard Lonergan*. Ph.D. diss., Boston College, 1991.

Coslet, Dorothy Gwayne. *Madame Jeanne Guyon, Child of Another World*. Fort Washington, PA: Christian Literature Crusade, 1984.

Cropper, Margaret. *Evelyn Underhill*. New York: Longmans, Green, 1958.

Crowe, Frederick E. S.J. *Appropriating the Lonergan Idea*. Edited by Michael Vertin. Washington D.C.: The Catholic University Press of America, 1989

_____. "An Exploration of Lonergan's New Notion of Value." In *Appropriating the Lonergan Idea*. Edited by Michael Vertin. Washington D.C.: The Catholic University Press of America, 1989

_____. *Lonergan*. Collegville, MN: Liturgical Press, 1992.

_____. *Method in Theology: An Organon for Our Time*. Milwaukee: Marquette University Press, 1980.

_____. "Origin and Scope of *Insight*." In *Appropriating the Lonergan Idea*. Edited by Michael Vertin. Washington D.C.: The Catholic University Press of America, 1989.

de Certeau, Michel. *La fable mystique: XVIe - XVIIe Siècle*. France: Éditions Gallimard, 1982.
_____. "The Weakness of Believing: From the Body to Writing, a Christian Transit." In *The Certeau Reader*. Edited by Graham Ward. Oxford: Blackwell Publishers, 2000.

Delekat, Friedrich. "Zur Theologie von Dorothee Sölle." *Kerygma und Dogma* 16:2 (1970): 130-143.

Doran, Robert, S.J. "Bernard Lonergan and the Functions of Systematic Theology." *Theological Studies* 59 (1998): 569-607

_____. "Psychic Conversion." In *Theological Foundations*, 2 vols. Milwaukee: Marquette University Press, 1995.

_____. *Subject and Psyche*, 2nd ed. Marquette Studies in Theology, vol. 3, ed. Andrew Tallon. Milwaukee, WI: Marquette University Press, 1994.

_____. *Theology and the Dialectics of History*. Toronto: University of Toronto Press.

Dunne, John, C.S.C. "Insight and Waiting on God." In *Creativity and Method: Essays in Honor of Bernard Lonergan, SJ*. Edited by Matthew L. Lamb, 3-9. Milwaukee: Marquette University Press, 1981.

Dunne, Tad, SJ. "Consciousness in Christian Community." In *Creativity and Method: Essays in Honor of Bernard Lonergan, SJ*. Edited by Matthew L. Lamb, 291-303. Milwaukee: Marquette University Press, 1981.

Dunne, Tad. *Lonergan and Spirituality: Towards a Spiritual Integration*. Chicago: Loyola University Press, 1985.

Dupré, Louis. *The Deeper Life: An Introduction to Christian Mysticism*. New York: Crossroad, 1981.

_____. *Passage to Modernity: An Essay in the Hermeneutics of Nature and Culture*. New Haven: Yale University Press, 1993.

Egan, Harvey D. *Christian Mysticism: The Future of a Tradition*. New York: Pueblo, 1984.

Eliade, Mircea. *Myths, Dreams, and Mysteries: The Encounter between Contemporary Faiths and Archaic Realities*. New York: Harper & Row, 1960.

Ellis, Marc, H. and Otto Maduro, eds. *Expanding the View: Gustavo Gutiérrez and the Future of Liberation Theology*. Maryknoll, NY: Orbis Books, 1990.

_____. *The Future of Liberation Theology: Essays in Honor of Gustavo Gutiérrez*. Maryknoll, NY: Orbis Books, 1989.

Evans, G.R. *Bernard of Clairvaux*. New York: Oxford University Press, 2000.

Field, Lester L. *Liberty, Dominion and the Two Swords: On the Origins of Western Political Theology*. Notre Dame, IN: Univeristy of Notre Dame Press, 1998.

Flanagan, Sabina. *Hildegard of Bingen, 1098-1179: A Visionary Life*. New York: Routledge, 1989.

Fluri, Phlipp. *Einsicht in Insight: Bernard J.F. Lonergans Kritische-Realistische Wissenschafts- und Erkenntnistheorie*. Frankfurt am Main: Haag & Herchen, 1988.

Fortini, Arnaldo. *Francis of Assisi*, 2 vols. Translated by Helen Moak. New York: Crossroad, 1981.

Fox, Matthew, ed. *Hildegaard of Bingen's Book of Divine Works with Letters and Songs*. Translated by Robert Cunningham, Ronald Miller, Jerry Dybdal, and Matthew Fox. Santa Fe, NM: Bear & Co., 1987.

Fox, George. *The Journal of George Fox*. Edited by Rufus M. Jones. Richmond, IN: Friends United Press, 1976.

Fraser, Nancy. *Justice Interuptus: Critical Reflections on the "Postsocialist" Condition*. New York: Routledge, 1997.

Furse, Margaret Lewis. *Mysticism: Window on a World View*. Nashville: Abingdon Press, 1977.

Geffré, Claude. "Le non-lieu de la théologie chez Michel de Certeau." In *Michel de Certeau ou la différence chrétienne*. Edited by Claude Geffré, 157-180. Paris: Cerf, 1991.

Gendlin, Eugene. *Focusing*. New York: Bantam Books, 1991.

Gilkes, Cheryl. *If It Wasn't for the Women--: Black Women's Experience and Womanist Culture in Church and Community*. Maryknoll, NY: Orbis Books, 2001.

Gilson, Etienne. *The Mystical Theology of Bernard of Clairvaux*. Translated by A.H.C. Gilson. Kalamazoo: Cistercian Publications, 1990.

_____. *Le théologie et histoire de la spiritualité*. Leçon inaugurale de la chaire d'histoire de spiritualité prononcée à l'institut catholique de Paris, le 15 Novembre 1943. Paris:Vrin, 1943.

Going, Cathleen. "'Persons as Originating Values': A Primer (Reader) from Lonergan's Thought on the Topic of Values." In *Lonergan Workshop* vol. 3. Edited by Frederick Lawrence, 25-32. Chico, CA: Scholars Press, 1982.

Gonzalez, Justo L. *A History of Christian Thought*, 3 vols. Rev. ed. Nashville: Abingdon Press, 1987.

Goodier, Alban. *The Life That Is Light*, 3 vols. London: Burns, Oates, & Washbourne, 1935.

Granfield, David. *Heightened Consciousness: The Mystical Difference*. New York: Paulist Press, 1991.

Grant, Patrick. *Literature of Mysticism in Western Tradition*. New York: St. Martin's Press, 1983.

Greene, Dana. *Evelyn Underhill: Artist of the Infinite Life*. New York: Crossroad, 1990.

Gregson, Vernon, ed. *The Desires of the Human Heart: An Introduction to the Thought of Bernard Lonergan*. New York: Paulist Press, 1988.

_____. "The Desire to Know: Intellectual Conversion." In *The Desires of the Human Heart: An Introduction to the Thought of Bernard Lonergan*. Edited by Vernon Gregson. 16-35. New York: Paulist Press, 1988.

_____. "The Faces of Evil and Our Response: Ricouer, Lonergan, Moore." In *Religion in Context: Recent Studies in Lonergan*. Edited by Timothy P. Fallon, SJ and Philip Boo Riley. College Theology Society Resources in Religion no. 4. 125-129. Lanham, MD: University Press of America, 1988.

_____. *Lonergan, Spirituality, and the Meeting of Religions*. College Theology Society Studies in Religion, vol. 2. Lanham, MD: University Press of America, 1985.

Guibal, Francis. "The force subversive de l'evangile: sur la pensee theologique de Gustavo Gutiérrez." *Recherches de science religieuse* 77:4 (1989): 483-508.

Gurber, Jacques. "La 'Representation' de Dorothee Sölle." 2 parts, *Revue d'histoire et de philosophie religieuses* 66 (2 Ap, 1986): 179-210.

_____. "La 'Representation' de Dorothee Sölle." 2 parts, *Revue d'histoire et de philosophie religieuses* 66 (3 Jl, 1986): 287-318.

Gutiérrez, Gustavo. *The Density of the Present: Selected Writings*. Maryknoll, NY: Orbis Books, 1999.

_____. *Essential Writings*. Edited by James B. Nickoloff. Maryknoll, NY: Orbis Books, 1996.

_____. "Freedom and Salvation: A Political Problem." In Gustavo Gutiérrez and Richard Schaull, *Liberation and Change*. Edited by Ronald H. Stone. 2-94. Atlanta: John Knox Press, 1977.

_____. *The God of Life*. Translated by Matthew J. O'Connell. Maryknoll, NY: Orbis Books, 1991.

_____. *Las Casas : In Search of the Poor of Jesus Christ*. Translated by Robert R. Barr. Maryknoll, NY: Orbis Books, 1993.

_____ and Richard Schaull, *Liberation and Change*. Edited by Ronald H. Stone. Atlanta: John Knox Press, 1977.

_____. "Liberation and Development: A Challenge to Theology." Translated by Margaret Wilde, in *The Density of the Present: Selected Writings*. Maryknoll: Orbis, 1999.

_____. *On Job: God-Talk and the Suffering of the Innocent*. Translated by Matthew J. O'Connell. Maryknoll, NY: Orbis Books, 1987.

_____. *The Power of the Poor in History*. Translated by Robert R. Barr. Maryknoll: Orbis Books, 1983.

_____. "Theology: A Critical Reflection." In *Gustavo Gutiérrez: Essential Writings*. Edited by James B. Nickoloff. Maryknoll: Orbis, 1996.

_____. *A Theology of Liberation: History, Politics, and Salvation*, rev. ed. Maryknoll, NY: Orbis Books, 1988.

_____. "Toward the Fifth Centenary." Translated by Dinah Livingstone. In *The Density of the Present: Selected Writings*. Maryknoll, Orbis Books, 1999.

_____. *We Drink from Our Own Wells: The Spiritual Journey of a People*. Translated by Matthew J. O'Connell. Maryknoll, NY: Orbis Books, 1984.

Harkness, Georgia. *Mysticism: Its Meaning and Message*. Nashville: Abingdon Press, 1973.

Hausammann, Susi. "Atheistisch zu Gott beten: Eine Auseinandersetzung mit D. Sölle." *Evangelische Theologie* 31 (1971): 414-436.

Heiler, Friedrich. "The History of Religions as a Preparation for the Cooperation of Religions." In *The History of Religions*, eds. Mircea Eliade and J. Kitagawa, 142-153. Chicago: University of Chicago Press, 1959.

Henry Suso: The Exemplar with Two German Sermons. Edited and Translated by Frank Tobin. The Classics of Western Spirituality: A Library of the Great Spiritual Masters. New York: Paulist Press, 1989.

Higgins, Jean. "Redemption." In *The Desires of the Human Heart: An Introduction to the Thought of Bernard Lonergan*. Edited by Vernon Gregson. 201-221. New York: Paulist Press, 1988.

Higginson, Richard. "From Carl Schmitt to Dorothee Sölle: Has Political Theology Turned Full Circle?" *Churchman* 97:2 (1983): 132-140.

Hildegard of Bingen: Scivias. The Classics of Western Spirituality: A Library of the Great Spiritual Masters. Translated by Mother Columba Hart and Jane Bishop. Mahwah: Paulist Press, 1990.

Hogan, Kevin. "The Experience of Reality: Evelyn Underhill and Religious Pluralism." *Anglican Theological Review* 74 (1992): 334-347.

Hopkinson, Arthur W. *Mysticism: Old and New*. Port Washington, NY: Kennikat Press, 1971.

Ignatius of Loyola: Spiritual Exercises and Selected Works. Edited by George E. Ganss, S.J. Translated by Parmananda R. Divarkar, S.J., George E. Gannss, S.J., Edward J. Malatesta, S.J., Martin E. Palmer, S.J. The Classics of Western Spirituality: A Library of the Great Spiritual Masters. Mahwah: Paulist Press, 1991.

James, William. *Varieties of Religious Experience*. New York: Penguin Books, 1982.

Janet, Paul. *Fénelon: His Life and Works*. Translated by Victor Leuliette. Port Washington, N.Y.: Kennikat Press, 1970.

Jantzen, Grace M. "The Legacy of Evelyn Underhill." *Feminist Theology* 4 (1993): 79-100.

Jaoudi, Maria. *Christian Mysticism East and West: What the Masters Teach Us*. New York: Paulist Press, 1998.

John of the Cross. *The Collected Works of John of the Cross*, Rev. ed. Translated by Kieran Kavanaugh, O.C.D. and Otilio Rodriguez, O.C.D. Washington, D.C.: ICS Publications, 1991.

Johnson, Donald H. "Lonergan and the Redoing of Ethics: [Application of Transcendental Method Described]." *Continuum* 5 (1967): 211-220.

Johnston, William. *Arise My Love: Mysticism for a New Era*. Maryknoll: Orbis, 2000.

_____. *Christian Mysticism Today*. San Francisco: Harper & Row, 1984.

_____. *Christian Zen*. San Francisco: Harper & Row, 1979.

_____, ed. *The Cloud of Unknowing*. New York: Doubleday, 1973.

_____. *The Inner Eye of Love: Mysticism and Religion*. San Francisco: Harper & Row, 1978.

_____. *Letters to Contemplatives*. Maryknoll, NY: Orbis Books, 1991.

_____. *The Mirror Mind: Spirituality and Transformation*. San Francisco: Harper & Row, 1981.

_____. *Mystical Theology: The Science of Love*. Maryknoll: Orbis, 1998.

_____. *The Mysticism of the Cloud of Unknowing: A Modern Interpretation*. St. Meinrad, IN: Abbey Press, 1975.

_____. *Silent Music: The Science of Meditation*. New York : Harper & Row, 1974.
_____. *The Still Point: Reflections on Zen and Christian Mysticism*. New York: Fordham University Press, 1970

_____. *The Wounded Stag: Christian Mysticism Today*. New York: Harper & Row, 1984. Reprint, New York: Fordham University Press, 1998.

Jonsson, Ulf. *Foundations for Knowing: Bernard Lonergan's Foundations for Knowledge of God and the Challenge from Antifoundationalism.* New York: Peter Lang, 1999.

Julian of Norwich: Showings. Translated by Edmund Colledge, OSA and James Walsh, SJ. New York: Paulist Press, 1978.

Kainz, Howard P. *Democracy and the "Kingdom of God."* Marquette Studies in Philosophy, no. 6. Milwaukee, WI: Marquette Univeristy Press, 1995.

Kavanaugh, Kieran, O.C.D. "Introduction." In *Teresa of Avila: The Interior Castle.* The Classics of Western Spirituality. Translated by Kieran Kavanaugh, O.C.D, 1-29. New York: Paulist Press, 1979.

Kee, Alistair. *A Reader in Political Theology.* Philadelphia: Westminster Press, 1975.

Kerby-Fulton, Kathryn. "Prophet and Reformer 'Smoke in the Vineyard.'" In *Voice of the Living Light: Hildegard of Bingen and Her World.* Translated by Barbara Newman, 70-90. Berkely: University of California Press, 1998.

Komonchak, Joseph A. "Lonergan's Early Essays on the Redemption of History." In *Lonergan Workshop.* vol 10. Edited by Frederick Lawrence, 159-177. Boston: Boston College, 1994.

Kress, Robert. "Theological Method: Praxis and Liberation." *Communio* 6 (1979): 113-134.

Lakeland, Paul. *Freedom in Christ: An Introduction to Political Theology.* New York: Fordham University Press, 1986.

Lamb, Matthew. "Generalized Empirical Method and Praxis." In *Creativity and Method: Essays in Honor of Bernard Lonergan, SJ.* Edited by Matthew L. Lamb, 53-77. Milwaukee: Marquette University Press, 1981.

_____. *Solidarity with Victims: Toward a Theology of Social Transformation.* New York: Crossroad, 1982.

Lämmerman-Kuhn, Heidemarie. *Sensibilität für den Menschen: Theologie und Anthropologie bei Dorothee Sölle.* Würzburger Studien zur Fundamentaltheologie, Bd. 4. Frankfurt am Main; New York: Lang, 1988.

Lash, Nicholas. *Easter in Ordinary: Reflections on Human Experience and the Knowledge of God.* Notre Dame, University of Notre Dame Press, 1988.

Lanzetta, Beverly. *The Other Side of Nothingness: Toward a Theology of Radical Openness.* Albany: State University of New York Press, 2001.

Lawrence, Frederick. "The Horizon of Political Theology." In *The Trinification of the World: A Festschrift in Honour of Frederick E. Crowe in Celebration of his 60th Birthday.* Edited by Thomas A. Dunne and Jean M. Laporte, 46-70. Toronto: Regis College Press, 1978.

_____. "Lonergan as Political Theologian." In *Religion in Context: Recent Studies in Lonergan*, eds. Timothy P. Fallon, S.J. and Philip Boo Riley, College Theology Society Resources in Religion, vol. 4. 1-21. Lanham, MD: University Press of America, 1988.

_____. "Political Theology and 'The Longer Cycle of Decline.'" In *Lonergan Workshop*, vol. 1. Edited by Frederick Lawrence. 223-255. Missoula, MT: Scholars Press, 1978.

Liddy, Richard M. *Transforming Light: Intellectual Conversion in the Early Lonergan*. Collegville, MN: The Liturgical Press, 1993.

Little, Katherine Day. *François de Fénelon: Study of a Personality*. New York: Harper, 1951.

Lonergan, Bernard. *Caring about Meaning: Patterns in the Life of Bernard Lonergan*. Edited by P. Lambert, C. Tansey, and C. Going. Montreal: Thomas More Institute, 1982.

_____. *Collected Works of Bernard Lonergan*, vol. 3, *Insight: A Study of Human Understanding*. 5th rev. ed. Edited by Frederick E. Crowe and Robert M. Doran. Toronto: University of Toronto Press, 1992.

_____. *Collected Works of Bernard Lonergan*, vol. 5, *Understanding and Being: The Halifax Lectures on "Insight."* Edited by Frederick E. Crowe and Robert M. Doran. Toronto: University of Toronto Press, 1990.

_____. *Collected Works of Bernard Lonergan*, vol. 6, *Philosophical and Theological Papers 1958-1964*. Edited by Robert C. Croken, Frederick E. Crowe, and Robert M. Doran. Toronto: University of Toronto Press, 1988.

_____. *Collected Works of Bernard Lonergan*, vol. 10, *Topics in Education*. Edited by Robert M. Doran and Frederick E. Crowe. Toronto: University of Toronto Press, 1993.

_____. *Collection: Papers by Bernard Lonergan, S.J.* Edited by F.E. Crowe, S.J. Montreal: Palm Publishers, 1967.

_____. *De Deo Trino*, 3rd ed., 2 vols. Rome: Gregorian University Press, 1956 (CWL 9).

_____. *Doctrinal Pluralism*. Milwaukee: Marquette University Press, 1971.

_____. "Finality, Love, Marriage." *Theological Studies* 4 (1943): 477-510.

_____. *Grace and Freedom: Operative Grace in the Thought of St. Thomas Aquinas*. Edited by J. Patout Burns. London: Darton, Longman, & Todd, 1974 (CWL 1).

_____. "The Human Good." *Humanitas* 15 (1979): 113-126.

_____. "Merging Horizons: System, Common Sense, Scholarship." *Cultural Hermeneutics* 1 (1973): 87-99.

_____. *Method in Theology*, 2nd ed. New York: Herder and Herder, 1973; reprint, Toronto: University of Toronto Press, 1990, 1994, 1996.

_____. "Philosophy and the Religious Phenomenon." *Method: Journal of Lonergan Studies* 12 (1994): 121-146.

_____. *Philosophy of God, and Theology: The Relationship between Philosophy of God and the Functional Specialty, Systematics*. St. Michael's Lectures. Gonzaga University, Spokane, WA. London: Darton, Longman & Todd, 1972.

_____. "Reality, Myth, Symbol." In *Myth, Symbol, and Reality*. Edited by Alan M. Olson, 31-37. Notre Dame: University of Notre Dame Press, 1980.

_____. *A Second Collection*. Edited by William F.J. Ryan, S.J. and Bernard J. Tyrrell, S.J. Philadelphia: The Westminster Press, 1974.

_____. *A Third Collection*. Edited by Frederick E. Crowe. New York: Paulist Press, 1985.

Louth, Andrew. *The Origins of Christian Mysticism: From Plato to Denys*. Oxford: Clarendon, 1981.

Loy, David R. "The Religion of the Market." In *Visions of a New Earth: Religious Perspectives on Population, Consumption, and Ecology*. Edited by Harold Coward and Daniel C. Maguire, 15-28. Albany: State University of New York Press, 2000.

Maloney, George. *The Breath of the Mystic*. Denville, NJ: Dimension Books, 1974.

Manenshijn, Gerrit. "'Jesus Is the Christ': The Political Theology of Leviathan." Translated by John Vriend. *Journal of Religious Ethics* 25 (1997): 35-64.

Marsh, James L. "Praxis and Ultimate Reality: Intellectual, Moral, and Religious Conversion as Radical Political Conversion." *Ultimate Reality and Meaning* 13 (1990): 222-240.

Martinez, Gaspar. *Confronting the Mystery of God: Political, Liberation, and Public Theologies*. New York: Continuum, 2001.

Matthews, William. "Method and the Social Appropriation of Reality." In *Creativity and Method: Essays in Honor of Bernard Lonergan, S.J.* Edited by Matthew L. Lamb, 425-441. Milwaukee: Marquette University Press, 1981.

Maurer, Armand A., C.S.B., *Medieval Philosophy*, 2nd ed. The Etienne Gilson Series, Vol. 4. Toronto: Pontifical Institute of Mediaeval Studies, 1982.

Maurer, Reinhart. "Thesen zur politischen Theologie: Augustinsche Tradition und heutige Probleme." *Zeitschrift fur Theologie und Kirche* 79:3 (1982): 349-373.

McGuire, Brian Patrick. *The Difficult Saint: Bernard of Clairvaux and His Tradition*. Cistercian Studies Series, no. 126. Kalamazoo: Cistercian Publications, 1991.

McIntosh, Mark Allen. *Mystical Theology: The Integrity of Spirituality and Theology*. Challenges in Contemporary Theology. Malden, MA: Blackwell, 1998.

McManners, John, ed., *The Oxford History of Christianity*. New York: Oxford University Press, 1990.

McNamara, William. *Christian Mysticism: A Psychotherapy*. Chicago: Franciscan Herald Press, 1981.

McGinn, Bernard. *The Presence of God: A History of Western Christian Mysticism*, 5 vols. New York: Crossroad, 1991-.

McShane, Phillip. *The Shaping of the Foundations: Being at Home in the Transcendental Method*. Washington, DC: University Press of America, 1977.

Merton, Thomas. *The Ascent to Truth*. New York: Harcourt & Brace, 1981.

_____. *Contemplation in a World of Action*. Notre Dame, IN: University of Notre Dame Press, 1998.

Metz, Johann Baptist. *Followers of Christ: The Religious Life of the Church*. Translated by Thomas Linton. New York: Paulist Press, 1978.

_____. *A Passion for God: The Mystical-Political Dimension of Christianity*. Translated and Edited by J. Matthew Ashley. New York: Paulist Press, 1998.

_____. *Theology of the World*. Translated by William Glen-Doepel. New York: The Seabury Press, 1973.

Mews, Constant J. "From *Scivias* to the *Liber Divinorum Operum*: Hildegard's Apocalyptic Imagination and the Call to Reform." *Journal of Religious History* 24/1 (Feb 2000): 44-56.

Meynell, Hugo Anthony. "Lonergan's Method: Its Nature and Uses." *Scottish Journal of Theology* 27 (1974): 162-180.

Mitchem, Stephanie Y. *Introducing Womanist Theology*. Maryknoll, NY: Orbis Books, 2002.

Monks, Gottfried and Theodoric. *The Life of Holy Hildegard*. Translated from Latin to German with Commentary by Adelgundis Führkötter, OSB. Translated from German to English by James McGrath. Collegeville: The Liturgical Press, 1995.

Morelli, Elizabeth A. *Anxiety: A Study of the Affectivity of Moral Consciousness*. Lanham, MD: University Press of America, 1985.

_____. "A Reflection on Lonergan's Notion of the Pure Desire to Know." *Ultimate Reality and Meaning* 13 (1990): 50-60.

Morelli, Mark D. "Horizonal Diplomacy." In *Creativity and Method: Essays in Honor of Bernard Lonergan, S.J.* Edited by Matthew L. Lamb, 459-474. Milwaukee: Marquette University Press, 1981.

Morrill, Bruce T. *Anamnesis as Dangerous Memory: Political and Liturgical Theology in Dialogue.* Collegeville, MN: Liturgical Press, 2000.

Murray, Joyce. "Liberation for Communion in the Soteriology of Gustavo Gutiérrez." *Theological Studies* 59 (1998): 51-59.

Mynarek, Hubertus. *Mystik und Vernunft: Zwei Pole einer Wirklichkeit.* Olten: Walter-Verlag, 1991.

Naickamparambil, Thomas. *Through Self-Discovery to Self-Transcendence: A Study of Cognitional Self-Appropriation in B. Lonergan.* Tesi Gregoriana Serie Filosofia, no. 5. Rome: Gregorian University Press, 1997.

Naudé, Beyers. *Hope for Faith: A Conversation.* Risk Book Series, no. 31. Geneva: WCC Publications; Grand Rabids, MI: Eerdmans, 1986.

Nickoloff, James B. "The Ecclesiology of Gustavo Gutiérrez." *Theological Studies* 54 (1993): 512-535.

Niebuhr, Reinhold. "Love and Law in Protestantism and Catholicism." In *The Essential Reinhold Niebuhr: Selected Essays and Addresses.* Edited by Robert MacAfee Brown. New Haven: Yale University Press, 1986.

_____. *Moral Man and Immoral Society: A Study in Ethics and Politics.* New York: Charles Scribner's Sons, 1932.

Oakley, Francis. *Politics and Eternity: Studies in the History of Medieval and Early-Modern Political Thought.* Studies in the History of Christian Thought, vol. 92. Leiden; Boston: Brill, 1999.

Oberg, Delroy. "Head v. Heart: Mysticism and Theology in the Life of Evelyn Underhill." *St. Mark's Review* 149 (1992): 7-14.

O'Donovan, Oliver. *The Desire of the Nations: Rediscovering the Roots of Political Theology.* New York: Cambridge University Press, 1996.

O'Keefe, Mark, O.S.B. *Becoming Good, Becoming Holy: On the Relationship of Christian Ethics and Spirituality.* New York: Paulist Press, 1995.

Price, James Robertson III. "Lonergan and the Foundation of a Contemporary Mystical Theology." In *Lonergan Workshop*, vol. 5. Edited by Fred Lawrence. 163-195. Chico, CA: Scholars Press, 1985.

Plotinus, 7 vols. Translated by A.H. Armstrong, LC. Cambridge, MA: Harvard University Press, 1966-1988.

Principe, Walter. "Toward Defining Spirituality." *Sciences Religieuses/Studies in Religion.* 12:2 (1983): 127-141.

Rahner, Karl. "Reflections on the Unity of the Love of Neighbour and Love of God." In *Theological Investigations*, vol. 6. Translated by Karl – H. & Boniface Kruger. New York: Crossroad, 1982.

Ramsey, Michael and A.M. Allchin, *Evelyn Underhill: Two Centenary Essays.* Oxford: S.L.G. Press, 1977.

Rende, Michael L. *Lonergan on Conversion: The Development of a Notion.* Lanham, MD: University Press of America, 1991.

Rixon, Gordon. "Lonergan and Mysticism." *Theological Studies* 62 (2001), 479-497.

Robert, Pierre. "The Spiritual Subject: Lonergan's Categories and Perspectives." In *Lonergan Workshop*, vol 11. Edited by Frederick Lawrence, 145-163. Boston: Boston College, 1995.

Robinson, John A.T. *The Body: A Study in Pauline Theology.* Philadelphia: Westminster Press, 1952.

Rouner, Leroy S., ed., *Civil Religion and Political Theology.* Boston University Studies in Philosophy and Religion, vol. 8. Notre Dame, IN: University of Notre Dame Press, 1986.

Roy, Louis. "La contribution de Bernard Lonergan à la théologie contemporaine." *Studies in Religion/Sciences Religieuse* 14 (1985): 475-485.

Saxer, Ernst. *Vorsehung und Verheissung Gottes: Vier theologische Modelle (Calvin, Scleiermacher, Barth, Sölle) une ein systematischer Versuch.* Studien zur Dogmengeschichte und systematischen Theologie, Bd. 34. Zürich: Theologischer Verlag, 1980.

Scharper, Stephen B. *Redeeming the Time: A Political Theology of the Environment.* New York: Continuum, 1997.

Sellner, Edward C. *Mentoring: The Ministry of Spiritual Kinship.* Notre Dame, IN: Ave Maria Press, 1990.

Sheldrake, Philip. "Unending Desire: De Certeau's 'Mystics.'" *The Way: Supplements* 102 (2001): 38-48.

Siebert, Rudolf J. *From Critical Theory to Communicative Political Theology: Universal Solidarity.* American University Studies VII, Theology and Religion, vol. 52. New York: Peter Lang, 1989.

Siker, Jeffrey S. "Uses of the Bible in the Theology of Gustavo Gutiérrez: Liberating Scriptures of the Poor." *Biblical Interpretation* 4 (1996): 40-71.

Smalley, Susan J. "Evelyn Underhill and the Mystical Tradition." In *Scripture, Tradition and Reason*. Edited by Richard Bouckham and Benjamin Drewery, 266-287. Edinburgh: T&T Clark, 1998.

Sölle, Dorothee. "Eine Erinnerung um der Zukunft willen." In *Mystik und Politik: Theologie im Ringen um Geschichte und Gesellschaft; Johann Baptist Metz zu Ehren zum 60. Geburtstag*. Edited by Edward Schillebeeckx, 13-18. Mainz: Matthias-Grünewald-Verlag, 1988.

_____. *Gegenwind: Errinerungen*. Hamburg: Hoffmann und Campe, 1995.

_____. and Fulbert Steffensky, *Not Just Yes and Amen: Christians with a Cause*. Translated by Rowohlt Taschenbuch Verlag. Philadelphia: Fortress Press, 1985.

_____. *On Earth as in Heaven: A Liberation Spirituality of Sharing*. Translated by Marc Batko. Louisville, KY: Westminster/John Knox Press, 1993.

_____. *Political Theology*. Translated by John Shelley. Philadelphia: Fortress Press, 1974.

_____ and Fulbert Seffensky, eds., *Politisches Nachtgebet in Köln*, 2 vols. Stuttgart/Mainz: Kreuz/Grünewald, 1971.

_____. *The Silent Cry: Mysticism and Resistance*. Translated by Barbara and Martin Rumscheidt. Minneapolis: Fortress Press, 2001.

_____. *Stellvertretung: Ein Kapitel Theologie nach dem "Tode Gottess."* Stuttgart: Kreuz-Verlag, 1965.

Sommerfeldt, John R. *The Spiritual Teachings of Bernard of Clairvaux: An Intellectual History of the Early Cistercian Order*. The Cistercian Fathers Series, no. 125. Kalamazoo: Cistercian Publications, 1991.

Sontag, Frederick. *Love Beyond Pain: Mysticism within Christianity*. New York: Paulist Press, 1977.

Stebbins, Michael J. *The Divine Initiative :Ggrace, World-Order, and Human Freedom in the Early Writings of Bernard Lonergan*. Toronto: University of Toronto Press, 1995.

Streeter, Carla Mae. "Aquinas, Lonergan, and the Split Soul." *Theology Digest* 32 (1985): 326-340.

Sturm, Douglas. "Praxis and Promise: On the Ethics of Political Theology." *Ethics* 92 (1982): 733-750.

Tastard, Terry. "Divine Presence and Human Freedom: The Spirituality of Evelyn Underhill Reconsidered." *Theology* 94 (1991): 426-432.

Tekippe, Terry J. "The Crisis of the Human Good." In *Lonergan Workshop* vol. 7. Edited by Frederick Lawrence, 313-329. Atlanta: Scholars Press, 1988.

Teresa of Avila, *The Collected Works of St. Teresa of Avila*, 3 vols. Translated by Kieran Kavanaugh, O.C.D. and Otilio Rodriguez, O.C.D. Washington D.C.: ICS Publications, 1980.

Thérèse of Lisieux, *The Story of a Soul: The Autobiography of St. Thérèse of Lisieux*, 3rd ed. Translated by John Clarke, O.C.D. Washington, D.C.: ICS Publications, 1996.

Thurman, Howard. "Excerpt from 'Mysticism and Social Change,'" In *A Strange Freedom: The Best of Howard Thurman on Religious Experience and Public Life*. Edited by Walter Earl Fluker and Catherine Tumber. Boston: Beacon Press, 1998.

Timmerman, Joan. "The Sacramentality of Human Relationships." *The Way Supplement* 94 (1999): 11.

Tracy, David. "Theologies of Praxis." In *Creativity and Method: Essays in Honor of Bernard Lonergan, S.J.* Edited by Matthew L. Lamb, 35-51. Milwaukee: Marquette University Press, 1981.

Underhill, Evelyn. *An Anthology of the Love of God: From the Writings of Evelyn Underhill.* Edited by Lumsden Barkway and Lucy Menzies. Wilton, CN: Morhouse-Barlow, 1976.

_____. *Collected Papers of Evelyn Underhill.* Edited by Lucy Menzies. New York: Longmans, Green, and Co, 1946.

_____. *Concerning the Inner Life.* Oxford: Oneworld, 1999.

_____. *Daily Reading with a Modern Mystic: Selections from the Writings of Evelyn Underhill.* Edited by Delroy Oberg. Mystic, CN: Twentythird Publications, 1993.

_____. *The Essentials of Mysticism and other Essays.* New York: AMS Press, 1976.

_____. *Evelyn Underhill: Modern Guide to the Ancient Quest for the Holy.* Edited by Dana Greene. Albany: SUNY Press, 1988.

_____. *Fragments from an Inner Life: The Notebooks of Evelyn Underhill.* Edited by Dana Greene. Harrisburg, PA: Morehouse, 1993.

_____. *The Fruits of the Spirit.* New York: Longmans, Green, 1949.

_____. *The Letters of Evelyn Underhill.* Edited by Charles Williams. Westminister, MD: Christian Classics, 1989.

_____. *Life as Prayer and other Writings of Evelyn Underhill.* Edited by Lucy Menzies. Harrisburg, PA: Morehouse, 1991.

_____. *The life of the Spirit and the Life of Today.* San Francisco: Harper & Row, 1986.

_____. *Man and the Supernatural.* New York: E.P. Dutton & Co., 1928.

_____. *Mixed Pasture: Twelve Essays and Addresses*. London: Methuen & Co., 1933.

_____. *The Mount of Purification, with Meditations and Prayers, 1949, and collected Papers, 1946*. London: Longmans, 1960.

_____. *Mysticism: The Nature and Development of Spiritual Consciousness*, 12th ed. Oxford: Oneworld, 1999.

_____. *Mysticism and War*. London: J.M. Watkins, 1915.

_____. *The Mystic Way: A Psychological Study in Christian Origins*. Kila, MT: Kessinger Publishing, 1998.

_____. *The Mystics of the Church*. New York: Schocken Books, 1964.

_____. *Practical Mysticism*. Columbus, OH: Ariel Press, 1986.

_____. *The Soul's Delight: Selected Writings of Evelyn Underhill*. Edited by Keith Beasley. Nashville, TN: Upper Room Books, 1998.

_____. *The Spiritual Life*. Oxford: Oneworld, 1993.

_____. *The Ways of the Spirit*. Edited by Grace A. Brame. New York: Crossroad, 1993.

Vincent, John J. "Doing Political Theology." *Drew Gateway* 50:2 (1979): 32-43.

Vogel, Arthur A. *The Power of His Resurrection: The Mystical Life of Christians*. New York: Seabury Press, 1976.

von Hildebrand, Dietrich. *Christian Ethics*. New York: David McKay, 1953.

von Hügel, Friedrich. *The Mystical Element of Religion as Studied in Saint Catherine of Genoa and Her Friends*, 2nd ed. 2 vols. London: J.M. Dent & Sons, 1961.

von Molnár, Géza. "Mysticism and a Romantic Concept of Art: Observations on Evelyn Underhill's Practical Mysticism and Novalis' Heinrich von Ofterdingen." *Studia Mystica* 6 (1983): 66-75.

Watts, Alan. *Behold the Spirit: A Study in the Necessity of Mystical Religion*. New York: Pantheon Books, 1971.

INDEX

A

Alexander, Jon, 4-5

B

bias. *See* dramatic bias; group bias; individual bias

C

common sense, 72, 77-78, 106-110, 121-122
communal self-appropriation, 184-185
conversion: general notion, 20, 131-142; intellectual, 20, 131, 133; moral, 20, 132, 134-140; relationship between the conversions, 140-142; religious, 20, 78-80, 131, 134, 164-165
coordination of human activity, 173-174
cultural decline, 171
culture, 169-172

D

de Certeau, Michel, 11, 13
decision, 14, 110-112
dialectic of contradictories, 143
dialectic of contraries
dialectic of the subject, 142-147
differentiation of consciousness, 19-20, 97, 120-121
Doran, Robert, 74-75, 113-119, 142-142. *See also* psychic conversion
Dunne, Tad, 1, 15, 80-81, 121-124
Dupré, Louis: on modernity, 3

E

economics, 169-170
education, 169-170
experience, 13, 14, 99

F

feelings, 73-75, 135-138
foundational reality, 15, 131-132, 150-151, 197-198
foundations, 20
Francis of Assisi, 7, 149-150

G

group bias, 74
Gutiérrez, Gustavo: conversion to the neighbor, 48; eschatology, 46-47; liberation, 46-47; political theology, 9, 44-49, 55; praxis, 48-49; salvation, 47

H

healing vector, 144-150
Hegel, Georg Wilhelm Friedrich, 159-161
horizonal diplomacy, 185-187
human freedom, 3-4, 76, 111-112, 144

I

Ignatius of Loyola, 123-124, 150. *See also* spiritually integrated subject; *Spiritual Exercises*
individual bias, 74
intersubjectivity of mystical experience, 84-86

J

James, William: on mysticism, 5, 8, 12; on passivity, 12; on transiency, 5, 8
Johanine literature, 1, 136, 146, 181
Johnston, William: acquired contemplation, 40; affective prayer, 40; dark night, 40-41; Eastern religions, 38-39; mystical theology, 38-43, 55; mysticism as journey of prayer, 38-40; orientation to the mystery of Christ, 40; prayer of